CW01486559

U.S. NAVY

U.S. MARINE CORPS

NWP 3-02.12

MCRP 3-31.1A

EMPLOYMENT OF LANDING CRAFT AIR CUSHION (LCAC)

DEPARTMENT OF THE NAVY
OFFICE OF THE CHIEF OF NAVAL OPERATIONS AND
HEADQUARTERS U.S. MARINE CORPS

0 4 1 1 L P 0 0 9 8 9 3 0

PCN 144 000018 00

1 (Reverse Blank)

ORIGINAL

DEPARTMENT OF THE NAVY
NAVAL DOCTRINE COMMAND
1540 GILBERT STREET
NORFOLK VA 23511-2785

February 1997

LETTER OF PROMULGATION

1. NWP 3-02.12/MCRP 3-31.1A, Employment of Landing Craft Air Cushion (LCAC), is an Unclassified naval warfare publication. It shall be handled by Department of the Navy holders in accordance with the administrative procedures contained in NWP 1-01.

2. NWP 3-02.12/MCRP 3-31.1A is effective upon receipt and cancels COMSURFWARDEVGRU TACMEMOs PZ0057-1-93, Air Cushion Landing Craft (LCAC) Vulnerability Reduction (U), and PZ2021-1-94, Employment of Landing Craft Air Cushion (LCAC) in Expeditionary Warfare.

3. This publication may be made readily available to the public upon request.

Paul K. Van Riper

PAUL K. VAN RIPER
Lieutenant General, U.S. Marine Corps
Commanding General
Marine Corps Combat Development Command
Quantico, Virginia

G. S. HOLDER
Rear Admiral, U.S. Navy
Commander, Naval Doctrine Command

U. S. Marine Corps distribution: PCN 144 000018 00.

PUBLICATION NOTICE   ROUTING

1. NWP 3-02.12/MCRP 3-31.1A, Employment of Landing Craft Air Cushion (LCAC), is available in the Naval Warfare Publications Library. It is effective upon receipt.

2. Summary: NWP 3-02.12/MCRP 3-31.1A is the single source of doctrine for planning and executing LCAC employment during amphibious and other operations. It serves as a guide for operational staffs, unit commanders, detachment officers-in-charge, LCAC craftmasters and crews, and school commands.

3. This publication complements NWP 3-02.2M, Ship-to-Shore Movement, the U.S. Navy and Marine Corps doctrine for ship-to-shore movement during the assault phase of an amphibious operation.

Naval Warfare Publications Custodian

Naval warfare publications must be made readily available to all users and other interested personnel within the U.S. Navy.

Note to Naval Warfare Publications Custodian

This notice should be duplicated for routing to cognizant personnel in accordance with NWP 1-01.

DOCTRINAL STATEMENT

The contents of this publication provide baseline tactics that establish the preferred beginning point for the tactical commander. Options to the baseline tactics are also presented. Tactical commanders will use baseline tactics to build the tactical innovation necessary for success in naval warfighting. Baseline tactics herein will be used as the basic structure for training.

EMPLOYMENT OF LANDING CRAFT AIR CUSHION (LCAC)

CONTENTS

Page No.

CHAPTER 1 – CONCEPT

1.1	PURPOSE	1-1
1.2	BACKGROUND	1-1
1.2.1	LCAC Overview	1-1
1.2.2	LCAC Operational Impact	1-13
1.3	CONCEPT OF LCAC OPERATIONS	1-17
1.3.1	Planning	1-17
1.3.2	Preassault Operations and Amphibious Raids	1-17
1.3.3	Ship-to-Shore Movement	1-17
1.3.4	Sustainment of LF Operations Ashore	1-17
1.3.5	Other LCAC Employment	1-17
1.3.6	LCAC Operations in Extreme Environmental Conditions	1-18

CHAPTER 2 – PLANNING

2.1	PURPOSE	2-1
2.2	BACKGROUND	2-1
2.3	AMPHIBIOUS OPERATION PLANNING	2-1
2.4	PREPARATION OF DOCUMENTS	2-2
2.5	ORGANIZATION OF THE LANDING AREA	2-2
2.5.1	Sea Operating Areas	2-2
2.5.2	LCAC Beach and Inland Operating Areas	2-5
2.5.3	Operating Area Selection Responsibilities	2-6
2.6	LCAC SHIP-TO-SHORE MOVEMENT PLANNING	2-6
2.6.1	LCAC Available	2-6
2.6.2	LCAC Standard Load	2-7
2.6.3	Total Lifts Required	2-8
2.6.4	Number of LCAC Cycles	2-8
2.6.5	Cycle Time	2-8
2.6.6	Rate of Combat Power Buildup Ashore	2-9

9

2.6.7   Efficient LCAC Employment. 2-9

2.7   MISSION PLANNING PROCEDURE. 2-10
2.7.1   Craft Factors 2-10
2.7.2   Other Factors 2-11

2.8   LCAC NIGHT AND LOW VISIBILITY SHIP-TO-SHORE MOVEMENT 2-11
2.8.1   Advantages 2-11
2.8.2   Disadvantages. 2-11
2.8.3   Sea State Concerns 2-11
2.8.4   Planning Emphasis 2-11

CHAPTER 3 – PREASSAULT OPERATIONS AND AMPHIBIOUS RAIDS

3.1   PURPOSE. 3-1

3.2   PREASSAULT OPERATIONS. 3-1
3.2.1   LCAC's Role in Reconnaissance and Special Warfare 3-1
3.2.2   LCAC's Role in Mine Warfare 3-3
3.2.3   LCAC's Role in Tactical Deception 3-3

3.3   AMPHIBIOUS RAIDS 3-3
3.3.1   Delivery of a Raid Force Directly Ashore 3-3
3.3.2   Delivery of a Mechanized Raid Force to a Launch Point 3-4
3.3.3   Delivery of a Boated Raid Force to an Insertion Point 3-4

3.4   LCAC PLANNING FOR PREASSAULT OPERATIONS AND
          AMPHIBIOUS RAIDS 3-4

3.5   CONTROL OF LCAC IN PREASSAULT OPERATIONS AND
          AMPHIBIOUS RAIDS 3-4

CHAPTER 4 – SHIP-TO-SHORE MOVEMENT

4.1   INTRODUCTION 4-1

4.2   LCAC SHIP-TO-SHORE MOVEMENT ORGANIZATION AND CONTROL 4-1
4.2.1   Organization 4-1
4.2.2   LCAC Control Areas 4-4
4.2.3   Control 4-7

4.3   COMMUNICATIONS. 4-9
4.3.1   Control Ship Coordination Net. 4-10
4.3.2   Primary Control Net 4-10
4.3.3   LCAC Operations Net 4-10
4.3.4   LCAC Control Net 4-10
4.3.5   Beach Boat Control (ALFA) Net 4-10

4.3.6   Beach Boat Operations (BRAVO) Net... 4-10
4.3.7   CLZ Control Net... 4-10

4.4   LCAC DEBARKATION 4-10
4.4.1   LCAC Debarkation Sequence and Procedures.................................. 4-10
4.4.2   LCAC Well Deck Operations.. 4-10

4.5   LCAC DISPATCH TO THE BEACH... 4-12
4.5.1   LCAC Waves 4-12

4.6   LCAC NAVIGATION 4-15

4.7   TURNAROUND AT THE BEACH AND RTF 4-18

4.8   GENERAL UNLOADING... 4-19

CHAPTER 5 – LCAC VULNERABILITY AND PROTECTION DURING SHIP-TO-SHORE MOVEMENT

5.1   PURPOSE.. 5-1

5.2   LCAC VULNERABILITY... 5-1
5.2.1   Vulnerability to Detection.. 5-1
5.2.2   Vulnerability to Enemy Attack... 5-2

5.3   LCAC SELF-DEFENSE.. 5-4
5.3.1   LCAC Armament 5-4
5.3.2   Embarked Vehicle/Troop Weapons 5-5
5.3.3   LCAC Operational Capabilities 5-6

5.4   PROTECTIVE SUPPORT MEASURES.. 5-6
5.4.1   Naval Surface Fire Support... 5-6
5.4.2   Close Air Support 5-6
5.4.3   AH-1 Cobra Helicopter Escort 5-6
5.4.4   AAW/ASUW Support... 5-6

CHAPTER 6 – SUSTAINMENT OF LF OPERATIONS ASHORE

6.1   INTRODUCTION 6-1

6.2   LFSP OPERATIONS 6-1
6.2.1   Craft Landing Zone Support Team.. 6-1
6.2.2   CLZ Control Team 6-3
6.2.3   Command Relationship.. 6-5

6.3   SEABASING 6-5

ORIGINAL

6.4   BULK FUEL/WATER TRANSFER 6-5

6.5   MEDICAL EMERGENCY EVACUATION 6-5

CHAPTER 7—OTHER LCAC OPERATIONS

7.1   INTRODUCTION 7-1

7.2   LCAC CONFIGURATION FOR PERSONNEL TRANSFER 7-1
7.2.1   Vehicle Configurations for Personnel Transfer. 7-1
7.2.2   MCESS Configuration of LCAC 7-3
7.2.3   PTM Configuration of LCAC 7-8

7.3   SUPPORT OF NEO. 7-11
7.3.1   LCAC NEO Roles 7-12
7.3.2   LCAC NEO Employment Considerations. 7-12

7.4   SUPPORT OF ATF CHOKE-POINT TRANSIT 7-12
7.4.1   LCAC in a Scouting Role. 7-13
7.4.2   LCAC Extension of ATF Radar Coverage 7-13
7.4.3   LCAC in Military OPDEC. 7-13

7.5   SUPPORT OF MIO 7-13

7.6   SUPPORT OF ATF MILITARY OPDEC. 7-13
7.6.1   CADS Van 7-13
7.6.2   SSQ-74 Van 7-14
7.6.3   Deception Van-Configured LCAC Employment Considerations 7-14

7.7   SUPPORT OF AOA MCM 7-14
7.7.1   Mechanical Minesweeping. 7-14
7.7.2   Acoustic and Magnetic Minesweeping 7-14
7.7.3   SZ Lane Breaching. 7-14
7.7.4   MCM-Configured LCAC Employment Considerations 7-14

7.8   SUPPORT OF HA AND DISASTER RELIEF OPERATIONS 7-15
7.8.1   LCAC's General Support Role 7-15
7.8.2   LCAC's Role in HA and Disaster Operations At Sea and Ashore 7-15
7.8.3   LCAC HA Disaster Operations Support Considerations. 7-15

CHAPTER 8 – LCAC OPERATIONS IN EXTREME ENVIRONMENTAL CONDITIONS

8.1   INTRODUCTION 8-1

8.2   OPERATIONS IN COLD WEATHER. 8-1
8.2.1   LCAC Cold-Weather Kit 8-1
8.2.2   Effects on LCAC Performance 8-2

8.2.3   Effects on Personnel Embarked in LCAC 8-6
8.2.4   Effects on LCAC Well Deck Operations 8-6

8.3   OPERATIONS IN HIGH-HEAT/ HIGH-AIRBORNE PARTICLE
         ENVIRONMENTS.. 8-7
8.3.1   Effects on LCAC Performance... 8-7
8.3.2   Effect on Personnel Embarked in LCAC 8-8
8.3.3   Effects on LCAC Well Deck Operations 8-8

8.4   OPERATIONS IN HEAVY WEATHER 8-8
8.4.1   LCAC Heavy-Weather Operations Conducted Over Water 8-9
8.4.2   LCAC Heavy-Weather Operations Conducted Over Land 8-11

APPENDIX A – OTHER LCAC OPERATIONAL AND ADMINISTRATIVE CONSIDERATIONS

A.1   PURPOSE... A-1

A.2   COMPONENTS AND CHARACTERISTICS A-1
A.2.1   LCAC Hull System A-1
A.2.2   LCAC Skirt System.. A-1
A.2.3   LCAC Cold Weather Kit.. A-1
A.2.4   LCAC Operational Characteristics.. A-1

A.3   MAINTENANCE, REPAIR, AND DOCKING A-1
A.3.1   LCAC Maintenance and Repair A-1
A.3.2   LCAC Docking A-5

A.4   SALVAGE, TOWING, AND DISABLED CRAFT LAUNCH AND RECOVERY
         OPERATIONS A-6
A.4.1   LCAC Salvage Operations A-7
A.4.2   LCAC Towing Procedures A-7
A.4.3   Disabled LCAC Launch and Recovery A-7

A.5   MOORING AND ANCHORING... A-7
A.5.1   LCAC Well Deck Mooring.. A-7
A.5.2   LCAC Mooring to a Ship A-7
A.5.3   LCAC Mooring to a Pier... A-8
A.5.4   LCAC Mooring to a Buoy A-11
A.5.5   LCAC Anchoring A-11

A.6   ADMINISTRATIVE SUPPORT AND CRAFT MANNING...................... A-12
A.6.1   LCAC Administrative Support.. A-12
A.6.2   LCAC Manning.. A-14

APPENDIX B – ATF SURFACE OFFLOAD CONSIDERATIONS

B.1   PURPOSE B-1

ORIGINAL

B.2   LANDING CRAFT ALLOCATION CONSIDERATIONS AND OBJECTIVES B-1
B.2.1   Surface Offload Considerations B-1
B.2.2   Efficient Surface Offload Objectives B-2

B.3   LCAC VERSUS LCU ADVANTAGES B-2
B.3.1   LCAC Advantages Over LCU B-2
B.3.2   LCU Advantages Over LCAC B-4

B.4   LHA 1 SHIP CLASS SURFACE OFFLOAD CONSIDERATIONS B-4
B.4.1   LCAC Well Deck Time B-5
B.4.2   LHA 1 Class Ship Offload by LCAC B-5
B.4.3   LHA 1 Class Ship Offload by LCU B-5
B.4.4   LHA 1 Offload by LCAC or LCU B-6

APPENDIX C – LCAC LOADING AND UNLOADING OPERATIONS

C.1   PURPOSE C-1

C.2   LCAC LOADING CHARACTERISTICS AND CONSIDERATIONS C-1
C.2.1   Loading Characteristics C-1
C.2.2   Loading Considerations C-1

C.3   LCAC LOADING/UNLOADING LOCATIONS AND MEANS C-7
C.3.1   In Well Decks C-7
C.3.2   Alongside Ships C-7
C.3.3   At Causeways and RO/RO Facilities C-7
C.3.4   In Beach/Inland Areas C-7
C.3.5   At Sea C-7

C.4   LCAC STANDARD LOADS C-7

APPENDIX D – LCAC IDENTIFICATION LIGHTS, MARKERS, AND SIGNALS

D.1   GENERAL D-1

D.2   LCAC NAVIGATION LIGHTS D-1

D.3   LCAC BEACH MARKERS D-1

D.4   HAND SIGNALS D-1

INDEX Index-1

LIST OF ILLUSTRATIONS

CHAPTER 1 – CONCEPT

Figure 1-1.   LCAC 1-2
Figure 1-2.   LCAC Support Ship Capabilities 1-4
Figure 1-3.   LCAC, LCU, and AAV Lift Capabilities..................................... 1-5
Figure 1-4.   LCAC Operational Characteristics Summary 1-6
Figure 1-5.   Rough Terrain Capabilities.. 1-7
Figure 1-6.   Maximum Allowable Speed to Avoid Structural Damage...................... 1-8
Figure 1-7.   Plow-in Avoidance Speeds... 1-9
Figure 1-8.   LCAC On-Cushion Operation in Surf 1-10
Figure 1-9.   LCAC Casualty Mission Impact.. 1-11
Figure 1-10.   Landing Craft Capabilities 1-16

CHAPTER 2 – PLANNING

Figure 2-1.   Listing of LCAC-Related Ship-to-Shore Movement Documents 2-2
Figure 2-2.   LCAC Operating Areas in the Landing Area................................. 2-3
Figure 2-3.   Operating Area Selection Responsibilities Matrix 2-6
Figure 2-4.   Maximum Speed for Planning LCAC Transit Times........................... 2-8
Figure 2-5.   Maximum Number of LCAC to Assign to a Ship for Unloading 2-10

CHAPTER 4 – SHIP-TO-SHORE MOVEMENT

Figure 4-1.   LCAC Ship-to-Shore Movement Control Organization........................ 4-2
Figure 4-2.   LCAC Control Areas in the Landing Area................................... 4-5
Figure 4-3.   Example of a CCP Used as a DP 4-6
Figure 4-4.   LCAC Voice Communications Matrix....................................... 4-9
Figure 4-5.   Example of an LCAC Launch Timetable..................................... 4-12
Figure 4-6.   Example of an LCAC Recovery Timetable 4-12
Figure 4-7.   LCAC Formations... 4-13
Figure 4-8.   Maximum Allowable Sideslip 4-16
Figure 4-9.   Reaction Times at LCAC Standard Distance 4-16
Figure 4-10.   LCAC Deceleration Performance... 4-16
Figure 4-11.   LCAC Acceleration Performance... 4-17
Figure 4-12.   Estimated Turn Radii for Various Turn Rates (Sideslip Neglected) 4-17
Figure 4-13.   Maximum Limits for Turns Together and Wheels............................ 4-18

**CHAPTER 5 – LCAC VULNERABILITY AND PROTECTION DURING
                SHIP-TO-SHORE MOVEMENT**

Figure 5-1.   Expected Mine Threat by Location Within the Landing Area.................. 5-3

Figure 5-2.   LCAC 1 Through 33 Firing Arcs.. 5-4
Figure 5-3.   LCAC 34 Through 84 Firing Arcs... 5-5
Figure 5-4.   5 Inch/54 Caliber Gun NSFS Capabilities................................. 5-6

CHAPTER 6 – SUSTAINMENT OF LF OPERATIONS ASHORE

Figure 6-1.   Basic LFSP Organization... 6-2
Figure 6-2.   Basic CCT Organization 6-4
Figure 6-3.   The Effect of CLZ Location on CCT and CST Command Relationship 6-6

CHAPTER 7 – OTHER LCAC OPERATIONS

Figure 7-1.   LCAC Troop-Carrying Potential 7-2
Figure 7-2.   Knockdown MCESS Shelter and Major Components........................ 7-4
Figure 7-3.   MCESS Shelter Assembly Process 7-5
Figure 7-4.   MCESS Shelter Configurations 7-6
Figure 7-5.   Six-Section PTM-Configured LCAC with Major Components 7-9
Figure 7-6.   PTM-Configured LCAC Assembly... 7-10
Figure 7-7.   LCAC PTM Cross Sectional View 7-10
Figure 7-8.   PTM-Configured LCAC... 7-11

CHAPTER 8 – LCAC OPERATIONS IN EXTREME ENVIRONMENTAL CONDITIONS

Figure 8-1.   Effects of Cold Weather on LCAC Operations.............................. 8-1
Figure 8-2.   Ice Topographical Features 8-5
Figure 8-3.   LCAC Load as a Function of Ambient Temperature.......................... 8-8
Figure 8-4.   Wave Height Compared to LCAC.. 8-9
Figure 8-5.   Estimating Sea States 8-10

APPENDIX A – OTHER LCAC OPERATIONAL AND ADMINISTRATIVE CONSIDERATIONS

Figure A-1.   LCAC Primary Features... A-2
Figure A-2.   3-Dimensional LCAC Skirt Component Drawing............................ A-3
Figure A-3.   LCAC Cold Weather Kit Component Location............................. A-4
Figure A-4.   LCAC Operational Characteristics.. A-5
Figure A-5.   LCAC Docking Block and a Typical Tiedown Configuration A-6
Figure A-6.   LCAC Emergency Well Deck Recovery.................................... A-8
Figure A-7.   LCAC Tiedown in Well Deck A-9
Figure A-8.   LCAC Mooring to a Ship... A-10
Figure A-9.   LCAC Mooring to a Pier A-11
Figure A-10.   LCAC Mooring to a Buoy A-12
Figure A-11.   LCAC Operational and Administrative Chains of Command While Deployed..... A-13

APPENDIX B – ATF SURFACE OFFLOAD CONSIDERATIONS

Figure B-1.   Number of LCAC for Single Ship Offload B-2
Figure B-2.   Average Landing Craft Speeds (LCAC and LCU) B-3

Figure B-3.   Average Landing Craft Cycle Times (LCAC and LCU) B-3
Figure B-4.   Carrying Capacity for Landing Craft B-4
Figure B-5.   Landing Craft Efficiency in Transporting Vehicles........................... B-5
Figure B-6.   LCAC Refueling Frequency... B-5
Figure B-7.   Estimated Time to Offload an LHA by LCAC (LCU Deliver LCU Preloads) B-6
Figure B-8.   Estimated Time to Offload an LHA by LCU or LCAC (LCU Deliver LCU
              Preloads When LCAC Assigned)... B-7
Figure B-9.   Estimated Time to Offload an LHA by LCU or LCAC (LCAC Deliver LCU
              Preloads When LCAC Assigned)... B-7

APPENDIX C – LCAC LOADING AND UNLOADING OPERATIONS

Figure C-1.   LCAC Deck Load Diagram C-2
Figure C-2.   LCAC Cargo Deck Grid C-2
Figure C-3.   Weight and Square Footage of USMC Vehicles and Equipment. C-4
Figure C-4.   Dimensions and Weights of LCAC-Compatible Containers C-5
Figure C-5.   Estimating Times for Backing Versus Driving Vehicles Forward onto LCAC. C-5
Figure C-6.   Combined Times for Various LCAC Loading and Griping Sequences............ C-6
Figure C-7.   LCAC Standard Loads and Standard Load Equivalents C-8

APPENDIX D – LCAC IDENTIFICATION LIGHTS, MARKERS, AND SIGNALS

Figure D-1.   LCAC Beach Markers (From Seaward)..................................... D-2
Figure D-2.   LCAC Maneuvering Hand Signals... D-3

RECORD OF CHANGES

Change No. and Date of Change	Date of Entry	Page Count Verified By (Signature)

ORIGINAL

RECORD OF CHANGES (continued)

Change No. and Date of Change	Date of Entry	Page Count Verified By (Signature)

ORIGINAL

LIST OF ACRONYMS AND ABBREVIATIONS

A

AIMD	aviation intermediate maintenance depot
AAV	assault amphibious vehicle
AAVP	assault amphibious vehicle, personnel
ACU	assault craft unit
ACV	air cushion vehicle
AMCM	airborne mine countermeasures
AMW	amphibious warfare
AOA	amphibious objective area
APU	auxiliary power unit
ARG	amphibious ready group
ARHU	attitude reference heading unit
ARP	airborne relay platform
ATF	amphibious task force
ATP	Allied tactical publication
AW	air warfare

B

B&A	boat and aircraft
BG	battle group
BGC	boat group commander
BMU	beachmaster unit
BWC	boat wave commander

C

C2WGRU-LANT	Command and Control Warfare Group, Atlantic
C2WGRU-PAC	Command and Control Warfare Group, Pacific
C3	command, control, and communications
CAP	combat air patrol
CAS	close air support
CATF	commander, amphibious task force
CBR	chemical, biological, and radiological
CCA	craft collection area
CCO	central control officer
CCP	craft control point
CCT	craft landing zone (CLZ) control team
CDP	craft departure point
CG	center of gravity
CHA	craft holding area
CLA	craft launch area
CLF	commander, landing force
CLS	craft landing site
CLZ	craft landing zone
CPP	craft penetration point
CRRC	combat rubber raiding craft
CRTS	casualty receiving and treatment ship
CSS	combat service support
CST	craft landing zone (CLZ) support team

ORIGINAL

D

DFM	defense fuel, marine
DP	decision point
DR	dead reckoning

E

EA	electronic attack
EMCON	emission control
EPW	enemy prisoner of war
ES	electronic warfare support
EW	electronic warfare

F

FAV	fast attack vehicle
FM	frequency modulation
FMC	fully mission-capable craft
FMFM	fleet Marine Force Manual
FOD	foreign object damage

G

GCE	ground combat element
GPS	global positioning system

H

HA	humanitarian assistance
HF	high frequency
HLZ	helicopter landing zone
HMMWV	high mobility, multipurpose wheeled vehicle
HQ	headquarters
HSVL	high-speed velocity log

I

IFF	identification friend or foe
IR	infrared
ISO	international standards organization
ITG	initial terminal guidance
IVCU	internal voice communications unit

L

LAV	light armored vehicle
LCAC	landing craft air cushion
LCO	LCAC control officer
LCS	LCAC control ship
LCU	landing craft utility
LF	landing force
LFSP	landing force support party
LHA	general purpose amphibious assault ship
LHD	general purpose amphibious assault ship (w/internal dock)
LOD	line of departure
LPD	amphibious transport dock
LSD	landing ship, dock
LVS	logistics vehicle system
LWC	LCAC wave commander

M

MAGTF	Marine air-ground task force
MBT	main battle tank
MC	mission-capable craft
MCAC	multimission craft air cushion
MCM	mine countermeasures

ORIGINAL

MCESS	Marine Corps expeditionary shelter system	OTH	over-the-horizon

MEDEVAC	medical emergency evacuation	PCO	primary control officer
MEF (FWD)	Marine expeditionary force (forward)	PCS	primary control ship
MEU	Marine expeditionary unit	PIRAZ	positive identification radar advisory zone
MHE	material handling equipment		
MILVAN	military van	PLRS	Position Location Reporting System
MIO	maritime interception operation	PMS	planned maintenance system
MOMS	man-on-the-move system	PTM	personnel transport module
MOPP	mission-oriented protective posture	PUK	pack-up kit
MPP	mission planning procedure		

N

R

		RECON	reconnaissance
NBG	naval beach group	RO/RO	roll-on/roll-off
NDI	navigation data integrator	RTCH	rough terrain container handler
NEO	noncombatant evacuation operation	RRDF	roll-on/roll-off (RO/RO) discharge facility
NMC	not mission-capable		
NSE	naval support element	RTF	return to force
NSFS	naval surface fire support		

S

NTDS	Naval Tactical Data System	SACC	supporting arms coordination center
NVG	night vision goggle	SCO	secondary control officer
NWP	naval warfare publication	SCS	secondary control ship
		SEAL	sea-air-land team

O

		SEAOPS	safe engineering and operations
OIC	officer in charge	SRP	seaward recovery point
OMFTS	operational maneuver from the sea	SOC	special operations capable
OPDEC	operational deception	SUW	surface warfare
OPORD	operation order	SW	shallow water
OPSEC	operations security	SZ	surf zone
OPTASK	operational tasking		

T

OPTASK AMPHIB	operational tasking amphibious	TACLOG	tactical-logistics group

TRAP	tactical recovery of aircraft and personnel

U

UHF	ultrahigh frequency

V

VHF	very high frequency
VSW	very shallow water

PREFACE

NWP 3-02.12/MCRP 3-31.1A, Employment of Landing Craft Air Cushion (LCAC), is the single source of doctrine for planning and executing LCAC employment during amphibious and other operations. It serves as a guide for operational staffs, unit commanders, detachment officers-in-charge, LCAC craftmasters and crews, and school commands. This NWP complements NWP 3-02.2M, Ship-to-Shore Movement.

Throughout this publication, references to other publications imply the effective edition.

Report any page shortage by letter to:

DIRECTOR
NAVY TACTICAL SUPPORT ACTIVITY
WASHINGTON NAVY YARD
BLDG 200
901 M STREET SE
WASHINGTON DC 20374-5079

Send a copy to:

COMMANDER
NAVAL DOCTRINE COMMAND
1540 GILBERT STREET
NORFOLK VA 23511-2785

ORDERING DATA

Order a new publication or change, as appropriate, through the Navy supply system. Make changes/revisions to the distribution list in accordance with NWP 1-01.

RECOMMENDED CHANGES

Submit routine changes to this publication at any time using the accompanying format.

All units and stations submit recommendations to:

COMMANDER
SURFACE WARFARE DEVELOPMENT GROUP
2200 AMPHIBIOUS DRIVE
NORFOLK VA 23521-2896

In addition, forward two copies of all recommendations to Director, Navy Tactical Support Activity at the address listed previously.

URGENT CHANGE RECOMMENDATIONS

Submit urgent changes (including matters of safety) in accordance with the accompanying sample message format. Information addressees should comment as appropriate. (See NWP 1-01.)

INFORMATION CUTOFF DATE

Information in this publication is current as of 1 August 1996. Change information received after this date will be reflected in the next change/revision to this publication.

CHANGE SYMBOLS

Revised text in changes is indicated by a black vertical line (change symbol) in either margin of the page, like the one printed next to this paragraph. The change symbol shows where there has been a change. The change might be material added or information restated. A change symbol in the margin, by the chapter number and title, indicates a new or completely revised chapter.

WARNINGS, CAUTIONS, AND NOTES

The following definitions apply to warnings, cautions, and notes found throughout this publication:

WARNING

An operating procedure, practice, or condition that may result in injury or death if not carefully observed or followed.

CAUTION

An operating procedure, practice, or condition that may result in damage to equipment if not carefully observed or followed.

ORIGINAL

Note

An operating procedure, practice, or condition that is essential to emphasize.

WORDING

The concept of word usage and intended meaning adhered to in this publication is :

"Shall" is used only when application of a procedure is mandatory.

"Should" is used only when application of a procedure is recommended.

"May" and "need not" are used only when application of a procedure is optional.

"Will" is used only to indicate futurity, never to indicate any degree of requirement for application of a procedure.

ORIGINAL

(CLASSIFICATION)

ROUTINE CHANGE TO: ___NWP 3-02.12/MCRP 3-31.1A___   **DATE:** _____
(PUBLICATION NUMBER/REVISION/CHANGE)

LOCATION: _____   _____   _____   _____
(PAGE)   (PARAGRAPH)   (LINE)   (FIGURE NUMBER)

TYPE OF CHANGE: ADD ☐   DELETE ☐   MODIFY ☐   TEXT ☐   FIGURE ☐

EXACT CHANGE RECOMMENDED: (USE ADDITIONAL SHEETS IF NEEDED. GIVE VERBATIM TEXT CHANGES. IF FIGURE IS TO BE ADDED, SUPPLY ROUGH SKETCH OR IDENTIFY SOURCE. IF FIGURE IS TO BE CHANGED, INCLUDE A MARKED-UP COPY OF EXISTING FIGURE.)

RATIONALE:

SUBMITTED BY: _____   _____
(ORIGINATING COMMAND)   (ORIGINATOR SEQUENCE NUMBER)

_____   _____
(POINT OF CONTACT)   (PHONE - IDENTIFY DSN OR COMMERCIAL)

PRA ACTION: ACCEPTED ☐   MODIFIED ☐   REJECTED ☐
(GIVE REASON)

REMARKS: (USE ADDITIONAL SHEETS IF NEEDED)

_____   _____
(PRA POINT OF CONTACT)   (PHONE - IDENTIFY DSN OR COMMERCIAL)

CONFERENCE DATE: _____   **CONFERENCE AGENDA ITEM NO.:** _____

| (CLASSIFICATION) | PAGE _____ OF _____
|---|

```
FM      ORIGINATOR
TO      COMSURFWARDEVGRU LITTLE CREEK VA//N52//
INFO    COMNAVDOCCOM NORFOLK VA//JJJ//
        CG MCCDC QUANTICO VA//JJJ//
        CINCPACFLT PEARL HARBOR HI//JJJ// or CINCLANTFLT NORFOLK VA//JJJ//
        COMNAVSURFLANT NORFOLK VA//N6/65//
        COMNAVSURFPAC SAN DIEGO CA//N8/N71//
        NAVSAFECEN NORFOLK VA//JJJ//
        NAVTACSUPPACT WHITE OAK MD//TT40//
        COMSURFWARDEVGRU DET WEST CORONADO CA//N58//
        (Others as appropriate)

CLASSIFICATION//N03510//

MSGID/GENADMIN/ORIGINATOR//
SUBJ/URGENT CHANGE RECOMMENDATION FOR NWP 3-02.12/MCRP 3-31.1A//
REF/A/DOC/CNO/AUG 96//
AMPN/NWP 1-01//
REF/B/(as required)//
RMKS/

1. AN URGENT (SAFETY) CHANGE IS RECOMMENDED FOR NWP 3-02.12/MCRP 3-31.1A.

2. PAGE _____ PAR. NO. _____ LINE NO. _____ FIG. NO. _____

3. PROPOSED NEW TEXT (include classification)




4. JUSTIFICATION




                                              (Urgent change format)
```

CHAPTER 1

Concept

1.1 PURPOSE

The purpose of this NWP is to provide the doctrine and considerations for planning and executing LCAC employment during amphibious and other operations. This NWP describes LCAC's:

1. Characteristics, capabilities, support requirements, and limitations

2. Operational impact on warfighting and AMW, including operations from OTH

3. Effect on the decisions made by the CATF and CLF

4. Incorporation into the ATF and LF landing plan

5. Conduct of waterborne ship-to-shore movement

6. Role in supporting LF operations ashore

7. Employment in roles other than AMW and in extreme environmental conditions.

This NWP serves as a guide for operational staffs, unit commanders, detachment OICs, LCAC craftmasters and crews, and school commands. It is the single source of doctrine on the operational employment of LCAC. This NWP complements NWP 3-02.2M, "Ship-to-Shore Movement," the Navy and Marine Corps doctrine for ship-to-shore movement during the assault phase of an amphibious operation.

Note

The "Safe Engineering and Operations (SEAOPS) Manual for Landing Craft Air Cushion (LCAC)," Volumes I through VI, is the authoritative document for operating individual LCAC. All procedures and instructions contained therein are applicable to all personnel involved in LCAC operation, training, maintenance, support, and scheduling. Any digression from these procedures and instructions must first be recommended, reviewed, and incorporated into SEAOPS.

1.2 BACKGROUND

This paragraph provides an LCAC overview and discusses the operational impact of the LCAC.

1.2.1 LCAC Overview. The LCAC was developed to provide the Navy a high-speed landing craft to complement Marine Corps rotary wing aircraft (and ultimately, the MV-22 tilt-rotor aircraft) in the conduct of ship-to-shore movement from OTH. The LCAC, designed using modern air cushion technology, was introduced operationally to the fleet in the mid-1980s. The LCAC can transport equipment, personnel, cargo, and weapon systems from ships through the surf zone and across the beach to hard landing points beyond the high-water mark in a variety of environmental conditions. By combining the heavy lift capability of a surface assault craft with the high speeds of helicopterborne assault, the LCAC exposes more of the world's littoral regions to expeditionary operations from the sea. At OTH distances up to 100 nm (load and sea state permitting), LCAC offers a method to attain tactical surprise.

In addition to supporting amphibious operations, LCAC is a viable platform for use in a variety of other missions ranging from humanitarian assistance to MCM (see paragraph 1.3.5). Figure 1-1 is an artist's conception of the LCAC.

1.2.1.1 Characteristics and Capabilities. The LCAC, supported on a pressurized cushion of air, is

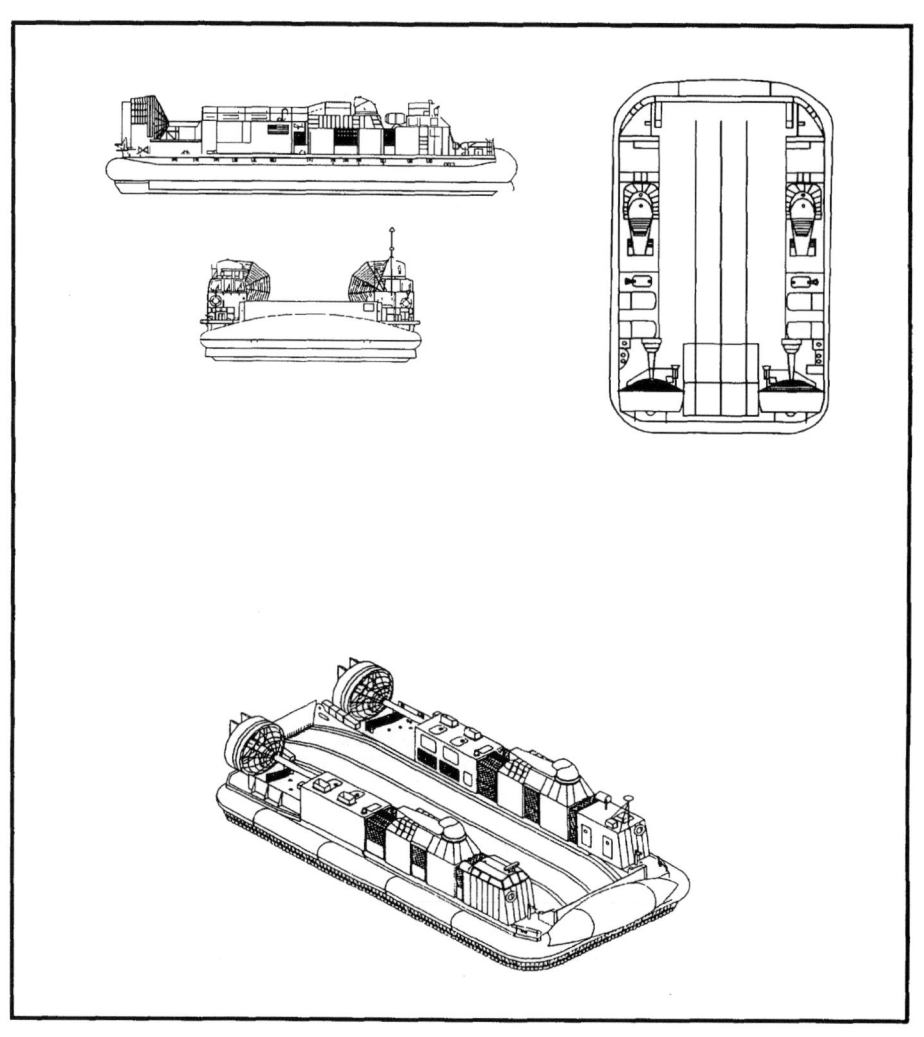

Figure 1-1. LCAC

ORIGINAL

much faster than displacement landing craft, traveling in excess of 40 knots (sea state permitting). Since the LCAC is not a displacement hull craft, it is less susceptible to mines and underwater ordnance, and is independent of tides and most hydrographic constraints that restrict maneuvering of displacement landing craft. Weather is less of a factor in LCAC operations than it is in conventional displacement craft operations, although the combined effect of seas, ambient temperature, and craft load must be taken into consideration in assault planning (refer to Volume V, Appendix C of SEAOPS). LCAC's high speed and long range significantly increase options for operations from OTH.

The LCAC has a compartmented flotation hull fabricated from welded aluminum alloy plates and beams forming watertight compartments. Port and starboard superstructures house craft equipment, propulsion machinery, crew stations, and passenger accommodations. The cargo deck accommodates a 60-ton payload of palletized and nonpalletized items (up to 75 tons in an overload condition), and roll-on, roll-off vehicular equipment up to the size of an M1A1 tank. Bulk cargo requires additional time to secure because of potential FOD to propellers and lift fans. Up to 24 passengers can be carried in designated seating in the cabin modules (16 port and 7 starboard) to avoid exposure to wind and spray during craft operation. Additional personnel may be embarked in armored vehicles or deck-installed portable structures.

Approximately 80 percent of the LCAC's propulsion is provided by two propellers mounted aft on the main deck and 20 percent by two controllable bow thrusters. Air for the bow thrusters and craft cushion is provided by four double-entry centrifugal lift fans. Four TF40B marine gas turbine engines drive both the propellers and lift fans. The maximum fuel capacity is approximately 6,000 gallons, expended at a rate of 1,000 gallons per hour during high consumption situations. A bag-and-finger seal around the sides of the craft and stability seals under the hull contain the cushion.

The propellers, rudders, and bow thrusters make the LCAC highly maneuverable and provide the craftmaster precise control to the extent of stationary rotation. Even so, it may require 500 yards to stop and 2,000 yards or more to turn. The craft is capable of entering and exiting amphibious ship well decks either on-

cushion or hullborne. The LCAC can be deployed on the following six amphibious ship classes:

1. LSD 41 (see paragraph 1.2.1.2.1)

2. LSD 49 (see paragraph 1.2.1.2.2)

3. LSD 36 (see paragraph 1.2.1.2.3)

4. LPD 4 (see paragraph 1.2.1.2.4)

5. LHA 1 (see paragraph 1.2.1.2.5)

6. LHD 1 (see paragraph 1.2.1.2.6).

Appendix A of this NWP and Volumes I through VI of SEAOPS provide additional details on LCAC operation, maintenance, and support.

1.2.1.2 Support Requirements. The LSD 41, LSD 49, and LHD 1 ship classes are designed specifically to operate and support LCAC. The LSD 36, LPD 4, and LHA 1 ship classes have been modified to conduct LCAC operations. The LSD 41 and, to a lesser extent, the LSD 49 ship classes have LCAC administrative and logistics support facilities and spaces designed into them. All other ship classes must be fitted with MILVANs to provide an acceptable level of logistics support. The use of MILVANs, however, must be weighed against the corresponding reduction of LF embarkation space. The AIMD capabilities of LHA 1 and LHD 1 class ships may reduce the number of MILVANs required by one.

Figure 1-2 summarizes LCAC support ship capabilities. Figure 1-3 summarizes the LCAC, LCU, and AAV lift capabilities for each amphibious ship class.

1.2.1.2.1 LSD 41 Class. The LSD 41 class was designed with the administrative and other working spaces to carry and support LCAC. The LSD 41 class can provide support to craft embarked in other, less capable LCAC-support ships.

The LSD 41 class well deck is 50 feet wide and 440 feet long. Clearance between the well deck and the helicopter deck above is 26 feet 8 inches forward of frame 92 and 30 feet 10 inches aft of frame 92. Four LCAC may be carried in the well deck with the portable vehicle ramp from the turntable in place. The

Service	LCAC Requirements	Support Ships					
		LSD 41	LSD 49	LSD 36	LPD 4	LHA 1	LHD 1
Compressed air	Maintenance and cleaning	125	125	125	120	125	125
Cranes	Cargo handling	60 ton B&A 20 ton B&A 7.5 ton (2) in well	30 ton B&A	56 ton B&A 17 ton B&A 2 ton in well	30 ton B&A 20 ton B&A 2 ton in well	30 ton B&A 3 ton in well	35 ton (Note 1) 3 ton (2) in well
Crew berthing (Note 2)	Crew (5 men) maintenance	42	42	32	27	25	32
Fuel (Note 3) DFM capacity (gal)	NA	563,800 (Note 3)	563,800 (Note 3)	872,424	743,862	1,843,990	1,800,000 (Note 3)
Delivery rate (gal/min)		275	275	250	500	700	250
JP-5 capacity (gal)		42,000	42,000	29,988	18,606	417,900	429,685
Delivery rate (gal/min)		50	50	250	75	150	250
Firefighting equipment in well deck	NA	AFFF	AFFF	AFFF	AFFF	AFFF	AFFF

Notes:
1. Tilley crane.
2. No crew berthing is specifically provided for LCAC personnel.
3. Two DFM LCAC service tanks each with a capacity of approximately 10,000 gallons.

Figure 1-2. LCAC Support Ship Capabilities

normal LCAC detachment consists of three craft. A watertight barrier can be raised between the forward one-third of the well and the aft two-thirds.

1.2.1.2.2 LSD 49 Class. The LSD 49 class ship was designed as a minimum modification "cargo variant" of the LSD 41 class with a shortened well deck to accommodate additional vehicle and cargo stowage. The LSD 49 class well deck is 180 feet long and can carry two LCAC. The LSD 49 class provides LCAC detachment administrative spaces and limited spaces for logistics support.

1.2.1.2.3 LSD 36 Class. The LSD 36 class has been modified (SHIPALT LSD 36-318K) to carry three LCAC. However, only two LCAC can be carried if the mezzanine deck is installed. No shops or storerooms are provided for maintenance support. Therefore, the em-

barked LCAC detachment is required to provide three MILVANs for logistics support and maintenance.

The LSD 36 class well deck is 50 feet wide and 252 feet long with the portable mezzanine deck removed. Clearance between the well deck and the helicopter deck above is 27 feet 4 inches. Clearance to the well deck catwalk is 20 feet 3 inches.

1.2.1.2.4 LPD 4 Class. Most of the LPD 4 class have been modified (SHIPALT LPD 916K) to accommodate one LCAC in the well deck with limited operational support. Due to well deck structural limitations the LCAC cannot be docked on blocks.

The LPD 4 class well deck is 50 feet wide and 164 feet long. The clearance from the well deck to the main deck above is 28 feet 9 inches. Clearance to the well deck catwalk is 20 feet 3 inches. The LPD 4 class

Ship Class	LCAC	LCU	AAV
LSD 41	4 (Note 1)	3	64
LSD 49	2	1	45
LSD 36	3 (Note 2)	3	49
LPD 4	1 (Note 3)	1	26
LHA 1	1 (Note 3)	4	-- (Note 4)
LHD 1	3	2	-- (Note 4)

Notes:
1. Five LCAC can be carried with the vehicle ramp lowered and stowed.
2. Three LCAC can be carried with the mezzanine deck removed and two LCAC with the mezzanine deck installed.
3. Installation of LCAC SHIPALTs required.
4. Tactical employment of AAVs is not normally conducted from the LHD or LHA.

Figure 1-3. LCAC, LCU, and AAV Lift Capabilities

well deck has a water barrier gate than cannot be raised with an LCAC on board.

1.2.1.2.5 LHA 1 Class. Most of the LHA 1 class have been modified (SHIPALT LHA 1-642K) to accommodate one LCAC in the well deck and provide power, fuel, and water services. This SHIPALT does not include modifications for spare parts and repair facilities. Without the SHIPALT installed, the LHA 1 class can serve as an LCAC emergency haven only.

The LHA 1 class well deck is 76 feet wide and 109 feet long from the stern gate sill to the aft end of the center island. Clearance between the well deck and the upper closure of the stern gate is 28 feet. The LCAC is stowed between the after end of the center island and the stern gate. There is insufficient clearance for

LCAC between the center island and the batterboards in the forward portion of the well deck.

1.2.1.2.6 LHD 1 Class. The LHD 1 class was designed to carry three LCAC. It has very limited support spaces available for the embarked LCAC detachment. A minimum of two MILVANs are required for logistic and administrative support during deployment.

The LHD 1 class well deck is 49 feet 5 inches wide forward of frame 91, gradually increases to 60 feet wide at the stern gate sill, and is 266 feet long. The stern gate is a watertight closure that consists of two gates, an upper gate that swings out and up and a lower gate that swings out and down. Clearance between the well deck and the upper closure of the stern gate is 28 feet.

ORIGINAL

1.2.1.3 Limitations. When employing LCAC there are a number of important limitations that must be considered by the CATF and CLF to maximize its performance and ensure its safety. The limitations will be discussed in the following paragraphs.

1.2.1.3.1 Operating Limits. Figure 1-4 summarizes LCAC operational characteristics including its operating limits in terms of maximum speed and terrain capabilities. Figure 1-5 depicts LCAC rough terrain capabilities.

1.2.1.3.2 Structural Limitations. The stress on LCAC's structure will become larger with an increase in gross weight, sea state, and forward speed at which the craft is operated. Figure 1-6 depicts the maximum allowable LCAC speed to avoid structural damage to the craft.

1.2.1.3.3 Maximum Craft Displacement. The maximum craft displacement weight of LCAC under any operating condition is 368,250 pounds (184 short tons). Since sea state and temperature affect LCAC speed, load must be limited to ensure sufficient speed to achieve hump transition (see paragraph 1.2.1.3.4) and obtain proper craft performance. An overloaded LCAC may have several operational impacts including:

1. Increased possibility of engineering system casualties

2. Higher fuel burn rates and decreased operating range

Characteristics	Maximum Speed (kt) (Note 2)
Sea State 0	50
Sea State 1	50
Sea State 2	42
Sea State 3 (80 °F and below)	35
Sea State 4 (80 °F and below)	5
Over Land (terrain dependent)	25
	Maximum Terrain
Slope (standing start)	5°
Step Up	4 ft vertical
Ditch (any width)	<4 ft deep
Ditch (span up to 15 ft)	<4 ft deep
Obstacle	4 ft high
Trees, several (Note 1)	4 in diameter, 18 ft tall
Trees, single (Note 1)	6 in diameter, 25 ft tall

Notes:
1. Some skirt and hull damage is likely. Rotating machinery damage is likely if tree branches are ingested by lift fans or propellers.
2. Actual speeds achieved depend on craft load, weather, sea state, and ambient temperature. See Volume V, Appendix C of SEAOPS for craft performance tables.

Figure 1-4. LCAC Operational Characteristics Summary

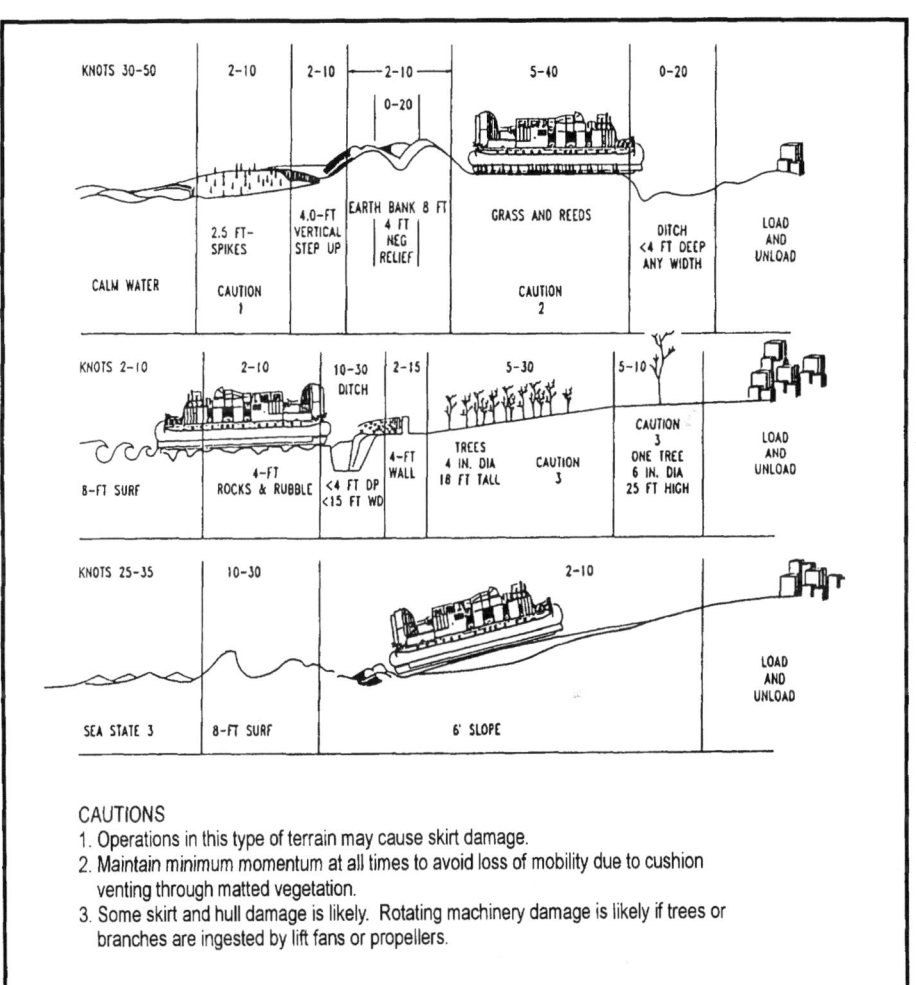

KNOTS 30-50	2-10	2-10	2-10		5-40	0-20
			0-20			
	2.5 FT-SPIKES	4.0-FT VERTICAL STEP UP	EARTH BANK 8 FT 4 FT NEG RELIEF		GRASS AND REEDS	DITCH <4 FT DEEP ANY WIDTH	LOAD AND UNLOAD
CALM WATER	CAUTION 1				CAUTION 2	

KNOTS 2-10	2-10	10-30 DITCH	2-15	5-30	5-10	
8-FT SURF	4-FT ROCKS & RUBBLE		4-FT WALL <4 FT DP <15 FT WD	TREES 4 IN. DIA 18 FT TALL	CAUTION 3 ONE TREE 6 IN. DIA 25 FT HIGH	LOAD AND UNLOAD
				CAUTION 3		

KNOTS 25-35	10-30		2-10	
SEA STATE 3	8-FT SURF	6' SLOPE		LOAD AND UNLOAD

CAUTIONS
1. Operations in this type of terrain may cause skirt damage.
2. Maintain minimum momentum at all times to avoid loss of mobility due to cushion venting through matted vegetation.
3. Some skirt and hull damage is likely. Rotating machinery damage is likely if trees or branches are ingested by lift fans or propellers.

Figure 1-5. Rough Terrain Capabilities

ORIGINAL

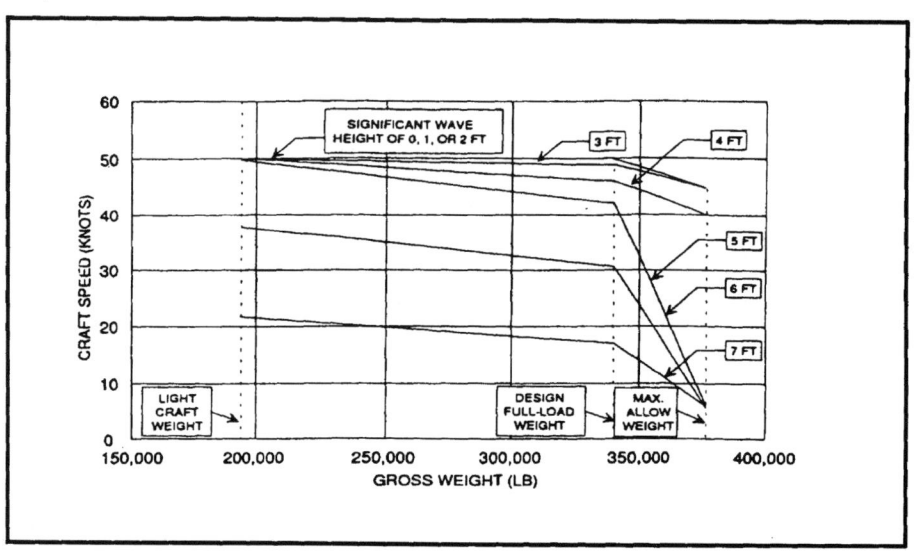

Figure 1-6. Maximum Allowable Speed to Avoid Structural Damage

3. Increased potential for serious bag deterioration

4. Decreased maneuverability during surf zone and over-beach transit.

1.2.1.3.4 Hump Transition. As the LCAC hovers over the water it creates a depression in the water surface directly beneath itself, equal in water volume to its weight. As the LCAC begins to move, the depression moves with it and creates a substantial wake. At certain speeds, craft resistance becomes relatively high. These critical speeds are referred to as "hump speeds" due to their "hump"-like appearance on a graph of speed versus resistance. At approximately 11 knots, a "secondary" hump occurs. At approximately 18 knots, the depression cannot keep up with the craft and the craft begins to "fly out" of the depression or "go over the hump." At approximately 20 knots, the depression no longer exists, and the LCAC creates little or no wake.

Operating considerations during hump transition are as follows:

1. Handling difficulty increases with sea state, craft load, and ambient air temperature.

2. LCAC operates easily in shallow water (less than 5 feet). The hump effect can be avoided by departing the beach at 18 knots or greater when surf and gradient permit.

3. Hump effect is amplified in critical water depths (approximately 8 to 20 feet), and craft may not have enough power to go over the hump if heavily loaded.

4. With sea states above 2, time must be added to the launch timetable to allow a fully loaded LCAC to turn either down- or cross-seas to go over the

1-8

hump before turning back to the initial leg of the planned track.

5. In operating environments of moderate to heavy sea states (2 to 4) and high headwinds, hump speeds will not always be possible even when craft are lightly loaded.

Because increased power is required to lift a more heavily loaded craft onto the cushion and go over the hump, there may be circumstances when the craft could be loaded so heavily that hump transit is not possible. Maximum weights for post-hump operations can be calculated for various combinations of air temperature, significant wave height, and wave period. Volume V, Chapter 3 of SEAOPS provides the procedures to calculate maximum weights.

1.2.1.3.5 Sea Conditions for Launch. To maximize the operational effectiveness of the LCAC, the craft must be loaded and operated in a manner that allows the craft to achieve speeds greater than hump speed.

It is quite possible to encounter a combination of payload weight, fuel weight, and environmental conditions which prohibit the craft from successfully performing hump transit. When the craft can not transit hump, the maximum achievable craft speed will be low (less than 20 knots) and the craft fuel consumption will be very high. When such a situation is encountered, the mission planner should use a shorter course that will require less fuel or reduce the weight of the payload if possible.

If the environment is particularly harsh (very large waves with associated high winds), the mission planner or the craft operator could be faced with a situation where the weight of payload and fuel cannot be reduced by a sufficient amount to allow the craft to transit the hump and achieve high speed operation. When this situation occurs, the craft should not be launched.

1.2.1.3.6 Plow-In Boundary. Plow-in describes a relatively sudden and large bow-down motion followed by a rapid deceleration. Under some conditions, the maximum LCAC speed may be limited to avoid plow-in.

When plow-in occurs, the forward skirt of the LCAC collapses inward causing excessive yawing and side slip. Unchecked, the cushion will degenerate and the hull will contact the water, resulting in high drag, rapid deceleration, and complete loss of cushion. The craft must subsequently retransition over hump to continue.

Plow-in generally occurs from excessive bow-down trim, coupled with extremely high speeds at high propeller pitch angles. Plow-in will normally occur during the beach-to-water transition into the surf. The potential for plow-in increases as surf height increases or the gradient of the beach steepens. Although plow-in normally does not occur at speeds below 50 knots in low sea states, it may occur at speeds as low as 30 knots in high sea states.

Recommended restrictions on maximum speed to avoid plow-in are depicted in figure 1-7.

Significant Wave Height (ft)	Speed Limitations to Avoid Plow-in (kt)
0	50
1	50
2	45
3	40
4	35
5	30

Figure 1-7. Plow-in Avoidance Speeds

1.2.1.3.7 Surf Zone Transitions. The LCAC is structurally designed to transit through a maximum surf height of 8 feet. Transition through surf heights between 8 and 12 feet should only be attempted in a situation of operational necessity, dependent upon the capability of the craftmaster, embarked load, and overall surf conditions. Figure 1-8 summarizes the operational considerations affecting LCAC on-cushion operation in the surf. Volume I, chapter 3 of SEAOPS provides detailed procedures for LCAC surf zone transitions.

1.2.1.3.7.a LCAC Beach Approach. During beach approach, there is a risk of taking plunging surf through the propellers, resulting in possible damage, and subsequent damage to the lift fans. In turn, these conditions could cause a possible operational loss of the craft. Beach approach should be timed by the craftmas-

Characteristics	Low Surf	Medium Surf	High Surf (Note 1)
Height	0 to 4 ft	4 to 8 ft	8 to 12 ft
Total Craft Weight	368,250 lb	338,250 lb	308,250 lb Negotiation of high surf depends on skill of operator (Note 2)
Heading to Surf Line	$90° \pm 10°$	$90° \pm 10°$	$90° \pm 10°$
Maximum Speed During Beach Approaches	50 kt (Note 2)	30 kt (Note 2)	20 kt (Note 2)
Maximum Speed During Beach Departures	25 kt (Note 3)	20 kt	10 kt

Notes:
1. The maximum surf height for structural design considerations is 8 feet. Transition through surf higher than 8 feet may result in damage to the craft structure or skirt.
2. Inside surf line, craft speed is adjusted taking into account wave speed, surf condition, beach gradient, beach terrain, and cargo load.
3. Speed should be reduced with a steep beach gradient to avoid plow-in and hard structure damage.

Figure 1-8. LCAC On-Cushion Operation in Surf

ter to ensure arrival just behind a wave crest. The craftmaster should maintain forward motion of the craft until safely beyond the high water mark, never allowing a wave to overtake the craft and break over its stern. Care must be taken once the LCAC clears the surf, since it will accelerate rapidly once on land and will need room to decelerate and stop.

CAUTION

Green water in the lift fans or propellers will cause failure of rotating equipment.

1.2.1.3.7.b LCAC Beach Departure. Due to propeller vulnerability, LCAC should always enter the surf bow-on. The major considerations during beach departure are the gradient of the beach and breaker height. The principle concern during beach departure is plow-in (see paragraph 1.2.1.3.6). The LCAC can be operated satisfactorily in a plunging surf. Beach departure should

be timed by the operator to arrive at the breaker line during a reduced wave period. An angle of approach to the breaker line of 10° off axis is required in heavy surf to reduce the possibility of plow-in. The maximum land-to-water transition speed is 25 knots.

CAUTION

To avoid propeller/duct damage, back down maneuvers shall never be executed into surf lines or areas with heavy debris concentrations.

1.2.1.3.8 Fuel Management. LCAC fuel consumption varies with load, speed, sea state, and ambient air temperature. Extensive operations below hump speed or involving high transition speeds consume fuel at the greatest rate. The LCAC uses 1,000 gph in high consumption situations.

To conserve fuel, LCAC should secure main engines during long delays on the beach or go off-cushion during long waits to enter the well deck.

The normal mission fuel load is 34,000 pounds (5,000 gallons) yielding a nominal running time of 4 hours 20 minutes with a 25 percent fuel reserve. Heavy loads or high sea states limit the allowable fuel quantity (see paragraph 1.2.1.3.5). Reserve fuel can be used to maintain the LCAC's trim.

CAUTION

Afloat LCAC refueling is not advisable except during benign weather conditions. LCAC are extremely vulnerable to damage when going alongside other craft or ships.

1.2.1.3.9 Casualty Mission Impact. Figure 1-9 details the extent of LCAC mission impact from various propulsion and skirt casualties. The ability to continue

Casualty	Mission Impact	Comments
One main engine lost	Reduce load or spread	May not be able to get over hump with full load
Two main engines lost (one each side)	Substantially reduced load or speed; reduced lift	Speed and maneuverability restricted (load/weather dependent)
Two main engines lost (the same side)	Not capable	Craft can salvage under own power
Three main engines lost	Not capable	Craft can salvage under own power (hull-borne only)
Slit in skirt < 10 ft	Slightly reduced lift and speed	Slit can increase to > 10 ft with continued operation
Slit in skirt > 10 ft	Substantially reduced lift and speed	Change in trim required
Large portion of skirt system missing	Not capable	Craft can salvage under own power (hull-borne only)
Lift fan lost (pair)	Reduced load, control, or speed	Results in loss of associated bow thruster, requires declutching and loss of one engine
One propeller lost	Substantially reduced speed and maneuverability	Speed restricted; offset thrust reduces speed and maneuverability (load/weather dependent)
Both propellers lost	Not capable	Craft can salvage under own power
Rudder control lost	Reduced speed and maneuverability	Restricted to propeller pitch and bow thruster control
One bow thruster lost	Reduced maneuverability	None
Two bow thrusters lost	Reduced maneuverability	Restricted to propeller pitch and rudder control
Loss of large segments of bag fingers (≥ 5)	Reduced maneuverability	Increased possibility of plow-in

Figure 1-9. LCAC Casualty Mission Impact

1-11

ORIGINAL

a mission will depend upon when the casualty occurs. See Volume I, chapter 4, of SEAOPS for recommended casualty report ratings.

1.2.1.3.10 Human Performance Guidelines and Health Standards.

Human performance guidelines and health standards have been established for LCAC crews and support personnel to enhance operational readiness and safety. Guidelines have been established for crew rest and sleep, crew day, and crew week to minimize the possibility of fatigue. Conditions which require operations outside the guidelines can decrease human performance and increase mishap potential. Volume I, chapter 6 of SEAOPS provides additional information on human performance and medical qualifications for LCAC personnel.

Note

The senior commander responsible for conduct of amphibious tactical operations may waive the SEAOPS human performance guidelines should operational necessity dictate. It must be recognized that such action increases the probability of crew fatigue, causing impaired judgment and reduced performance.

1.2.1.3.10.a Rest and Sleep.

Eight hours for sleep time should be made available for each crew member every 24-hour period. Time between operational missions should be adjusted to allow personnel to eat and obtain the required 8 hours of interrupted rest each day. LCAC crews should not be scheduled for continuous alert/standby (required awake) in excess of 18 hours. LCAC crew schedules shall be made with due consideration for watchstanding, detachment duties, training, and off-duty activities.

1.2.1.3.10.b Crew Day.

Crew day is the maximum safe operating time based upon optimum operating conditions. As operating conditions deteriorate, crew day is reduced. Since safe operations are dependent upon the mental and physical alertness of the crew, crew day is designed to minimize the effects of fatigue on crew alertness. Crew day should routinely be considered in planning safe LCAC operations.

The crew day for LCAC personnel under optimum conditions is 12 hours. The period commences with craft APU start and ends with the postmission craft requirements. APUs are normally started 30 minutes before the craft exits the well. If operations commence before dawn, they must end at dusk even if the 12-hour limit has not been exceeded. For night operations, the crew day is reduced to 8 hours. After each operating period, 8 hours of rest are required. Thereafter, a cycle of 8 hours of operations and 8 hours of rest will be followed.

1.2.1.3.10.c Crew Day Formulas for Planning Guidance.

Optimum conditions for a 12 hour crew day include daylight hours, no combat, clear weather, and calm seas. While the following formulas are provided as quantifiable guidance for planning LCAC operations, they do not replace the commander's judgment in determining safe craft operations. The following formula is used to determine maximum safe operating hours when LCAC operations start during the day and end before sunset, or start at night and end before sunrise:

$$CD = (12)(V/SS)$$

Where:

CD = Crew day (in hours)
V = Variable (from table below)
SS = Sea state (Note: for sea state (0) or overland, use (1) in the equation for sea state factor)

| | Variables | |
Sea State	Night	Day
3 (max)	1.5	2.0
2	1.33	2.0
1/0/Overland	0.66	1.0

The following formula is used to determine maximum safe operating hours when LCAC operations start at night and continue past sunrise: $TD = CD - (TN/CN) CD$.

Where:

TD = number of hours between sunrise and the end of crew day
CD = crew day for operations (from previous paragraph)
TN = number of hours between start of mission and sunrise

CN = crew day for night operations (from previous paragraph).

The following formula is used to determine maximum safe operating hours when LCAC operations start during the day and continue past sunset: TN = CN - (TD/CD) CN.

Where:

TN = number of hours between sunset and the end of crew day
CN = crew day for night operations (from previous paragraph)
TD = number of hours between start of mission and sunset
CD = crew day for day operations (from previous paragraph).

Note

In conditions of reduced visibility (fog, snow, heavy rain, divide the variable in the crew-day equation by (2) in solving the formula.

1.2.1.3.10.b Crew Week. Total weekly crew time operating an LCAC should not normally exceed 40 hours. When practical, personnel should not be assigned LCAC operational duties on more than six consecutive days. When the tempo of operations requires individuals to operate LCAC in excess of these guidelines, crew members should be closely monitored by the cognizant medical authority, and specific clearance for operations in excess of guidelines must then be given.

1.2.2 LCAC Operational Impact. LCAC has the potential to make a significant impact on all phases of amphibious operations and naval warfighting in general.

1.2.2.1 Maneuver Warfare. Maneuver warfare is a warfighting philosophy that seeks to shatter the enemy's cohesion through a series of rapid, violent, and unexpected actions which create a turbulent and rapidly deteriorating situation with which the enemy cannot cope.

As the focal point for improved waterborne ship-to-shore mobility, LCAC provides a means to apply maneuver warfare at sea in an amphibious operation. An LCAC-equipped ATF can threaten a larger area and project the LF inland far more rapidly than a displacement assault craft-equipped ATF. The LCAC's capability allows it to proceed to a larger number of potential landing sites and further inland than the traditional high water mark to discharge its cargo on dry, negotiable terrain. The LCAC contributes to tactical mobility and the operational speed and flexibility aspects of maneuver warfare that threaten the foundations of the enemy's antilanding doctrine.

1.2.2.2 Operational Maneuver From the Sea. OMFTS is a developing concept which applies the principles of maneuver warfare to a maritime campaign for projecting naval power ashore. OMFTS involves the seamless and continuous projection of self-contained, combined arms teams ashore in the face of an enemy threat of increased lethality and sophistication. OMFTS operations are designed to break the cohesion and integration of enemy defenses and rapidly attain campaign objectives while avoiding attrition through head-on attacks. The OMFTS concept emphasizes speed, deception, surprise, and other battlefield preparations that paralyze the enemy and create uncertainty and delay in its actions.

1.2.2.3 Amphibious Operations From OTH. Amphibious operations from OTH are operational initiatives launched from beyond visual and radar range of the shoreline.

The speed, range, and amphibious capabilities of LCAC provide a tremendous improvement in ship-to-shore mobility. The range of tactical options is expanded from a surface assault launched a few thousand yards from shore to an OTH launch of the initial waves in excess of 25 nm from shore. LCAC's capability potentially enhances the ATF's survivability during the initial assault because of the OTH standoff of key ships and the opportunity for dispersion. Combined with helicopterborne operations, LCAC OTH capability can provide increased tactical advantage to

CATF and CLF and a distance buffer to aid in countering the threats to the ATF.

1.2.2.4 Impact on Threat. The presence of an LCAC-equipped ATF complicates the enemy's efforts to mass an adequate force to repel a waterborne assault by increasing the number of potential landing sites along the expanse of shoreline to be defended. LCAC's unique speed, range, and mobility provide CATF and CLF a much wider range of options in the selection of landing sites. By landing over beaches that are less heavily defended, the LF can benefit from a more rapid buildup of combat power ashore.

1.2.2.5 Marine Expeditionary Unit Special Operations Capable. The presence of LCAC in an ARG with a MEU SOC embarked increases the range of options available to the ARG and MEU commanders for accomplishing most types of special operations. LCAC can be used to overcome geographic obstacles which might otherwise jeopardize completion of the mission.

In particular, LCAC can be a valuable asset in carrying out the following MEU SOC missions:

1. Amphibious raid (see paragraph 1.3.2 and chapter 3)

2. Limited objective attack

3. NEO (see chapter 7)

4. Show of force

5. Reinforcement operation

6. Civil action (see chapter 7)

7. Deception operation

8. TRAP

9. Clandestine recovery operation

10. In-extremis recovery operation.

1.2.2.6 Planning. The LCAC's unique capabilities must be considered carefully throughout the planning phase of an amphibious operation. Joint Pub 3-02, "Joint Doctrine for Amphibious Operations," provides guidance on the approach to planning and basic decisions for an amphibious operation.

1.2.2.6.1 Landing Area and Beach Selection. The following Navy landing area selection factors are influenced by LCAC availability.

1. Ability of the naval forces to support the landing and subsequent operation

2. Hydrographic features of the beach approaches as related to the size, draft, maneuverability, and beaching characteristics of the assault ships and craft involved

3. Hydrographic features of the offshore and near-shore areas

4. Extent of mineable waters

5. Conditions affecting the ability of the enemy to defeat MCM.

The following LF landing area selection factors are affected by LCAC availability:

1. Configuration of coastline

2. Terrain inland from the coastline

3. Requirements for combat service support.

The availability of LCAC also affects the formulation of the LF concept of operations particularly in the selection of landing beaches. For example, an LCAC can successfully cross beaches inaccessible by displacement craft; however, the required force build-up rate ashore may require that the beach be accessible by displacement landing craft as well. Other factors in selection of landing beaches influenced by LCAC availability are as follows:

1. Capacity for landing supplies and equipment

2. Suitability for beaching landing ships, landing craft, and amphibious vehicles

3. Beach trafficability

4. Suitability of offshore approaches

5. Number, location, and suitability of beach support areas and beach exits

6. Location, type, and density of beach obstacles, including underwater obstacles

7. Nature of terrain immediately inland from beach

8. Suitability of beach from the standpoint of expected weather and tidal conditions.

1.2.2.6.2 Intelligence Planning. Since the OTH capability of LCAC establishes a need for detailed information on potential landing areas over a wider frontage than that using displacement landing craft only, LCAC availability affects intelligence planning. Intelligence plays a critical role because LCAC tactical employment decisions depend on accurate and timely information on the enemy and area of operations. Because the operational tempo of LCAC operations is much faster than that of displacement landing craft operations, intelligence planning must provide for expeditious processing and dissemination of information.

1.2.2.6.3 C3 Systems Support Planning. Greater ATF dispersion and an increased requirement for long-range communications are significant factors in planning for C^3 support of LCAC OTH operations. Both Navy and LF C3 requirements must be considered carefully in planning the allocation of shipboard equipment and the outfitting of landing craft.

1.2.2.6.4 Supporting Arms Planning. The LCAC's speed, mobility, and ability to access a wider range of coastline complicate supporting arms planning from a time and distance perspective. The use of LCAC may necessitate the enlargement of the AOA to accommodate operations from OTH. Longer distances and wider areas of coverage are factors. Higher LCAC speeds substantially reduce the safety margins associated with fire support timing over those associated with much slower displacement landing craft. As a result, craftmasters in initial surface assault waves must drive the planned timeline, passing through control points on schedule and CPPs at precisely H-hour. Both air and naval surface fire support planning must consider these reduced safety margins and planned craft timelines to the beach when LCAC is employed.

NWP 22-2/FMFM 1-7, "Supporting Arms in Amphibious Operations," provides detailed guidance to naval commanders for coordinating the planning and delivery of supporting fire.

1.2.2.6.5 Logistic/CSS Planning. The availability of LCAC significantly affects planning for logistic/CSS of the LF ashore. The incorporation of LCAC in the designed logistic/CSS system can add to the system's responsiveness, simplicity, flexibility/ mobility, economy, attainability, sustainability, and survivability. LCAC's presence is also a key factor in planning the sustained support of LF operations ashore through the seabasing concept.

1.2.2.6.6 Ship-to-Shore Movement Planning. The presence of LCAC significantly increases the options available in planning the ship-to-shore movement of the LF. Operational implications of having LCAC available are as follows:

1. LCAC can be employed from OTH to achieve tactical surprise.

2. LCAC is not constrained by tidal conditions and most hydrographic features.

3. LCAC complements the vertical assault by providing combat support that is not helicopter deliverable.

4. Alternate beaches can be included to tactically employ LCAC's speed and mobility.

5. LCAC operations beyond the high water mark could influence the scheme of maneuver ashore.

6. A beach separation of 500 yards from displacement landing craft is required unless a lesser distance is approved by the CATF.

The available mix of LCAC and displacement landing craft is a significant factor in the formulation of detailed plans to support the ship-to-shore movement. Figure 1-10 provides a summary of LCAC and LCU capabilities that can be useful in the ship-to-shore movement planning process. Appendix B provides ATF surface offload considerations which include comparisons between LCAC and LCU tactical load capacities and transit, beach, and cycle times. Appen-

	LCAC	LCU	AAV
Average speed with cargo:			
Over water (kt)	35 (Note 1)	11	6
Over land (mph)	10	NA	25
Onload time (min) (Note 2)			
Mobile cargo	25	30	NA
Bulk cargo	45	60	NA
Refueling time (min)	15	15	10
Average operating time before refueling is required (hr)	4	40	7
Maximum cargo:			
Weight (short tons)	60 (Note 3)	180	5
Square footage	1,809	2,300	NA
Personnel	24 (Note 4)	400	18

Notes:
1. At designed overload.
2. Includes nominal griping time. Actual onload times will vary based on type of load, experience of personnel, and operating environment. Bulk cargo time assumes cargo is palletized.
3. 75 short tons at design maximum overload.
4. Hand carried baggage/equipment can significantly reduce the troop carrying capability of the LCAC.

Figure 1-10. Landing Craft Capabilities

dix B also provides offload considerations for employment of assault craft mixes with LHA 1 class ships.

1.2.2.6.7 CBR Defense Planning. A CBR defense plan is prepared when the risk level is suspected or higher. A CBR defense plan should consider the development of an alternate landing plan to exploit LCAC's speed and maneuverability to avoid contaminated areas.

1.2.2.7 Embarkation. Traditional approaches to combat loading and craft assignment during the embarkation phase of amphibious operations must be reconsidered when LCAC assets are added to the force. Craft refueling, cargo capacity, and cycle times are embarkation planning factors affected by the use of LCAC. The landing craft capabilities data provided in figure 1-10 can be useful, as well, in the embarkation planning process. The embarkation plan should make best use of LCAC as follows:

1. To support the LF landing plan, scheme of maneuver ashore, and plan for landing supplies

2. To provide the highest possible degree of unit self-sufficiency

3. To provide for dispersion of critical units and supplies

4. To expedite unloading of the assault echelon to attain a rapid and responsive buildup of combat power ashore.

Joint Pub 3-02.2, "Joint Doctrine for Amphibious Embarkation," provides general guidance concerning amphibious embarkation from the perspective of CATF and CLF.

Appendix C provides information on LCAC loading and unloading operations which should be considered in embarkation planning.

1.3 CONCEPT OF LCAC OPERATIONS

LCAC adds high speed and long range to surface assault operations. LCAC's ability to operate independently of tides and hydrographic constraints provides additional flexibility, and supports the rapid buildup of forces ashore on beaches not accessible by displacement landing craft. Although weather may affect LCAC operations, it is less of a factor than for displacement landing craft. CATF/CLF options for operations from OTH are enhanced. LCAC complements LF delivery assets during both OTH and nearshore ship-to-shore movement. Conceptually, LCAC operations should be viewed as a part of a single integrated evolution, rather than a parallel operation to conventional surface assault and helicopterborne assault.

Tactical surprise achieved through the use of LCAC can result in fewer losses in landing and can permit rapid buildup of the LF ashore prior to contact with the enemy main antilanding units. When LCAC is used in an amphibious raid, it may be possible to conduct the entire operation and withdraw before enemy forces can react.

1.3.1 Planning. The detailed planning for LCAC operations is an integral part of the planning for waterborne amphibious operations. Chapter 3 of NWP 3-02.2M covers the planning process for amphibious ship-to-shore movement. Chapter 2 of this NWP addresses and expands on the LCAC portion of ship-to-shore movement planning.

1.3.2 Preassault Operations and Amphibious Raids. The unique capabilities of LCAC make it a viable platform for use in a variety of preassault operations, including the clandestine insertion of reconnaissance and special warfare assets. Similarly, LCAC is an effective platform for the long-range insertion of forces in an amphibious raid. Therefore, planning for preassault operations should include gathering information to support LCAC operations ashore, as well as the need for craft ITG into CLZs. The fact that LCAC is not constrained by tidal conditions and most hydrographic features does not diminish the need for reconnaissance of beach and inland areas to identify landing sites and ingress and egress routes.

Chapter 3 addresses preassault operations in support of LCAC and, conversely, LCAC support of both advance force operations and amphibious raids.

1.3.3 Ship-to-Shore Movement. Tactics for conducting the waterborne ship-to-shore movement focus on underway launch of AAVs and displacement landing craft in the nearshore area and the launch of LCAC from OTH as a complement to the helicopterborne assault. Together, the nearshore and OTH launches provide CATF/CLF with greater flexibility in conducting an amphibious operation.

Chapter 4 of NWP 3-02.2M discusses the range of options available to CATF for initiating LF debarkation and the ship-to-shore movement. Chapter 4 of this NWP expands on the LCAC portion of ship-to-shore movement and chapter 5 discusses LCAC's vulnerability and protection during ship-to-shore movement.

1.3.4 Sustainment of LF Operations Ashore. LCAC can play a major role in the sustainment of LF operations after the scheduled assault waves are ashore. The LCAC is a viable platform for supporting LFSP operations by moving troops, equipment, and supplies ashore. The craft can be of great value in the concept of seabasing, for transfer of bulk fuel and water ashore, and for the emergency MEDEVAC of casualties from the beach.

Chapter 6 addresses LCAC support of LFSP operations and the use of LCAC in the seabasing concept, bulk fuel/water transfer, and emergency MEDEVAC.

1.3.5 Other LCAC Employment. LCAC's unique capabilities can be exploited for a number of operational missions beyond the traditional range of ship-to-shore operations. Chapter 7 addresses each of the following missions in more detail:

1. Configuration for personnel transfer (see paragraph 7.2)

2. Support of NEO (see paragraph 7.3)

3. Support of ATF choke point transit (see paragraph 7.4)

4. Support of MIO (see paragraph 7.5)

5. Support of ATF military OPDEC (see paragraph 7.6)

6. Support of AOA MCM (see paragraph 7.7)

7. Support of HA and disaster relief operations (see paragraph 7.8).

1.3.6 LCAC Operations in Extreme Environmental Conditions. LCAC can operate in most environmental conditions. However, precautions may have to be taken and equipment limitations imposed for LCAC operations in extreme cold weather, high sea state, and high heat and dust environments. Chapter 8 addresses LCAC operations in extreme environmental conditions.

CHAPTER 2

Planning

2.1 PURPOSE

This chapter provides guidance on the selection of LCAC areas, control points, transit lanes, and ingress/egress routes and the planning necessary for LCAC ship-to-shore movement. LCAC doctrine and terminology in this chapter supplement that found in NWP 3-02.1, Ship-to-Shore Movement, and provide the basic building blocks for planning amphibious operations involving LCAC.

2.2 BACKGROUND

LCAC can be used independently or in coordination with displacement landing craft to land troops, equipment, and supplies during the waterborne ship-to-shore movement. Although this chapter reflects the planning for a MEF FWD-size ATF operation, it can be used for any size operation.

Detailed planning for the ship-to-shore movement begins after the LF concept of operations ashore is approved by CATF and is conducted at both the operational level and the mission level. The ship-to-shore movement plan is the integrated sum of detailed plans, tables, diagrams, and schedules that are prepared by Navy and LF commanders. These documents provide the instructions for conducting the ship-to-shore movement and are issued by CATF and CLF as an appendix to the amphibious operations annex to the OPORD, message OPORD supplements, or an APP 4, "Allied Tactical Messages (U)" formatted message such as the OPTASK AMPHIB. The ship-to-shore movement plan is integrated with the plan for supporting fires and provides for the requisite CSS to the LF during the early stages of the assault. Together the documents composing the ship-to-shore movement, supporting fires, and CSS constitute the landing plan.

Chapter 3 of NWP 3-02.1 details the planning sequence CATF and CLF follow to land troops, equipment, and supplies at prescribed times and places. It also provides the ATF landing organization required to support the LF scheme of maneuver ashore, the formats for the naval landing plan (contained in CATF's OPORD) and the LF landing plan (contained in CLF's OPORD), and the contribution of each plan in developing the ship-to-shore movement plan. NWP 3-02.1 also discusses the organization of the landing area to show the inter-relationship between the planning process and the establishment of operating areas and control points to systematically and efficiently conduct amphibious operations.

2.3 AMPHIBIOUS OPERATION PLANNING

Planning for an amphibious operation involves co-ordination between all levels of the parallel chains of command established to support CATF and CLF. Commander's guidance, based on the LF concept of operations ashore, is provided to subordinate commanders. The means to land the LF are tabulated and apportioned. Subordinate commanders prepare individual plans, tables, schedules, and diagrams for approval and consolidation into the Naval and LF landing plans.

Chapter 3 of NWP 3-02.1 delineates the overall planning sequence for developing the landing plan. It consists of the naval landing plan and the LF landing plan and describes how the AOA and landing area are organized to facilitate amphibious operations. It further discusses the arrangement of LF troops, equipment, and supplies into five movement categories for delivery ashore. These categories include scheduled waves, on-call waves, nonscheduled units, prepositioned emergency supplies, and remaining LF supplies. The documents, organization of the landing area, and operational and mission level planning involved in the waterborne ship-to-shore movement of these five categories of troops, equipment, and supplies ashore by LCAC are presented in the remainder of this chapter.

2.4 PREPARATION OF DOCUMENTS

The documents prepared by Navy and LF commanders to plan the ship-to-shore movement, the document preparation sequence, and the relationship between the documents are described in chapter 3 of NWP 3-02.1. Documents necessary to plan waterborne ship-to-shore movement that include LCAC are listed in figure 2-1. Some or all of the documents listed in figure 2-1 may be included in the OPORD/OPTASK AMPHIB. Figure 2-1 has been annotated to indicate the applicable figure numbers in NWP 3-02.1 that provide samples of Navy and LF planning documents.

2.5 ORGANIZATION OF THE LANDING AREA

The landing area is that part of the AOA within which the landing operations of the ATF are conducted. It includes the sea echelon area, transport areas, approaches to the beach, the beach, land areas over which the LF must advance inland to the initial objective, and the air space occupied by close supporting aircraft. All LCAC ship-to-shore operations are conducted within the landing area.

Sea, beach, and inland operating areas in the landing area are selected to meet tactical requirements and facilitate control of the ship-to-shore movement. Chapter 3 of NWP 3-02.1 describes the complete organization of the landing area. The following paragraphs discuss the sea, beach, and inland organization of the landing area that LCAC operations affect. Figure 2-2 depicts the landing area and its LCAC-related components.

2.5.1 Sea Operating Areas. Sea operating areas in the landing area are established to minimize the possibility of mutual interference among elements of the ATF or supporting forces during amphibious operations. Sea operating areas in the landing area are established by CATF and promulgated in the OPORD/OPTASK AMPHIB.

Prepared by Navy	
Naval Landing Plan (figure 3-5) Landing Craft Availability Table (figure 3-6) Landing Craft Employment Plan (figure 3-7) Debarkation Schedule (prepared jointly by ship's CO and CO of troops) (figure 3-8) Approach Schedule (figure 3-10)	Assault Wave Diagram (figure 3-11) Landing Area Diagram (figure 3-12) Transport Area Diagram (figure 3-13) Sea Echelon Area Plan (figure 3-15) Landing Control Plan
Prepared by Landing Force	
LF Landing Plan (figure 3-16) Landing Craft and Amphibious Vehicle Assignment Table (figure 3-18) Landing Diagram (figure 3-19)	LF Serial Assignment Table (figure 3-20) LF Landing Sequence Table (figure 3-23) Assault Schedule (figure 3-24) GCE Landing Plan (figure 3-30)
Note: Figure numbers are from NWP 3-02.1.	

Figure 2-1. Listing of LCAC-Related Ship-to-Shore Movement Documents

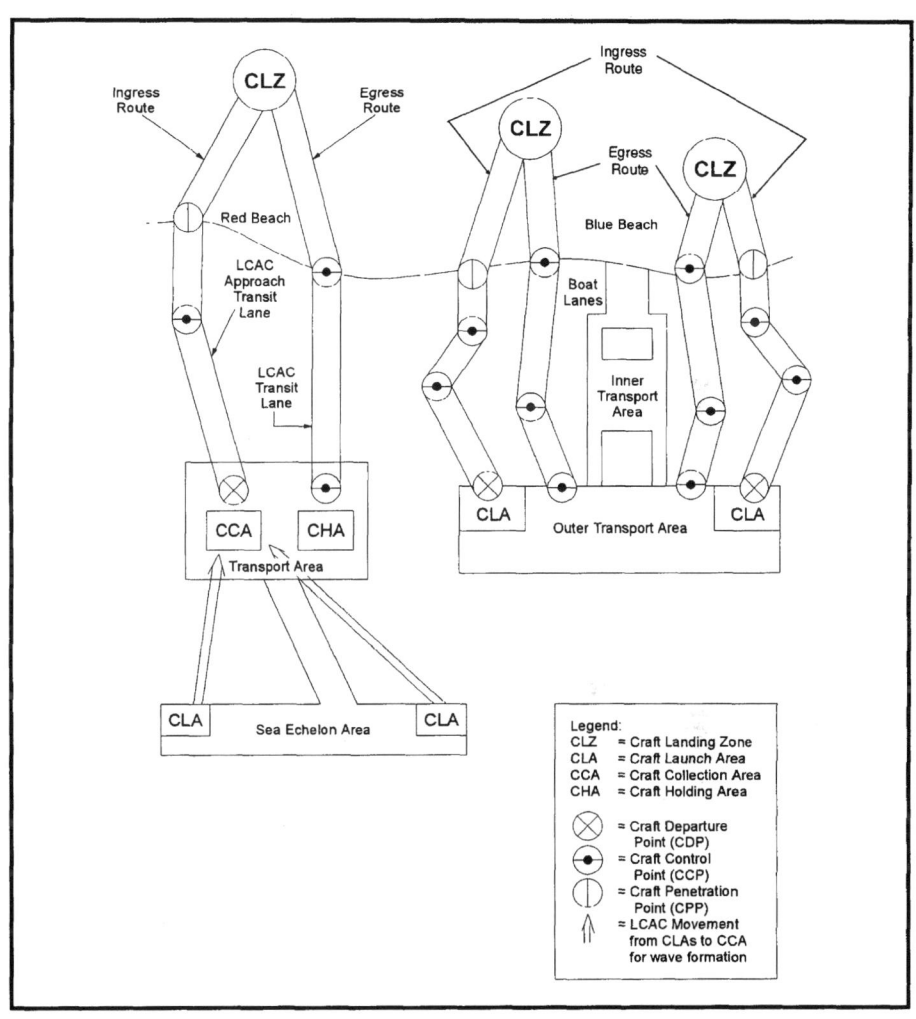

Figure 2-2. LCAC Operating Areas in the Landing Area

ORIGINAL

2.5.1.1 Transport Area. The transport area is an area assigned to a transport organization for the purpose of debarking troops and equipment. This area may be divided into inner and outer areas and includes the helicopter transport area. A transport area supports one or more colored beaches, depending on the distance between beaches, and their supporting CLZs or HLZs.

2.5.1.1.1 Outer Transport Area. The outer transport area is an area to which assault shipping proceeds upon entering the AOA. This area is located sufficiently seaward of landing beaches to be beyond shore battery range. Assault shipping remains underway in the outer transport area and may initiate an assault from OTH or proceed into the inner transport area for a near-shore assault. LCAC may be launched or recovered in the outer transport area.

2.5.1.1.2 Inner Transport Area. The inner transport area is used to expedite unloading and is located as close to the landing beach as the depth of water, navigational hazards, boat traffic, and enemy action permit. LCAC may be launched or recovered in the inner transport area.

2.5.1.2 LCAC Areas, Control Points, and Transit Lanes. The location of LCAC areas, transit lanes, and control points is based primarily on the tactical situation, geography, timing, and safety considerations involved in the operation. While chapter 4 of this NWP explains their use in the control of the LCAC ship-to-shore movement, the following paragraphs provide guidance on locating LCAC areas, transit lanes, and control points. CATF, or his designated representative within the landing control organization, selects LCAC areas, control points, and transit lanes.

2.5.1.2.1 Craft Launch Area and Craft Departure Point. The CLA is where LCAC launch occurs and is located anywhere in the landing area from several thousand yards to 100 nm seaward. The CLA is connected to the CPP (see paragraph 2.5.2.1) by LCAC transit lanes through various control points. The CDP is the geographic position marking the seaward end of the LCAC transit lane. The CLA usually encompasses the CDP and is sized to provide ample LCAC maneuvering room between the launching ship and the CDP. However, during OTH operations, CLAs may be located at substantial distances seaward from the CDP to facilitate the independent transit of LCAC from multiple CLAs

to a common CCA where LCAC waves can be formed prior to passing through the CDP.

As the initial control point in the LCAC transit lane, the CDP should be positioned at least 500 yards from other transit lanes to preclude interference. Other considerations in CDP selection include:

1. Distance from the beach (to permit LCAC tactical maneuvering)

2. Desired proximity to the well deck ships

3. Mission parameters including payload, environment, and time line

4. Enemy threat including the proximity to minefields.

2.5.1.2.2 LCAC Transit Lane. An LCAC transit lane is the sea route between the CDP and the CPP. The length of the transit lane is dependent upon the number and position of control points through which it passes. Its width should allow sufficient maneuvering room for LCAC transiting in formation, and it should approach other landing craft transit lanes no closer than 500 yards. A separate return transit lane is normally provided. To allow for LCAC sideslip and beach marking identification, the final leg of the approach transit lane should be 1 to 5 nm long depending on the severity of the turn from the previous leg.

2.5.1.2.3 Craft Control Point. CCPs are points along the LCAC transit lanes through which LCAC will pass proceeding to and from the beach. CCPs usually mark LCAC course changes made for the following reasons:

1. Tactical (deception or evasive maneuvers)

2 .Environmental/geographical conditions (i.e., go around an island, avoid head wind or sea conditions, cross the surf perpendicular to waves)

3. Traffic control (i.e., go around traffic, establish a traffic pattern)

4. Rendezvous or decision point

5. Timing approach with scheduled friendly fire.

When possible, CCPs should be positioned to minimize the length of the transit lane. They should also be positioned to preclude large course changes, particularly when LCAC are transiting in formation/in the vicinity of other landing craft. Smaller course changes will minimize side-slip and reduction in speed during the turn, and will help LCAC maintain track and time line. If the angle of the surf allows, the final leg of the transit lane should be straight and as close to perpendicular to the beach as possible.

2.5.1.2.4 Craft Holding Area. CHAs can be used when there are multiple CLAs and there is a need to clear LCAC from CLZs for tactical reasons or to make room for follow-on waves. When required, CHAs should be located seaward of the CDP and equidistant from the CLAs. Use of CHAs increases LCAC cycle times and routine use of CHAs is, therefore, not recommended. Proper planning will facilitate dispatch of LCAC from the beach directly to the locations of the next loads. LCAC should not loiter at sea while waiting for further tasking.

2.5.1.3 Sea Echelon Area. The sea echelon area is located in the landing area seaward of the transport area. The ATF operates in the sea echelon area for dispersion and mobility. Assault shipping from the sea echelon area may be phased in and out of transport areas as the assault progresses. The sea echelon area may contain multiple CLAs to support LCAC operations. Chapter 3 of NWP 3-02.1 provides additional information on the sea echelon concept of operations.

2.5.2 LCAC Beach and Inland Operating Areas. CLF, in coordination with CATF, selects the location of LCAC beach and inland operating areas beyond the high water mark. LCAC beach and inland areas include CPPs, CLZs, CLSs, and ingress and egress routes. Extreme care should be exercised in the selection of LCAC beach and inland areas to avoid interference with other beach and inland area operations.

Note

The CPPs, CLZs, and ingress/egress routes should be separated from AAV and displacement landing craft areas by at least 500 yards. Where beach separation of 500 yards is not feasible, LCAC, displacement landing craft, and AAVs may land across the same beach. However, sufficient time must exist between scheduled waves to preclude LCAC overtaking slower vehicles/craft and avoid a beach congestion/LCAC turnaround problem.

2.5.2.1 Craft Penetration Point. A CPP is the geographic position where LCAC crosses the high water mark at the landward end of an LCAC transit lane. The selection of CPPs is influenced by a variety of factors, including ease of identification, tactical scheme of maneuver ashore, local topography, and suitability of nearby CLZs. Selection should be based upon adequate and current intelligence. Although CATF selects CPPs and CLF selects the corresponding ingress and egress routes and CLZs, their selection is interdependent. In general, CPPs are selected based on the type of surf, beach obstacles, and the availability of suitable routes to and from the CLZs to permit safe craft operation.

2.5.2.2 Ingress and Egress Routes. Ingress and egress routes are the paths LCAC must traverse from the CPP to the CLZ and from the CLZ back to the beach. Separate ingress and egress routes are desirable. CLF selects ingress and egress routes with CATF's concurrence.

The following terrain features may preclude using otherwise suitable areas as ingress/egress routes:

1. Large areas covered with tall grass and reeds

2. Trees greater than 4 inches in diameter and taller than 18 feet

3. A single tree greater than 6 inches in diameter and taller than 25 feet

4. Wooden or metal spikes taller than 2.5 feet

5. Earth banks wider than 8 feet, and vertical step-ups and negative relief greater than 4 feet

6. Ditches greater than 4 feet deep and 15 feet wide

7. Littoral bands of boulders, rocks, and rubble wider than 4 feet

8. Walls taller than 4 feet

9. Flat up-slope gradients greater than 6°.

2.5.2.3 Craft Landing Zone. A CLZ is the area on the beach or inland in which LCAC come off-cushion to offload or onload personnel, equipment, and cargo. It is connected with the CPP by an ingress route. CLZs are selected based on a variety of factors supporting the LF scheme of maneuver ashore. These factors include proximity to other landing operations to facilitate the rapid uniting of forces and material, number of LCAC required simultaneously in the CLZ, type of cargo discharged, proximity to HLZs/colored beaches when troop and equipment assembly is required, general terrain features, trafficability, absence of mines, and avoidance of bottlenecks leading into and out of CLZs. A CLZ should be of sufficient size to accommodate the number of LCAC to be offloaded simultaneously. The same terrain features that affect route selection also affect CLZ selection (see paragraph 2.5.2.2). CLF selects CLZs with CATF's concurrence. CLZs will be named for the beach on which they are located; for example, CLZ Blue would be the CLZ on Blue Beach. If more than one CLZ is located on a colored beach then each CLZ will also receive a numerical designation such as CLZ Blue One.

2.5.2.4 Craft Landing Site. A CLS is an individual LCAC landing spot within the CLZ. As a planning estimate, at least a 150-foot diameter area is required for each LCAC. The size of the CLS must be increased for sloping terrain, weather conditions, or other natural or man-made features which require greater LCAC maneuvering room.

2.5.3 Operating Area Selection Responsibilities. Figure 2-3 provides a matrix which summarizes CATF and CLF responsibilities for selecting operating areas within the landing area.

2.6 LCAC SHIP-TO-SHORE MOVEMENT PLANNING

The scheme of maneuver ashore drives the ship-to-shore movement. The assets required to execute the ship-to-shore movement depend on how much is to be landed, how fast, and by what means. Ship-to-shore movement planning must consider the number of available LCAC, LCAC standard loads, total lifts required, LCAC cycles, and required rate of build up.

2.6.1 LCAC Available. The total number of LCAC available for the surface assault is a function of the number of LCAC carried by ATF ships (see figure 1-3)

Operating Areas within the Landing Area	Selection Responsibilities	
	CATF (Note 1)	CLF (Notes 1 and 2)
Outer Transport Area	X	
Inner Transport Area	X	
Craft Launch Area (CLA)	X	
Craft Collection Area (CCA)	X	
Craft Departure Point (CDP)	X	
LCAC Transit Lanes	X	
Craft Control Point (CCP)	X	
Craft Holding Area (CHA)	X	
Sea Echelon Area	X	
Craft Penetration Point (CPP)	X (Note 3)	
Ingress/Egress Routes		X
Craft Landing Zone (CLZ)		X
Craft Landing Site (CLS)		X

Notes:
1. CATF and CLF may designate representatives within their respective control organizations to select certain operating areas within the landing area.
2. All selections made by CLF are subject to review/concurrence by CATF from a supportability perspective.
3. Subject to review/concurrence by CLF from a scheme of maneuver supportability perspective.

Figure 2-3. Operating Area Selection Responsibilities Matrix

and the anticipated reliability of those craft. Based upon LCAC's operational record, an availability exceeding 90 percent can be expected throughout the initial surface assault. The total number of LCAC available, therefore, is the number of LCAC carried by the ATF less 10 percent.

2.6.2 LCAC Standard Load. An LCAC standard load is used in developing notional landing plans and is defined as a combination of troops, vehicles, and cargo that can be carried by LCAC under ideal conditions. It is based on an overload weight of 75 short tons and a usable deck area of 1,809 square feet. Use of standard loads ensures that the capacity of the LCAC is utilized as fully as possible, that loading the LCAC beyond design limits is avoided, and that an operationally feasible notional landing plan can be developed with minimum effort. A properly trimmed and loaded LCAC can carry cargo in excess of the 75 ton overload limitation if the LCAC maximum gross weight of 368,250 pounds is not exceeded and local environmental conditions allow. LCAC would be required to carry less fuel which, in addition to reducing range, reduces the ability of the crew to maintain proper trim. Loads approaching the maximum gross weight may also render the craft incapable of achieving and maintaining hump speed in high sea states or winds.

2.6.2.1 Environmental Conditions. The capability of LCAC to carry a standard load is affected by sea state and temperature. This capability assumes certain environmental conditions which include head seas, sea state 2, and 80° Fahrenheit. Increasing sea state or decreasing temperature below freezing will decrease LCAC's capability to carry a standard load. The effect of temperature and sea state on LCAC load capability can be computed using the MPP discussed in paragraph 2.7.

2.6.2.2 Load Considerations. When planning LCAC loads, the following should be considered:

1. As LCAC rides on an air cushion, the load center of gravity must correspond closely to the LCAC center of gravity. Therefore, cargo spotting is critical. Load distribution required to maintain balanced loads must be considered as well as weight and area limitations. LCAC has only a limited capacity to shift fuel to compensate for load imbalance. Volume IV, part 1, chapter 3 of the "Safe Engineering

and Operations (SEAOPS) Manual for Landing Craft Air Cushion (LCAC)" addresses LCAC cargo loading considerations.

2. Standard loads are defined to ensure the maximum capacity of LCAC is used in developing landing plans. Operational considerations may dictate the use of less than maximum capacity. For instance, although an LCAC may have the capacity to carry AAVs and HMMWVs simultaneously, carrying only AAVs in the first wave to seize CLZs preserves the tactical option of launching the AAVs at sea for the final leg of the transit to the beach.

3. In planning ship-to-shore movements, loads smaller than standard loads may be desired for a variety of operational reasons. When this occurs, the total number of LCAC sorties will increase and the ship-to-shore movement timing may be affected.

4. In planning LCAC preloads, routine craft loading over 60 short tons should be avoided to facilitate assault operations in a variety of environmental conditions. LCAC in an overloaded condition (60 to 75 short ton loads) may not be able to achieve hump speeds when less than optimum environmental conditions are encountered, necessitating lightening of loads and potential delays in the ship-to-shore movement. The ramifications of various preload configurations should be an integral part of preembarkation planning discussions between Navy and LF staffs.

2.6.2.3 Vehicle Weight and Area Requirements. The vehicle weights used in planning LCAC loads should include the weight of crew, troops, equipment, and fuel that is not an integral part of the vehicle. Appendix C provides the weights and area requirements for Marine Corps vehicles frequently embarked in LCAC.

2.6.2.4 Standard Load Equivalents. LCAC standard load equivalents are variations of LCAC standard loads. Appendix C provides examples of standard loads and standard load equivalents which may be used in the development of landing plans. See Volume IV of SEAOPS for additional guidance in LCAC load planning.

2.6.3 Total Lifts Required. Based on standard loads, the total number of LCAC lifts required is a function of the size and composition of the intended surface assault of the LF.

2.6.4 Number of LCAC Cycles. An LCAC cycle is defined as a single trip to the beach with a tactical load during the ship-to-shore movement. The number of LCAC cycles can be determined by dividing the total lifts required by the number of LCAC available.

2.6.5 Cycle Time. Cycle time is the total time for an LCAC to complete one mission. The time required to execute the LCAC ship to shore movement is measured from the first LCAC touchdown in the CLZ. Subsequent cycle times include offload in the CLZ, transit from the CLZ to the well deck, onload in the well deck, refueling if necessary, and transit from the well deck to the CLZ. Other considerations for cycle times based on variables such as LCAC and displacement landing craft mixes are discussed in appendix B.

2.6.5.1 Transit Considerations. Transit considerations and procedures to reduce cycle times are based primarily on sea state and its affect on LCAC speed (see paragraph 1.2.1.3.1), and craft loading and its affect on hump transition (see paragraph 1.2.1.3.4). While LCAC can exceed 40 knots in sea state 0 or 1, the combination of seas, swell, and wind in higher sea states can reduce LCAC maximum speed significantly. Transit considerations, most of which are taken into account in the MPP, include:

1. LCAC on-cushion operations are possible up to sea state 3, and under some combinations of wind and seas up to sea state 4.

2. Approximately 20 seconds are required for LCAC to go on- or off-cushion.

3. Maximum speeds over ground for planning LCAC transit times are depicted in figure 2-4. Actual LCAC transit speeds should be based on LCAC load, projected or observed sea state and ambient temperature in the area of operation. Transit speeds must be above hump speed and at least 25 knots. Assuming optimum environmental conditions and high transit speeds can result in LCACs not meeting ship-to-shore time line requirements.

Sea State	Speed (kt) (Overground)	
	Inbound	Outbound
0 to 1	45	50
2	38	42
3 (≥ 80 °F)	18	40
3 (≤ 80 °F)	18	35
4	5	5

Figure 2-4. Maximum Speed for Planning LCAC Transit Times

Time line and transit speeds may need to be adjusted based on changing weather conditions.

4. Transits directly into seas, wind, or swells may reduce maximum available speed in sea states 2 and 3 to as low as 8 knots, depending on the wave period.

5. The worst sea effect occurs when the crest-to-wave separation is near one craft length (approximately 90 feet). Effects can be minimized by putting the seas 25° to 45° relative off either bow.

6. Running downwind and with the seas can reduce maximum available speed, particularly when there are long, rolling swells. LCAC tend to surf down the front side of swells, plow-in at the bottom, and decelerate up the back side of the next swell. As a result, craft heading becomes difficult to maintain.

7. With a full load in sea state 3, LCAC may have to accelerate over hump on a downwind heading before turning to the transit course. Plan loaded LCAC transits to the beach when feasible with the seas and downwind to optimize LCAC's ability to achieve and maintain hump speed.

8. The higher the speed, the greater the turn radius for any major course change.

9. Drag buildup at speeds between 12 and 25 knots causes LCAC to become difficult to handle. Therefore, to avoid loss of maneuverability do not plan LCAC operations for speeds between 13 and 24 knots.

2.6.5.2 Other Procedures to Reduce Cycle
Times. Other procedures to reduce cycle times are primarily concerned with operations on the beach and in the well deck. Procedures to reduce cycle times, some of which are taken into account in the MPP, include:

1. Minimize the time well decks are empty.

2. Plan for the efficient use of LCAC but ensure that the estimated LCAC time in the well deck is not too short.

3. Verify the shipboard staging of subsequent LCAC loads against the desired beach offload sequence and correct errors in advance of LCAC onload.

4. Load and gripe equipment on LCAC simultaneously. Set gripes properly and use dedicated griping teams to reduce load and gripe times. All Marine Corps equipment crews are trained in griping their own equipment.

5. Position returning tractor-trailer combinations to ensure there will be no requirement for turnaround in the well deck.

6. Position LCAC in the well deck so that bow and stern ramps can be used to load and position vehicles.

7. Coordinate helicopter landings on ship flight decks to reduce interference with LCAC operations.

8. Minimize LCAC beach and inland area congestion, including awkward cargo and stuck vehicles.

9. Minimize cryptographic changes that might result in loss of communications with LCAC or delays in the delivery of new cryptographic material.

10. Incorporate LCAC refueling requirements into detailed planning.

11. Coordinate LCAC well deck operations with other boat and landing craft operations.

12. Plan for reduced visibility operations.

13. Maximize vehicle loads on LCAC.

14. Ensure palletized LCAC loads are banded securely and protected from water intrusion to avoid packaging deterioration which can lead to FOD.

15. Ensure LCAC are launched from the beach promptly to minimize the time between departure of one LCAC from the well deck and entry of the next one.

16. Lower and use both LCAC ramps to reduce CLZ onload time.

17. Conduct FOD inspections of all vehicles prior to loading.

2.6.6 Rate of Combat Power Buildup Ashore.
The LF must build up combat power ashore fast enough to meet the enemy threat of counterattack. Depending on intelligence estimates of a high, mid, or low threat of enemy counterattack, CLF can determine the rate of combat power buildup ashore necessary to meet the enemy threat. If it takes too long to build up sufficient combat power ashore, adjustments to LCAC loads/LCAC cycle times must be made to increase the rate of combat power delivery, or other tactical options must be explored to support the LF.

2.6.7 Efficient LCAC Employment.
It is possible to compute the maximum number of LCAC required to efficiently unload a ship given its standoff distance from the landing beach and the expected time in the well deck for each craft. Figure 2-5 provides a nomograph for use in planning the maximum number of LCAC to assign to a ship for unloading. The nomograph assumes an average LCAC transit speed of 40 knots, 15 minutes on the beach for each craft, and sequential entering of the well deck. The maximum number of LCAC can also be computed by dividing the cycle time by the time in the well deck (see appendix B for unloading data for specific classes of amphibious ships).

In some cases, two LCAC can perform an offload of an amphibious ship just as efficiently as three LCAC. When the length of time a single LCAC spends in the well deck is approximately the same as the time for a round trip transit to the CLZ and back, two LCAC can sustain full time well deck operations.

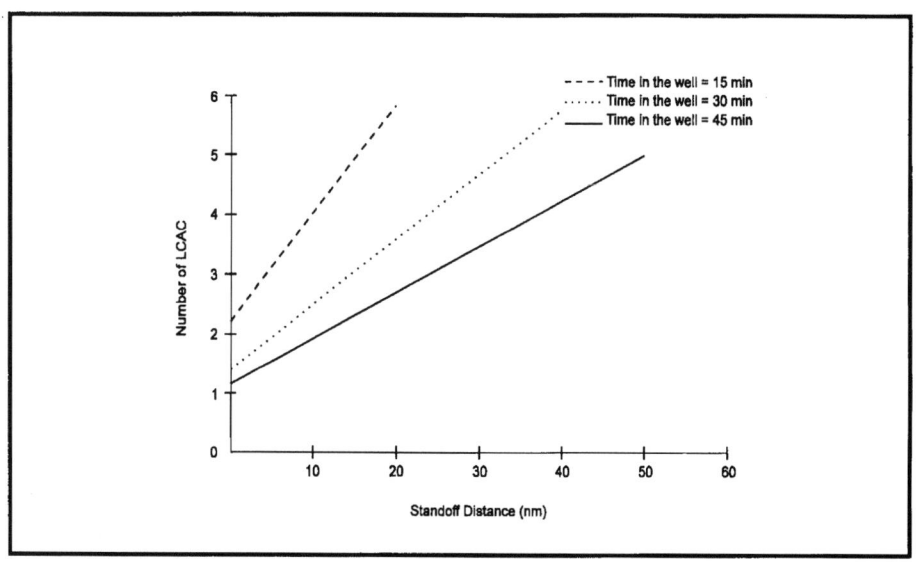

Figure 2-5. Maximum Number of LCAC to Assign to a Ship for Unloading

The use of a third LCAC results in excessive loiter time while waiting to enter the well deck.

2.7 MISSION PLANNING PROCEDURE

MPP is a step-by-step procedure that provides the LCAC mission planner an accurate means of estimating craft performance, fuel requirements, and performance limitations necessary to adequately plan a mission. MPP is contained in Volume 5 of SEAOPS.

The advantage of using the MPP is that the mission planner can determine not only craft performance, but also mission feasibility while ensuring craft and crew safety during LCAC operations. The MPP is applicable to all potential LCAC missions.

The staff planner can use the MPP to preplan specific missions using nominal data for a typical LCAC and assumed environmental conditions. The craftmas-

ter can use MPP to verify the craft's capability to fulfill the given mission based upon specific craft data and current environmental conditions.

MPP factors are derived from LCAC mission details; environmental conditions; and data on the surf zone, beach conditions, and overland terrain. MPP factors can be broken down into the categories of craft and other factors.

2.7.1 Craft Factors. Craft factors are those factors that affect LCAC's capability to accomplish its mission. The interaction of craft factors are analyzed in the MPP, resulting in an operational plan for the specified mission which includes maximum cargo capacity, fuel requirement, engine requirements, courses and speeds, distance traveled, and duration of the mission. Craft requirements include:

1. Geographic positions: launch, CLZ, recovery alternatives

2. Geographic considerations: CPP, ingress/egress routes, CLS

3. Distance to CLZ: inbound, over water and land; return, over land and water

4. Courses: inbound, outbound

5. Speed: inbound, over water and land; return, over land and water

6. Time: inbound (amount), depart ship (clock) and arrive CLZ (clock); return (amount), depart CLZ (clock) and arrive ship (clock)

7. Fuel: required percent capacity, required refuel sites

8. Payload: cargo weight, fuel weight, special considerations

9. Environmental factors: temperature, sea state, wind direction and velocity, visibility, surf conditions, terrain conditions, tidal status, current considerations

10. Craft status: crew, maintenance, repair, known limitations, armament.

2.7.2 Other Factors. Other factors are those derived from intelligence, communications, and operational factors which must be integrated with the MPP results to provide a complete LCAC mission plan. Intelligence factors include the status of the enemy threat en route, on, and beyond the beach and updates to geographic characteristics and environmental factors. Communications to support the LCAC mission plan are in accordance with the current ATF communications plan. Operational factors include the use of beach markers and lights, location of control points and transit lanes, and beach and shore party instructions.

2.8 LCAC NIGHT AND LOW VISIBILITY SHIP-TO-SHORE MOVEMENT

LCAC ship-to-shore operations at night and during periods of low visibility are subject to the same advantages and disadvantages as displacement landing craft.

2.8.1 Advantages. LCAC ship-to-shore movements are conducted at night to exploit the tactical advantages of landing under the cover of darkness. Similarly, low visibility conditions can be used to mask the movements of LCAC during the day. The principal tactical advantage of both is the reduced probability of detection by visual or electro-optical means.

2.8.2 Disadvantages. Disadvantages of LCAC ship-to-shore movements at night and during periods of low visibility may include a requirement for increased separation between LCAC and displacement landing craft operations, stricter LCAC movement control procedures, and changing the timing of LCAC assault waves. In general, night and low visibility operations take longer than operations in daylight and may result in a slower buildup of LF combat power ashore. The possibility of low visibility conditions existing in the landing area should be considered in developing alternative landing plans.

2.8.3 Sea State Concerns. During night and low visibility operations, the sea state is of greater concern to LCAC than during conditions of clear visibility in daylight. During daylight when visibility is clear or in extremely bright moonlight at night, the LCAC craftmaster can vary propeller pitch and other control inputs to lessen the impact of swells on his craft. At night/during low visibility, it is virtually impossible for the craftmaster to anticipate swells and wave action, even with the use of NVGs. As the sea state increases, the potential for damage to LCAC and its payload increases and LCAC speed must be reduced accordingly. In higher sea states, the LCAC may not be able to safely attain and maintain speeds for over the hump operation.

2.8.4 Planning Emphasis. In planning LCAC night and low visibility operations, additional emphasis should be placed on:

1. Time, distance, and route separation modifications

2. Anticipated effects of sea state on safe speed and achieving hump transition

3. Control procedure modifications

4. Anticipated ambient lighting, restricted/reduced visibility, and meteorological conditions

5. Anticipated illumination

6. LCAC group transit formations to be employed

7. LCAC lighting requirements

8. CLZ lighting requirements

9. Additional LCAC crew coordination requirements

10. Additional safety precautions for LCAC crew and embarked troops

11. EMCON relaxations.

CHAPTER 3

Preassault Operations and Amphibious Raids

3.1 PURPOSE

This chapter provides guidance on the employment of LCAC in preassault operations and amphibious raids.

3.2 PREASSAULT OPERATIONS

A preassault operation is an operation conducted in the AOA prior to the commencement of the assault phase. It may include reconnaissance, minesweeping, bombardment, underwater demolition, and destruction of beach obstacles.

Preassault operations are conducted by elements of the ATF which are normally organized as an advance force. Joint Pub 3-02, "Joint Doctrine for Amphibious Operations," provides guidance on the conduct of preassault operations, including advance force operations. The objectives of preassault operations may include:

1. Isolation of the landing area

2. Gaining information about the enemy

3. Preparing the landing area for the assault.

The unique capabilities of LCAC can be used to achieve any or all of these objectives. While assigned to the advance force, LCAC may be employed as a reconnaissance and special warfare asset or as an MCAC for mine warfare or tactical deception.

Note

The acronym MCAC has been mistakenly used in various tactical documents to represent an MCM-configured LCAC.

MCAC actually stands for multimission craft air cushion. When used in this NWP, MCAC is a collective term to describe LCAC configured to perform MCM, deception van, or personnel transport module missions.

3.2.1 LCAC's Role in Reconnaissance and Special Warfare. Reconnaissance and special warfare assets include ships, LF RECON teams, and SEAL teams assigned to conduct reconnaissance, hydrographic surveys, demolition of natural and man-made obstacles, and other special operations missions in the landing area.

LCAC's speed, range, and payload make it a viable platform for delivering RECON/SEAL teams from OTH ranges to dropoff points seaward of the enemy's shore. These teams can gather intelligence and prepare inland, beach, and beach approach areas for subsequent LCAC ship-to-shore movement. LCAC employed in such operations are normally assigned to the reconnaissance and special warfare group of the advance force. The use of LCAC in delivery of RECON/SEAL teams presupposes that the craft are not preloaded or that preloads were offloaded in ATF shipping.

3.2.1.1 Delivery of RECON and SEAL Teams. Clandestine delivery of RECON/SEAL teams from OTH may be desirable to avoid compromise of the landing plan. At the same time, delivery closer to the shore may be desirable to reduce the physical demands of long open-water transits in small boats. With its high speed and extended range, LCAC can be used for rapid, long-range delivery of RECON/SEAL teams in CRRC without substantial degradation to team physical readiness.

3.2.1.1.1 Concept of Operations. Each LCAC can transport up to 12 CRRC, including outboard motors, fuel tanks/bladders, and support equipment. Unaugmented, an LCAC may only carry 24 RECON/SEAL personnel. LCAC can be configured with MCESS shelters or PTM sections, as discussed in chapter 7, to increase the number of RECON/SEAL personnel carried. With one MCESS shelter or one PTM section embarked, LCAC can transport 63 or 54 personnel, respectively, in addition to approximately 10 CRRCs. The unique physical characteristics of CRRC mandate special underway securing procedures on LCAC which are described in Volume IV, Part 1, Chapter 5 of the "Safe Engineering and Operations (SEAOPs) Manual for Landing Craft Air Cushion (LCAC)" (LCAC Loadmasters Manual).

LCAC depart advance force ships positioned OTH, transit to dropoff points specified in the advance force plan, and launch CRRC with RECON/SEAL teams embarked. LCAC craftmasters provide each CRRC coxswain a magnetic heading to the selected landing point on the enemy's shore prior to the CRRC's departure. Upon completion of reconnaissance and special warfare operations ashore, LCAC may return to designated pickup points to recover the CRRC.

3.2.1.1.2 CRRC Launch and Recovery Operations. LCAC launch and recovery of CRRC must be conducted in sea state 3 or less. LCAC sequence for CRRC launch is:

1. Come off-cushion

2. Maneuver the bow into the seas at bare steerageway

3. Lower the stern ramp

4. Ungripe, position, load, and launch the CRRC.

LCAC sequence for CRRC recovery is:

1. Come off-cushion

2. Maneuver the bow into the seas at bare steerageway

3. Lower the stern ramp

4. Recover, unload, position, and secure the CRRC.

The LCAC Loadmaster Manual provides safety guidelines and detailed procedures for CRRC launch and recovery.

3.2.1.2 RECON and SEAL Team Support of LCAC Ship-to-Shore Movement. RECON/SEAL team preassault hydrographic, beach, and inland area reconnaissance may result in the collection of intelligence critical to the planning of subsequent LCAC ship-to-shore movement.

Hydrographic reconnaissance can detect and classify mine-like objects and obstacles in VSW and the SZ which might pose a threat to waterborne LCAC operations. Reconnaissance of beach and inland areas can identify suitable CPPs, ingress and egress routes, and CLZs; detect and classify mine-like objects and obstacles on the beach; and provide intelligence on lights, landmarks, or other prominent radar points to facilitate terminal guidance of LCAC during ship-to-shore movement. Chapter 2, paragraph 2.5.2.2 provides a description of beach and inland terrain features used to evaluate potential CPPs, ingress/egress routes, and CLZs.

RECON/SEAL teams can also provide direct landing support to LCAC ship-to-shore movement by:

1. Placing IR strobes to mark CPPs for night assaults

2. Providing initial terminal guidance of LCAC into CLZs

3. Calling for and adjusting supporting fires

4. Conducting limited mine clearance operations from the 21 foot curve to the seaward end of the SZ (SEALs only)

5. Verifying the effectiveness of surface and airborne mine countermeasures and placing buoys to mark cleared lanes through the SZ and VSW region

6. Neutralizing obstructions blocking otherwise suitable CLZs.

In addition, RECON/SEAL teams may provide laser designation in support of CAS for targets threatening LCAC/MCAC operations.

3.2.2 LCAC's Role in Mine Warfare. LCAC's speed, maneuverability, payload, air cushion capability, and sustainability make it a viable candidate for use in MCM. Preliminary test and evaluation indicates the MCM-configured LCAC is effective in minesweeping and mine hunting roles and as a launch platform for breaching the SZ with line charges (see chapter 7). If employed, MCM-configured LCAC are assigned to the mine warfare group of the advance force.

3.2.2.1 Minesweeping and Mine Hunting. The MCM-configured LCAC can stream, tow, operate, and recover the same mechanical and influence minesweeping and mine hunting equipment as AMCM helicopters. The time for MCM-configured LCAC to stream and recover that equipment appears to be comparable to AMCM helicopter times. However, the on-station time for the MCM-configured LCAC is greater than that of AMCM helicopters.

3.2.2.2 SZ Breaching. MCM-configured LCAC is an effective platform for firing M58 linear demolition charges to help establish breach lanes through the SZ and to further reduce the threat of mines to LCAC ship-to-shore movement. This employment of MCM-configured LCAC remains under development at the writing of this NWP.

3.2.3 LCAC's Role in Tactical Deception. LCAC's speed, range, and payload make it a viable platform for use in tactical deception operations in and en route the AOA. A deception van-configured LCAC may be employed in feints, amphibious demonstrations, or as an EA platform to deceive the enemy during amphibious operations. Chapter 7 describes deception van-configured LCAC in more detail.

3.3 AMPHIBIOUS RAIDS

An amphibious raid is an amphibious operation involving swift incursion into or temporary occupation of an objective followed by a planned withdrawal. It involves the use of LF assets which are relatively light, highly mobile, and tailored for a specific mission. The objectives of an amphibious raid may include:

1. Inflicting loss or damage

2. Securing information

3. Creating a diversion

4. Capturing or evacuating individuals/material

5. Executing deliberate deception operations

6. Destroying enemy information gathering systems to support OPSEC.

Surprise is most critical to the success of an amphibious raid. A raid force may be inserted by surface, subsurface, or air (helicopter, parachute, etc.) means. It may be launched from the advance force during pre-assault operations or from the ATF main body at any time during the amphibious operation.

LCAC, with its unique speed and endurance, can be used to deliver and withdraw a surface raid force. LCAC may be used to:

1. Deliver a raid force directly ashore

2. Deliver a mechanized raid force to a launch point seaward of the beach

3. Deliver a boated raid force to an insertion point seaward of the beach.

3.3.1 Delivery of a Raid Force Directly Ashore. LCAC can deliver a raid force directly ashore and/or extract the raid force upon completion of its mission. The raid force may consist of any combination of mechanized, motorized, waterborne, or foot mobile troops and equipment task organized to accomplish the assigned mission.

LCAC's speed and load capacity enable it to deliver equipment and personnel to an objective area quickly and effectively, particularly across swampy or low-lying areas or up rivers to inland CLZs. Once vehicles disembark, the LCAC can remain in the vicinity of the CLZ or relocate. By having LCAC skirt beach landing zones and transit up a flanking river or waterway, an LAV/FAV-equipped force can threaten an enemy with flanking movements and multiple fronts.

Each LCAC can carry two combat-loaded AAVs or four combat-loaded LAVs with a total of 42 and 24 troops, including crews, respectively. An additional 24 personnel can be accommodated in the port and starboard LCAC cabins.

3.3.2 Delivery of a Mechanized Raid Force to a Launch Point.
LCAC can deliver a mechanized raid force comprised of AAVs to a launch point seaward of the beach if required by the amphibious raid plan. Considerations for LCAC AAV launch at sea are:

1. Launch must be conducted in sea state 1 or less

2. Since launch is potentially hazardous to LCAC, AAV, and personnel, safety must be paramount

3. Extreme care must be taken throughout to secure all AAV equipment and antennas to prevent possible FOD to LCAC propellers and lift fans

4. Launch shall be conducted off the stern ramp only (this necessitates the loading of AAVs facing aft)

5. LCAC crew shall be augmented to a minimum of 7 to meet the additional safety requirements of AAV launch

6. LCAC cannot recover AAVs at sea and must extract the raid force from CLZs during the withdrawal phase of the operation.

The sequence for LCAC AAV launch is:

1. Come off-cushion and cease forward movement

2. Lower and rig the stern ramp

3. Remove tiedowns from the first AAV

4. Position the AAV

5. Get underway with a speed of approximately three knots

6. Launch the AAV

7. Inspect the stern ramp and rigging

8. Repeat the cycle for the remaining AAV.

The LCAC Loadmasters Manual describes rigging, launch procedures, and safety actions that must be implemented when conducting AAV launches from LCAC.

3.3.3 Delivery of a Boated Raid Force to an Insertion Point.
LCAC can deliver a boated raid force to an insertion point seaward of the beach for launch in CRRC. The procedures for launching and recovering CRRC are outlined in paragraph 3.2.1.1.2.

3.4 LCAC PLANNING FOR PREASSAULT OPERATIONS AND AMPHIBIOUS RAIDS

Planning for LCAC employment in preassault operations and amphibious raids is subject to the same guidance as planning for LCAC ship-to-shore movement. Chapter 2 of this NWP provides the guidance for planning LCAC employment. The LF space aboard ATF shipping needed to stow equipment used for the various LCAC configurations must be considered in the overall planning process. The reduction in the number of LCAC available for ship-to-shore movement due to LCAC multimission configuration operations must also be considered.

3.5 CONTROL OF LCAC IN PREASSAULT OPERATIONS AND AMPHIBIOUS RAIDS

Control of LCAC in preassault operations and amphibious raids is similar to control during LCAC ship-to-shore movement. LCAC control areas, organizations, and communications may be tailored to the requirements of the pertinent operations plan. Chapter 4 of this NWP provides guidance for the control of LCAC during ship-to-shore movement.

CHAPTER 4

Ship-to-Shore Movement

4.1 INTRODUCTION

The LCAC ship-to-shore movement, including movement from OTH, commences when the CATF executes the signal "Land the landing force" and concludes when all LCAC-capable ship loads have been delivered to the beach. The final preparations, approach, positioning, and landing sequence for an LCAC-equipped ATF are the same as those described in NWP 3-02.2M, "Ship-to-Shore Movement," chapter 4.

This chapter discusses LCAC ship-to-shore movement organization and control; communications; and procedures for debarking, dispatching, turnaround at the beach, return to force, and general unloading during ship-to-shore movement.

4.2 LCAC SHIP-TO-SHORE MOVEMENT ORGANIZATION AND CONTROL

The waterborne ship-to-shore movement control organization is the Navy control group. The CCO is designated by CATF to organize the Navy control group and to plan and conduct the overall waterborne ship-to-shore movement. The LCAC ship-to-shore movement control organization consists of personnel, ships, and landing craft within the Navy control group that are designated to plan and control the LCAC portion of the waterborne ship-to-shore movement.

4.2.1 Organization. The LCAC ship-to-shore movement control organization under the CCO is discussed in the following paragraphs and summarized in figure 4-1. The primary control group is composed of a PCO, PCS, LCO, LCS, boat control team, LCAC control team, LWCs, BGCs, and BWCs. BGCs and BWCs are part of displacement landing craft boat groups which are discussed in NWP 3-02.2M, chapter 4 along with PCSs and boat control teams.

4.2.1.1 Primary Control Officer. A PCO is designated for each colored beach. PCO responsibilities include:

1. Detailed planning to conduct the ship-to-shore movement

2. Maintaining current location and status of ships, landing craft, and boats assigned

3. Monitoring surf conditions and weather predictions, and recommending termination of boating when conditions warrant

4. Maintaining the status of embarkation and debarkation

5. Landing scheduled waves at the correct beach at the specified time.

When a separate LCO is not assigned, the PCO will also perform duties outlined in paragraph 4.2.1.4.

4.2.1.2 Primary Control Ship. The PCS supports the embarked PCO and provides a boat control team to track and control displacement assault craft and amphibious vehicles. When a separate LCS is not assigned, the PCS will also perform the duties outlined in paragraph 4.2.1.5.

4.2.1.3 Secondary Control Officer and Secondary Control Ship. The SCO embarks in the SCS and is the principal assistant to the PCO for controlling the ship-to-shore movement. The responsibilities of the SCO/SCS include maintaining readiness to assume PCO/PCS duties outlined in paragraphs 4.2.1.1 and 4.2.1.2 and/or LCO/LCS duties outlined in paragraphs 4.2.1.4 and 4.2.1.5, when directed.

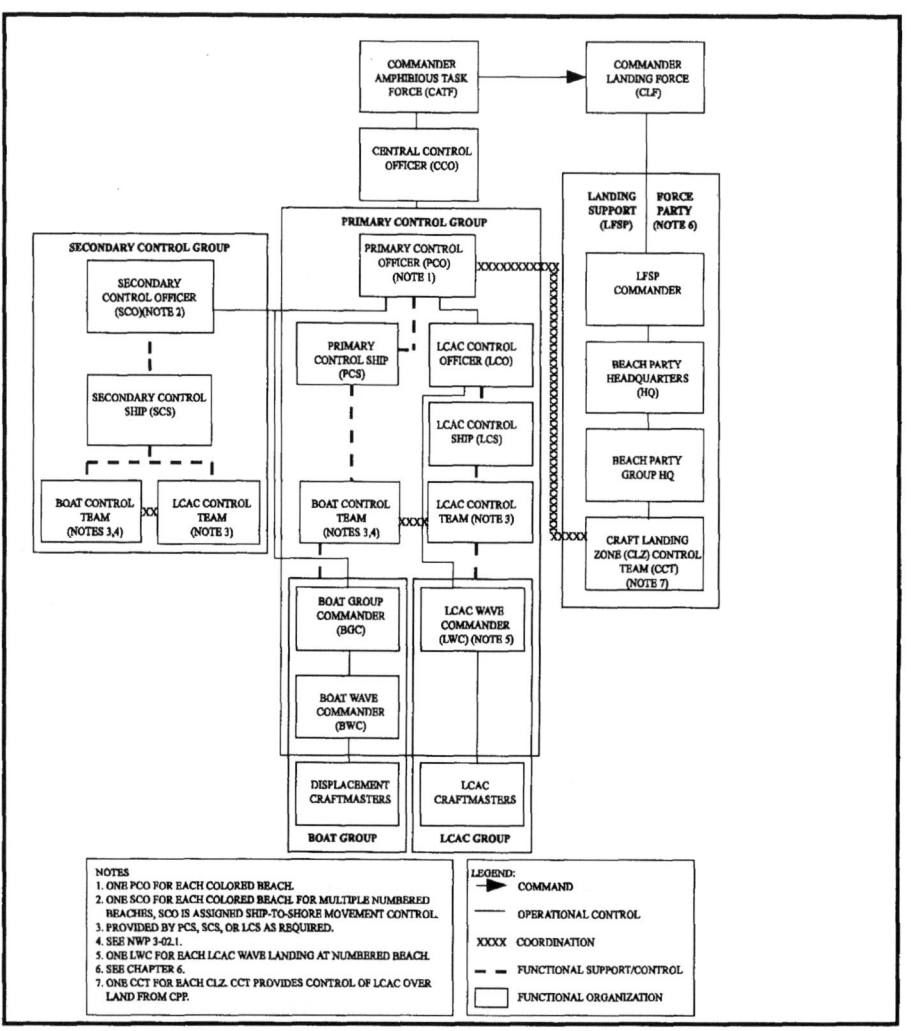

Figure 4-1. LCAC Ship-to-Shore Movement Control Organization

A secondary control group is composed of an SCO, SCS, LCAC/boat control teams, and any LWCs/BGCs/BWCs assigned.

4.2.1.4 LCAC Control Officer. The LCO embarks in the LCS and assists the PCO with detailed plans for and control of the LCAC ship-to-shore movement. The LCO reports to the PCO and is responsible for:

1. Providing detailed plans in the form of LCO Instructions to conduct the ship-to-shore movement of LCAC during amphibious operations

2. Controlling LCAC from the CLA to the CPP

3. Monitoring the location and status of assigned LCAC

4. Monitoring surf conditions and weather predictions and recommending to PCO the termination of LCAC operations when conditions warrant

5. Arranging for LCAC fueling and providing rest and food for LCAC crews

6. Coordinating LCAC salvage operations.

4.2.1.5 LCAC Control Ship. The LCS supports the embarked LCO and provides an LCAC control team to control LCAC waves from CLAs to CPPs.

4.2.1.6 LCAC Control Team. During the initial assault, the LCAC control team plots, tracks, and provides positive or advisory control to LCAC waves en route CPPs. During general offload, the team controls or monitors LCAC movements as directed by the LCO (PCO when a separate LCO is not assigned).

The LCAC control team is analogous to the boat control team discussed in NWP 3-02.2M, chapter 4. When the PCS is controlling LCAC and displacement craft concurrently, the functions of the LCAC and boat control teams can be combined where feasible to avoid redundancy. LCAC control team members include:

1. A supervisor/evaluator

2. Wave controllers

3. A plotter/computer workstation operator (for AN/KSQ-1)

4. Radio net operators

5. A radar/NTDS operator.

4.2.1.7 LCAC Wave Commander. An LCAC wave consists of two or more craft comprising a scheduled wave. An LWC is the tactical commander designated for each LCAC wave. The LWC is responsible to the LCO/PCO for directing the maneuvers of all craft under the LWC's command.

The LWC is normally an officer from the ACU LCAC detachment. The LWC is analogous to the BWC in a displacement landing craft wave of the boat group. An LWC embarks in an LCAC with an installed GPS and AN/KSQ-1 amphibious assault direction system (when available). The LWC's craft is the lead craft in all LCAC wave formations.

4.2.1.8 LCAC Craftmaster. An LCAC craftmaster is the person in charge of an individual LCAC. The craftmaster reports to the LWC and is responsible for the safety and well-being of the embarked personnel and equipment and efficient and safe operation of the craft. LCAC craftmasters are analogous to craftmasters of displacement landing craft.

4.2.1.9 Craft Landing Zone Control Team. A CCT provides LCAC terminal guidance from seaward of the CPP to a CLZ for unloading or loading, and then directs the LCAC back to the SZ for the return transit to ATF shipping. A CCT consists of personnel from the ACU/BMU, and is placed ashore as soon as practicable after the initial waterborne assault. LCAC ITG into the CLZ is provided by LF RECON/SEAL teams (see paragraph 3.2.1.2) until a CCT is established.

The CCT is subordinate to the Navy beach party component of the LFSP and is analogous to a beach party team within the beach party organization. Its counterpart in the CLZ for the unloading and movement of personnel, equipment, and supplies from LCAC is the CST, a subordinate of the shore party component of the LFSP. Chapter 6 describes in detail how these teams support the waterborne ship-to-shore movement and their command and organizational relationship with the LFSP.

4.2.2 LCAC Control Areas. LCAC control areas are established in the landing area to deconflict tactical operations, define transit lanes/routes for LCAC waves, and identify geographic positions for timing of the LCAC ship-to-shore movement. They include CLAs, CCAs, CDPs, LCAC transit lanes, CCPs, CPPs, ingress and egress routes, CLZs, CLSs, and CHAs. Figure 4-2 depicts an example of a landing area with only the LCAC control areas shown. These areas are described in chapter 2 and the following paragraphs delineate who is responsible for designating or selecting the area. When a separate LCO/LCS is not assigned, the PCO/PCS designates or selects the area.

4.2.2.1 Craft Launch Area. The CLA is designated by CATF and is where LCAC launch occurs. The LCO, using the LCAC control team in the LCS, takes operational control of LCAC in the CLA upon departure from the well decks of launching ships. The LCO either dispatches LCAC waves to the CDP in accordance with the approach schedule or monitors their independent transit to the CCA.

4.2.2.2 Craft Collection Area. The CCA is designated by the LCO and is where LCAC waves are formed by craft coming from multiple CLAs located OTH. The LCO dispatches LCAC waves to the CDP in accordance with the approach schedule. The positioning of the CCA relative to the CDP is critical in LCAC getting up to speed and over the hump prior to passing through the CDP. As discussed in paragraph 1.2.1.3.4, a heavily-loaded LCAC attempting to get over hump may need to turn down or cross-seas. This could be extremely hazardous when dealing with multiple waves of LCAC unless the CCA and CDP are properly positioned. Ideally, the CCA should be positioned upwind and up-seas of the CDP. Landing area planning must be flexible enough to facilitate CCA positioning on any axis from the CDP just prior to LCAC launch in order to ensure all craft obtain hump speed before passing through the CDP.

4.2.2.3 Craft Departure Point. The CDP is the geographic position designated by the LCO which marks the seaward end of the LCAC approach transit lane. It is analogous to the LOD for displacement landing craft and AAVs discussed in NWP 3-02.2M, chapter 4. Depending on the type of control used (see paragraph 4.2.3) the LCO, using the LCAC control team, or LWCs direct course and speed adjustments for LCAC waves

to conform to the LCAC transit lane and maintain the approach schedule.

CDPs are not loiter or rendezvous points. Launch and CLA/CCA dispatch timing should permit LCAC to proceed directly to and through the CDP to the next control point on schedule, with the craft already over hump speed and at the intended track speed.

4.2.2.4 LCAC Transit Lanes. LCAC transit lanes are the sea routes designated by the LCO to connect the control points through which LCAC must pass. Approach transit lanes connect CDPs to CPPs and may include one or more CCPs. Separate approach transit lanes for each LCAC wave or a single transit lane for all waves may be designated by the LCO based upon dispersion of the ATF. Separate return transit lanes may also be established to deconflict inbound and outbound LCAC flow.

4.2.2.5 Craft Control Point. A CCP is a geographic position established by the LCO along the LCAC transit lane to control the ship-to-shore movement of LCAC waves. The position of LCAC waves in the transit lane relative to CCPs can be used by the LCAC control team or LWCs to verify that the waves are on schedule or to adjust craft speed to regain the approach schedule. CCPs are sequentially numbered from sea to shore, i.e., the first CCP after the CDP is CCP1. Paragraph 4.2.3 discusses the types of LCAC control available.

A DP is a special type of CCP which marks a split in the LCAC approach transit lane, providing alternate routes to the shore. The use of a DP is directed by CATF to allow the tactical option of changing the CPP and CLZ in response to a changing tactical situation ashore. For instance, a DP may be necessary when a decision to land on one side or another of a terrain feature has to be made based on the direction of the enemy's deployment of forces. Figure 4-3 provides an example of this use of a DP. Terrain features such as hills or forested areas can also be used to mask the CLZ selected. A DP provides greater flexibility for CATF and the CLF but requires more coordination within the LCAC control organization.

4.2.2.6 Craft Penetration Point. A CPP is the geographic position where the LCAC wave crosses the high water mark. The CPP is selected by CATF and is the point at which operational control of LCAC waves shifts

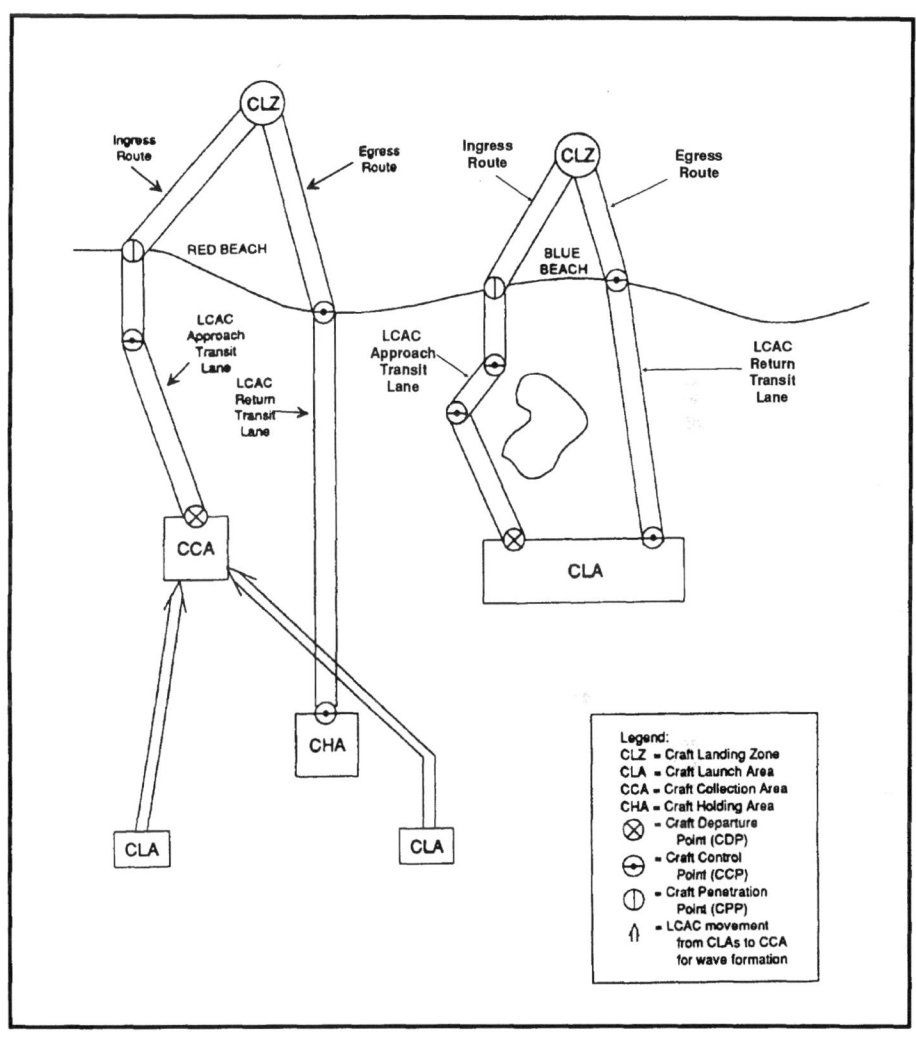

Figure 4-2. LCAC Control Areas in the Landing Area

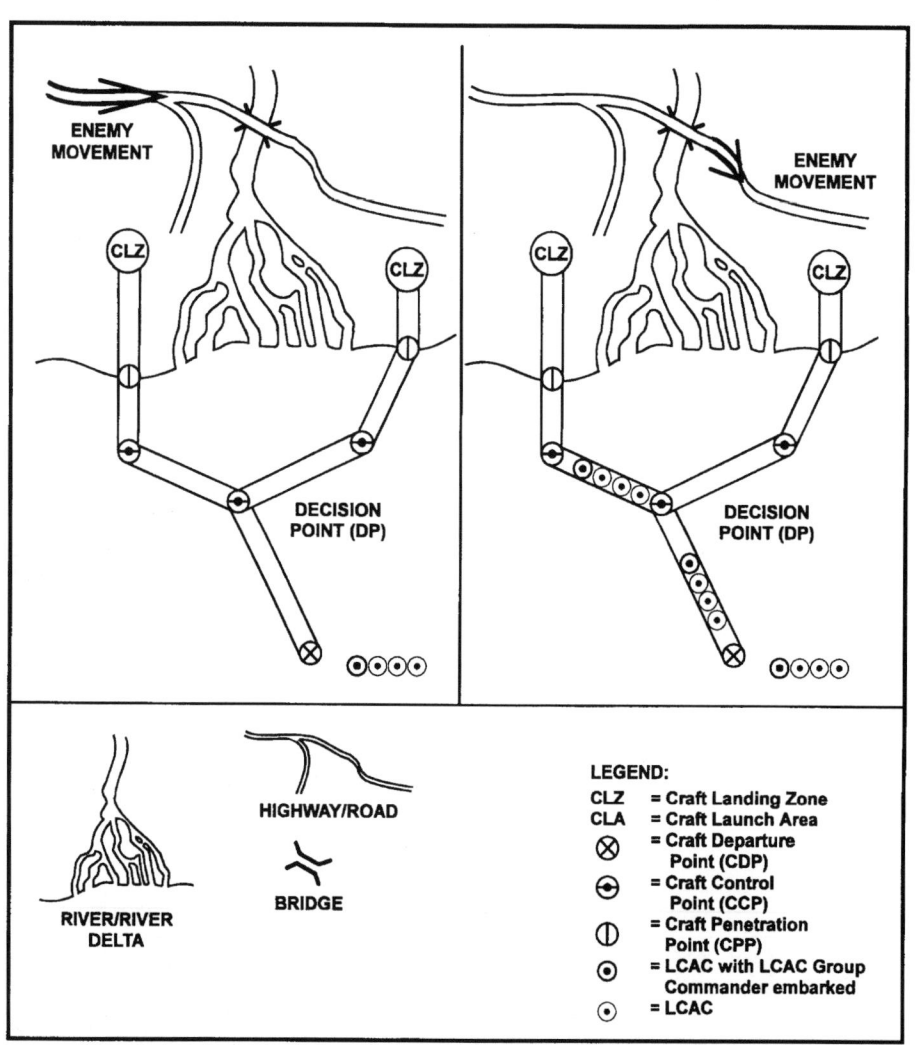

Figure 4-3. Example of a CCP Used as a DP

from the LCO to the CCT or RECON/SEAL teams providing ITG into the CLZ.

For night landings, the center and flanks of CPPs may be marked initially by lights/strobes placed during preassault operations. Later, beach party personnel (see chapter 6) will mark the flanks of CPPs and beginning of the ingress route with strobe lights affixed to poles at night and 6-foot by 6-foot markers with inverted international orange triangles during the day. The arrangement and characteristics of the markers are shown in appendix D.

4.2.2.7 Ingress and Egress Routes. Ingress and egress routes are the land paths selected by CLF over which LCAC waves traverse to and from CLZs. Separate ingress and egress routes may be selected to deconflict inbound and outbound LCAC traffic. The CCT controls LCAC wave movement along ingress and egress routes and relinquishes operational control during egress to the LCAC control team at the high water mark prior to entering the SZ.

4.2.2.8 Craft Landing Zone and Craft Landing Site. A CLZ is the beach or inland area selected by CLF where LCAC waves come off-cushion to off-load or on load personnel, equipment, and cargo. A CLS is an individual LCAC landing spot within the CLZ. The CCT controls LCAC wave movement into and out of CLZs and positions LCAC in an available CLS upon its arrival for off-load/on load by the CST. The RECON/SEAL teams may provide ITG into CLZs and CLSs until CCTs are in place.

4.2.2.9 Craft Holding Area. The CHA is the area designated by CATF to which LCAC waves may proceed upon return from the beach to await further assignment by the PCO. A SRP may be located in the CHA where individual LCAC rendezvous with and are recovered by amphibious shipping.

4.2.3 Control. The way the LCAC ship-to-shore control organization exercises control depends on the mission and tactical situation, the LCAC navigation suite installed, and the PCS command and control capabilities. The types of LCAC control, procedures for exercising control from OTH, and the AN/KSQ-1 amphibious assault direction systems under development to aid in LCAC movement are discussed in the following paragraphs.

4.2.3.1 Types of LCAC Control. The three types of LCAC control are advisory, independent, and positive.

4.2.3.1.1 Advisory Control. Advisory control involves minimal communications between the LCAC control team and the LWC and, for that reason, is the preferred type of LCAC control. The LCAC control team and LWC interact and exchange positional information as follows:

1. Two-way voice communications are maintained on the LCAC control net between the LCAC control team and the LWC.

2. LCAC are provided the launch position and a vector to the CDP or CCA by the launching ship.

3. The LWC takes tactical control of the wave en route the CDP or in the CCA via the MOMS voice radio system or another designated voice net.

4. The LCAC control team tracks the LCAC wave and periodically gives the LWC a current position and time early or late based on the approach schedule.

5. The LWC adjusts the wave's course and speed to pass through the next control point on schedule.

6. The LWC may mark passage through control points, course and speed changes, and the sighting of navigational aids over the LCAC control net if required.

7. More frequent positioning information may be needed from the control team while the LCAC wave is in the transit lane.

8. The voice communications procedures discussed in NWP 3-02.2M, appendix D are used when required.

4.2.3.1.2 Independent Control. Independent control involves emergency only use of voice communications between the LCAC control team and the LWC. It is used when assaults are conducted under restricted EMCON conditions. With GPS installed, LCAC are capable of independent movement from OTH to an unmarked CPP. Without GPS, the LWC must rely upon

DR from a known point at sea to a visually prominent or marked CPP. Transit from OTH under independent control by DR will likely result in navigation errors and negatively impact arrival time.

4.2.3.1.3 Positive Control. Positive control involves a continuous flow of communications from the LCAC control team to the LWC via voice or data link.

Radar is the primary sensor for determining an LCAC wave's position relative to the PCS. LCAC OTH operations may preclude positive control due to loss of radar coverage. Voice communications over the LCAC control net are used to provide positions and vectors to the LWC. The following procedures are employed in positive control:

1. An LCAC wave is launched and passes through the CDP at the designated time. LCAC may maneuver on a zigzag course, execute a 360° turn, or adjust speed to arrive at the CDP on time. Since LCAC will be over the hump (18 to 21 knots), speed should not drop below 25 knots.

2. Position information is provided by the LCAC control team every minute over the LCAC control net using the grid reference system procedures in NWP 3-02.2M, appendix D. Speed up and slow down commands are not used. For multiple leg transit lanes, the LCAC control team provides time and distance to turn. A 600 to 700 yard tactical diameter is used for computing turn points. If the LCAC wave is significantly off track, a left or right correction command in degrees is given ("come left 15°"). If the LCAC wave is more than 5 minutes early, a 360° turn to port or starboard is used to recover the timeline.

3. When running multiple legs to the beach in high sea state, it may be necessary to establish different notional speeds on each leg, or accept a time late or early on initial legs which can be made up or lost on subsequent legs. The effects of high sea state on multiple legs are considered in the MPP (see paragraph 2.7).

4.2.3.2 Procedures for LCAC OTH Control. When LCAC are launched from OTH, arrival at the CLZ or designated rendezvous position will require detailed planning, coordination by the PCO/LCO, and

precise navigation by LCAC crews. Procedures for LCAC OTH control include independent transit and aircraft relay if continuous radar coverage is required.

4.2.3.2.1 Independent Transit. LCAC independent transit is conducted under independent control and is the most frequently used method for transiting from OTH. LCAC equipped with GPS are capable of independent transit from OTH at high speed, passing through CCPs to the CPP and arriving at the CLZ on time. Additionally, LCAC crews can accurately navigate to RECON/SEAL drop-off points and amphibious raid launch points as discussed in chapter 3. Unless LCAC OTH operations are conducted under restrictive EMCON, the craft will remain under advisory control until passing beyond the radar horizon of the controlling ship. Considerations in LCAC independent transit planning include:

1. Navigation skills of LCAC crews

2. Availability and accuracy of GPS position updates in the area of operation

3. Advance coordination and detailed briefing of participants, particularly during EMCON transits

4. Shipping in or near LCAC transit lanes

5. Weather, visibility, current, and projected sea state

6. Radar navigation features in the vicinity of the CPPs

7. Criteria for operating LCAC radar in event of GPS failure during restrictive EMCON transits

8. RTF procedures.

4.2.3.2.2 Aircraft Relay. An ARP can be used to maintain the progress of the LCAC wave as it transits to the beach and relay the wave's position to the LCAC control team via voice or data link. An ARP can also be stationed "on top" the LCAC wave where it can be tracked on radar by the LCAC control team. The track/position of the ARP would accurately represent that of the LCAC wave.

4.2.3.3 AN/KSQ-1 Amphibious Assault Direction System. The AN/KSQ-1 system will enable the LCAC control team positive identification and continuous monitoring of LCAC position in the landing area during the ship-to-shore movement. A component of the AN/KSQ-1 is the USQ-90 PLRS.

4.3 COMMUNICATIONS

LCAC are capable of encrypted and unencrypted voice and limited visual communications.

Voice communication capabilities include HF, UHF, and VHF radios which may be each channelized for and quickly shifted. The LCAC crew, and the LWC if embarked, are connected on a craft IVCU which also permits access to any of the external radios. The IVCU can also access the MOMS voice radio system, a short range UHF walkie-talkie for communicating with well deck and CLZ personnel and between LCAC in formation. Figure 4-4 provides an LCAC voice communications matrix. The following paragraphs describe the voice nets available for LCAC ship-to-shore movement.

Note

The design of IVCU helmets worn by LCAC crewmembers facilitates receipt of transmissions over several nets through a common speaker. This creates potential operator confusion, necessitates maintenance of proper circuit discipline, and may require special call-up procedures to

Nets	\multicolumn{12}{c}{Stations}
	CCO	PCO	SCO	Boat Control Team	LCAC-Capable Ships	Displacement Lighterage	Med/Admin/Salvage Boats	LCAC Control Team	CLZ Control Team	LGCs/LCAC	Beach Party Team	ARP
Control Ship Coordination	C	X	X									
Primary Control		X	X	X				X			X	
LCAC Operations					X					X		
LCAC Control								C	X	X		W
Beach Boat Control (ALFA)		C	X	X			X	X	W	W		
Beach Boat Operations (BRAVO)		X	X	X		W	X	X	W	W	X	
CLZ Control									C	W	W	

Guard Legend:
  C - Net Control
  W - When Directed
  X - Guard

Figure 4-4. LCAC Voice Communications Matrix

distinguish nets within the bounds of OP-SEC.

Visual communications are limited to the use of hand signals while maneuvering in well decks and ashore. LCAC do not display any amphibious unique visual signals or insignias because of the FOD these devices could cause.

4.3.1 Control Ship Coordination Net. The control ship coordination net is a directed net used for overall coordination of the waterborne ship-to-shore movement.

4.3.2 Primary Control Net. The primary control net is a directed net used for coordinating ship-to-shore movement at a colored beach.

4.3.3 LCAC Operations Net. The LCAC operations net is a free net used by launching ships to control assigned LCAC until operational control of LCAC is assumed by the PCO on the LCAC control net. Multiple LCAC operations nets may be employed to provide individual or groups of LCAC-capable ships discrete frequencies.

4.3.4 LCAC Control Net. The LCAC control net is a directed voice UHF/HF net or data link used to control LCAC waves from launch to CPPs and during return to amphibious shipping. If AN/KSQ-1 is installed, the AN/KSQ-1 master station to LCAC user unit link may perform this function.

4.3.5 Beach Boat Control (ALFA) Net. The ALFA net is a directed net used to provide displacement landing craft and AAV control during the near shore ship-to-shore movement of scheduled waves for a numbered colored beach.

4.3.6 Beach Boat Operations (BRAVO) Net. The BRAVO net is a free net used to coordinate the launch of displacement landing craft and AAVs and the initial and general offload at a numbered colored beach.

4.3.7 CLZ Control Net. The CLZ control net is a directed net used to control LCAC from the CPP into and out of the CLZ at a numbered colored beach.

4.4 LCAC DEBARKATION

LCAC can be used to debark LF troops, equipment, and supplies from an LCAC-capable ship (see paragraph 1.2.1.2). LCAC debarkation may be accomplished with the ship underway, lying to, or at anchor. The following paragraphs discuss the LCAC debarkation process.

4.4.1 LCAC Debarkation Sequence and Procedures. The sequence for LCAC debarkation of the LF is defined in the landing craft employment plan, landing craft and amphibious vehicle assignment table, landing diagram, LF landing sequence table, and LF serial assignment table (see paragraph 2.4). The specific procedures and debarkation sequence for an LCAC-capable ship are detailed in:

1. The ship's debarkation bill/instruction which provides the standard operating procedures for assembling, moving, and loading troops and equipment aboard LCAC

2. The ship's debarkation schedule which lists each well deck debarkation station, the boat teams assigned to that station, and the sequence of LCAC in the well deck (see paragraph 2.4)

3. A supplemental diagram showing the location of each debarkation station and the boat team that loads at that station

4. A launch/recovery checklist (see paragraph 4.4.2.2)

5. Launch and recovery timetables (see paragraph 4.4.2.2).

4.4.2 LCAC Well Deck Operations. The efficiency of LCAC well deck operations can play a critical role in the timing of the LF waterborne debarkation and the subsequent ship-to-shore movement. By their nature, well deck operations are potentially hazardous. The efficiency with which LCAC are recovered, loaded, refueled, and launched must therefore be balanced with the concerns for safety.

LCAC are loaded, launched, and recovered in accordance with the sequence established in the debarkation schedule. LCAC well deck launches and recoveries are usually directed by voice radio rather than day and night visual signals, since LCAC physical characteristics preclude maintaining an effective visual watch. The MOMS voice radio system or the LCAC operations net is used. If required, LCAC may be launched in an EMCON condition using visual signals alone. Various well deck alignment means including painted day markings, night lights, and optical guidance systems aid LCAC craftmasters in well deck approaches. Day markings, night lights, and optical guidance systems applicable to each LCAC-capable ship class are discussed in the appendices of Volume III of the "Safe Engineering and Operations (SEAOPS) Manual for Landing Craft Air Cushion (LCAC)."

Once in the well deck, the movement of LCAC to designated spots are directed by the ship's ramp marshall using MOMS radio or approved hand signals. Approved hand maneuvering signals for LCAC are contained in appendix D. When maneuvering LCAC within the well deck either during the day or at night, conditions are considered to be "darkened." Therefore, only the darkened condition maneuvering signals shall be used for LCAC well deck operations.

Detailed loading, unloading, and refueling procedures and safety precautions for LCAC well deck operations are contained in Volume III of SEAOPS.

Specific LCAC launch and recovery procedures for each LCAC-capable ship class are contained in Volume III of SEAOPS. SEAOPS contains the current guidance on LCAC launch and recovery procedures and remains the authoritative guide. General LCAC launch and recovery considerations and launch and recovery timetables are discussed in the following paragraphs.

4.4.2.1 LCAC Launch and Recovery Considerations. Ship considerations for LCAC launch and recovery are:

1. Ship should be trimmed bow up to a maximum of 0.75° and ballasted to the sill with sterngate at minus 10°. No more than 6 inches of water above the sill is recommended to minimize spray into the well during entries and exits. Ballasting below the sill should be avoided to preclude LCAC skirt/finger damage.

2. Ship shall be headed into the wind and sea.

3. When wind and sea are from different directions, ship shall be headed into the sea. A course should be selected that minimizes roll and keeps the relative wind within 30° of the bow, if possible. Excessive rolling should be avoided.

4. Optimum speed for dry well deck operations is 10 to 12 knots (5 knots for LHA class ships). Dry well deck recoveries at speeds above 12 knots require LCAC to operate near maximum power settings when crossing the sill, backing off on power as soon as wake effects are cleared. This higher speed transition increases the potential for craft damage. Therefore, dry well deck recoveries at speeds above 12 knots should be avoided.

5. The limiting speed for wet well deck operations is 2 to 3 knots with sea state 1, determined by LCAC's maximum hullborne speed of 5 knots.

6. Ship course and speed for launch must be maintained constant until the LCAC navigation system has stabilized. This can take up to 20 minutes.

7. LCAC have a tendency to wallow in the ship's wake while following close astern, making well deck line up more difficult. The receiving ship should give LCAC permission to enter the well deck as quickly as possible to minimize time in the wake.

8. Wind sheer must be considered during LCAC well deck recoveries at anchor. When possible, maneuver the ship to keep the bow into the wind to minimize the wind sheer effect.

CAUTION

Conducting LCAC dry well deck operations in seas greater than sea state 3 or wet well deck operations in seas greater than sea state 1 is extremely dangerous and should be avoided unless operational necessity dictates. The decision to do so shall be made by the ship's commanding officer. There is no completely safe mode of operation in seas greater than sea state 3. Chapter 8 discusses LCAC operations in high sea states.

4.4.2.2 LCAC Launch/Recovery Checklist and Timetables.
The LCAC launch/recovery checklist contains sequential listings of the actions to be completed prior to and during well deck launch or recovery operations. Volume III of SEAOPS requires the use of the launch/recovery checklist and provides a standard checklist which may be modified as required.

Launch and recovery timetables supplement the debarkation schedule and launch/recovery checklist and assist in monitoring and controlling the well deck during LCAC operations. LCAC launch timing is based on the time of departure from the CDP required by the approach schedule (see paragraph 2.4) and the PCO instructions (see paragraph 4.2.1.1). LCAC recovery timing is based on the expected time of the first LCAC return to the well deck. Figure 4-5 and 4-6 are examples of LCAC launch and recovery timetables, respectively.

Time (min)	Event
D-100	Start LCAC premission checks
D-40	Man LCAC
D-25	Start APUs/shift to craft power
D-15	Start main engines
D-10	LCAC cross sill
D-5	LCAC wave forms
D-0	LCAC cross CDP
D = Departure time	

Figure 4-5. Example of an LCAC Launch Timetable

Time (min)	Event
R-60	Man LCAC stations/commence checkoff list
R-40	Commence FOD walkdown
R-20	Lower sterngate to - 10°
R-20	Conduct time check (1MC)
R-15	Maneuver ship to recovery course and speed
R-5	Establish communications with LCAC
R-0	LCAC cross sill
R = Recovery time	

Figure 4-6. Example of an LCAC Recovery Timetable

4.5 LCAC DISPATCH TO THE BEACH

As soon as LCAC are launched in the designated CLAs, the launching ship directs the LCAC to report to the PCO on the LCAC control net. The LCO (PCO when a separate LCO is not assigned) takes operational control of the LCAC and the LCAC control team dispatches the craft to the beach via CDPs. Depending on the type of control used, direction to proceed to the beach is provided over the LCAC control net or LCAC proceed without direction in accordance with the approach schedule timeline. En route CDPs, craft form into LCAC waves per the landing plan.

If the landing plan requires LCAC from dispersed CLAs to rendezvous in designated CCAs and form waves, the LCAC control team monitors craft transits to the CCAs and dispatches the LCAC waves from the CCAs to the beach via CDPs once the waves are formed.

4.5.1 LCAC Waves.
LCAC proceed to the beach in waves of two or more craft that pass through CDPs at the times prescribed in the approach schedule and proceed along LCAC approach transit lanes. LCAC waves use a variety of formations depending on the tactical situation or other maneuvering considerations. The LWC is always in the lead craft. LCAC formations and maneuvering considerations are discussed in the following paragraphs.

4.5.1.1 Formations.
LCAC formations include echelon, line abreast, wedge, and column as depicted in figure 4-7. LCAC formations during ship-to-shore movement are generally preplanned and account for the limited visibility of craftmasters on the port side of their craft. Changes to formations are either signaled by the LWC over the MOMS radio or LCAC control net or executed without signal as the LCAC wave passes through specified CCPs.

4.5.1.1.1 Echelon.
The echelon, or line of bearing, is the preferred formation for most transit situations. The echelon is formed on the starboard or port quarter of the lead LCAC and can be either steep or shallow depending on the angle abaft the lead craft's beam. An echelon right allows the LWC to see the entire formation, visibility permitting. An echelon left facilitates more efficient station-keeping by other craftmasters.

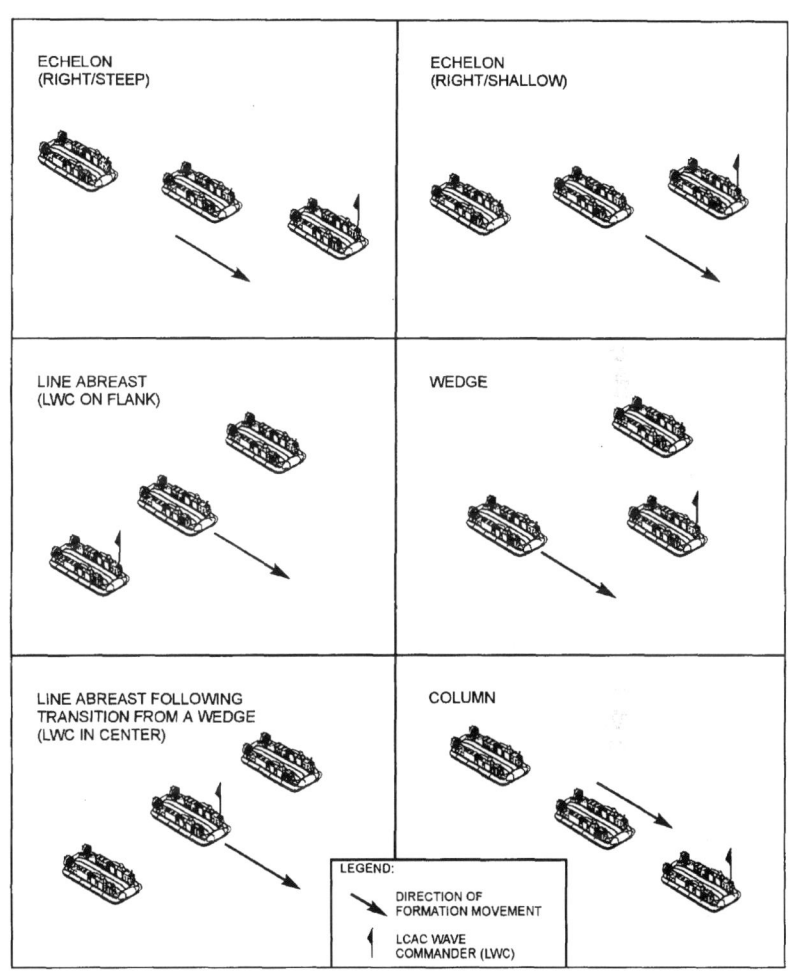

ECHELON
(RIGHT/STEEP)

ECHELON
(RIGHT/SHALLOW)

LINE ABREAST
(LWC ON FLANK)

WEDGE

LINE ABREAST FOLLOWING
TRANSITION FROM A WEDGE
(LWC IN CENTER)

COLUMN

LEGEND:

DIRECTION OF
FORMATION MOVEMENT

LCAC WAVE
COMMANDER (LWC)

Figure 4-7. LCAC Formations

4-13

The advantages of an echelon are:

1. Good visibility for all LCAC

2. Ease in maneuvering the wave

3. Rapid transition to most other formations.

The disadvantages of an echelon are:

1. Trailing LCAC may be far from the LWC depending on the number of LCAC in the wave and the interval used

2. Echelon formation requirements are not delineated in ATP-1C, Volume I, "Allied Maritime Tactical Instructions and Procedures (U)", but coincide with line of bearing restrictions therein.

4.5.1.1.2 Line Abreast. The line abreast formation is typically used during the final leg of a transit to allow all LCAC in the wave to penetrate the surf zone and cross the high water mark simultaneously. The lead LCAC is on either flank except when the line abreast is formed from a wedge formation, in which case the lead LCAC will be positioned in the center of the formation. LWC positioning on the right flank facilitates more efficient station-keeping by other craftmasters.

The advantages of the line abreast formation are:

1. Simultaneous landing of all LCAC, aiding rapid concentration of embarked LF equipment and personnel

2. An individual LCAC casualty has minimal effect on adjacent craft

3. Good visibility from all LCAC

4. Compounds enemy fire correction problems.

The disadvantages of the line abreast formation are:

1. Difficulty in stationkeeping in a large wave

2. CLZ may be too small to handle ingress of all LCAC at once

3. Wave presents large visual/radar cross section

4. Difficulty in maneuvering the wave

5. Cannot be used in a narrow approach lane or where mine threat is present.

4.5.1.1.3 Wedge. The wedge is used when a tight LCAC formation is desired. The wedge is composed of one or more craft in echelon off each quarter of the lead LCAC.

The advantages are:

1. Good visibility from all LCAC

2. Reduces size of visual/radar cross section

3. Reduces formation width for transit of narrower approach transit lanes

4. Facilitates easier ingress to CLZs.

The disadvantages are:

1. Difficulty in maneuvering the wave

2. Requires longer to transition to all formations except line abreast

3. Provides no abort option to the lead craftmaster without crossing the bow of the trailing LCAC.

4.5.1.1.4 Column. The column formation is used when LCAC are required to transit narrow approach transit lanes, swept/breached lanes through minefields, or channels. The LCAC with the LWC embarked is always the first craft in a column.

The advantages are:

1. Smallest visual/radar cross section

2. Ease in maneuvering the wave

3. Ease in transiting narrow approach lanes, including swept/breached lanes through near-shore mine-fields.

The disadvantages are:

1. Visibility of trailing LCAC restricted by spray from preceding craft, increasing possibility of collision

2. Does not facilitate rapid concentration of embarked LF elements in the CLZ.

4.5.1.2 Maneuvering Considerations. While maneuvering LCAC in formations/along narrow transit lanes, sideslip, standard distance, deceleration and acceleration distances, turn rate, and maximum degree of turns together and wheels must be considered. The actual distances between LCAC and turn rates used in maneuvering LCAC formations should take into account craftmaster proficiency and training, craft performance, formation, formation speed, wind and sea conditions, beach conditions, visibility, and the tactical situation.

4.5.1.2.1 Sideslip. Sideslip is a phenomena experienced by an LCAC on-cushion in which the craft develops a lateral motion component as it slides across the water's surface. Sideslip is the angle between the LCAC heading and the course made good and results from the interaction of wind, sea, and craft momentum. As wind, sea, and craft speed increase, the amount of sideslip increases. Excessive sideslip at higher speeds can result in plow-in (see paragraph 1.2.1.3.6). Figure 4-8 depicts sideslip and lists the MAS for various speeds to avoid plow-in.

4.5.1.2.2 Standard Distance. Standard distance between adjacent LCAC in formation is 100 yards. At higher speeds double and triple standard distance may be required. The principal determinant by which standard distance was selected is reaction time to avoid craft or obstacles directly ahead. Figure 4-9 lists reaction times at LCAC standard distance for various speeds.

4.5.1.2.3 Deceleration and Acceleration Distances. LCAC deceleration and acceleration distances must be considered while maneuvering in formations or when avoiding other craft or obstacles. LCAC deceleration distance can be affected by the use of propeller pitch and bow thrusters. Figures 4-10 and 4-11 list LCAC deceleration and acceleration characteristics, respectively.

4.5.1.2.4 Standard Turn Rate. Standard turn rate for LCAC maneuvering in formation is 2° per second. Turn and turn rate considerations include:

1. Avoid turn rates greater than 2° per second due to excessive sideslip and the increased possibility of plow-in.

2. Turn radius is a function of craft speed, turn rate, and sideslip (which varies with wind, sea, and craft momentum). The wind can tighten an upwind/headwind turn and extend a downwind turn to more than twice the normal radius.

3. Angles of sideslip greater than 15° should be avoided in turns.

4. Speed will tend to decay in turns, so additional propeller pitch must be used to maintain constant speed.

5. Turns at speeds of 25 knots and more are normally accomplished by the use of bow thrusters and rudders.

Figure 4-12 provides a nomograph for estimating turn radii for various turn rates neglecting the effects of sideslip.

4.5.1.2.5 Turns Together and Wheels. The execution of turns together and wheels by LCAC in formation are subject to limitations. Figure 4-13 lists the maximum limits for turns together and wheels for various LCAC formations.

4.6 LCAC NAVIGATION

LCAC navigation is achieved through a combination of electronic and visual means or through external information received from the control organization.

The LCAC electronic navigation suite may consist of the AN/ARN-151 GPS, LN-66 or CMR-90 surface search radar, LR-80 ARHU, a backup magnetic compass, Doppler radar HSVL, and LCAC NDI. The surface search radar provides ranges up to 32 nm. The ARHU and HSVL may be used to DR and compensate for currents, advance, and transfer. The NDI allows the craft crew to overlay geographic points and

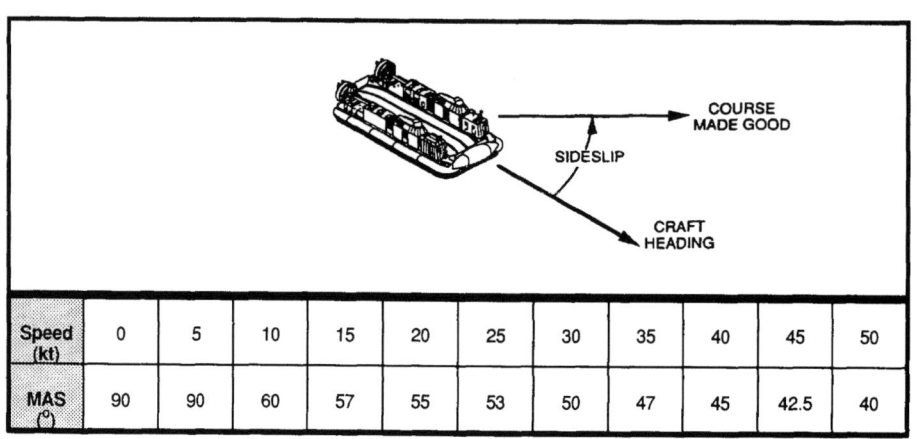

Speed (kt)	0	5	10	15	20	25	30	35	40	45	50
MAS (°)	90	90	60	57	55	53	50	47	45	42.5	40

Figure 4-8. Maximum Allowable Slideslip

Speed (kt)	25	30	35	40	45	50
Time (sec)	7.2	6.0	5.1	4.5	4.0	3.6

Figure 4-9. Reaction Times at LCAC Standard Distance

Prop Pitch 35° Reverse; Bow Thrusters, Forward											
Speed (kt)	50	45	40	35	30	25	20	15	10	5	0
Distance Traveled (yd)	535	430	340	270	195	140	100	66	40	20	0
Prop Pitch 0°; Bow Thrusters, Reverse											
Distance Traveled (yd)	505	410	320	250	185	130	90	58	40	20	0
Prop Pitch 35° Reverse; Bow Thrusters, Reverse											
Distance Traveled (yd)	410	330	260	200	150	105	70	45	25	10	0

Figure 4-10. LCAC Deceleration Performance

Speed (kt)	0	5	10	15	20	25	30	35	40	45	50
Time (sec)	0	3	8	18	28	40	52	63	75	87	96
Distance Traveled (yd)	0	30	100	250	600	1000	1600	2200	2800	3800	5400

Figure 4-11. LCAC Acceleration Performance

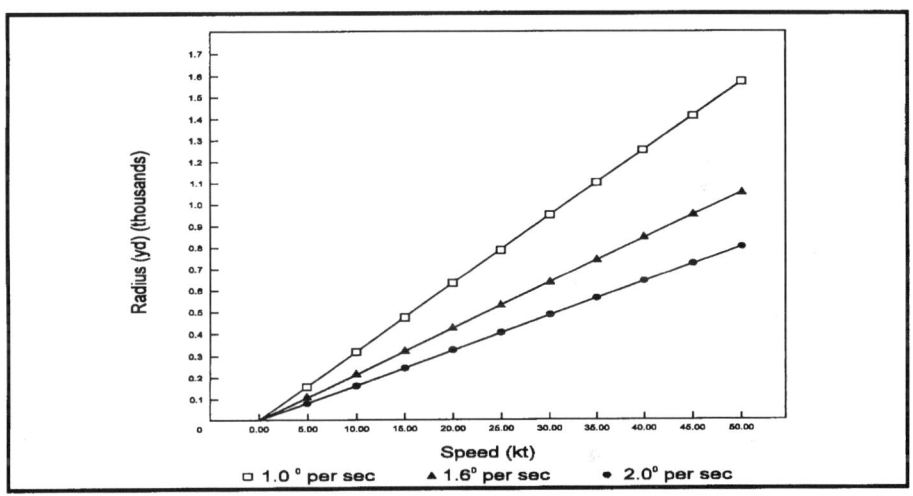

Figure 4-12. Estimated Turn Radii for Various Turn Rates (Sideslip Neglected)

integrates GPS with the radar. Not all LCAC are GPS or NDI equipped at the writing of this NWP.

LCAC visual navigation is limited to what can be viewed from the port and starboard modules. Whenever an LCAC is underway, a lookout shall be posted in the observer's dome on the port side passenger module. Personnel in the starboard side control module provide starboard side lookout coverage. NVGs may be used to enhance visibility at night. Lookouts can take rough visual bearings on aids to navigation and can detect beach markers identifying CPPs and CLZs.

Navigation considerations include:

1. LWCs should always embark in GPS-equipped LCAC, if available.

2. GPS-equipped LCAC are more desirable during operations in restricted EMCON environment.

3. For transits from OTH in a restricted EMCON environment without GPS, large course changes and frequent maneuvers should be avoided to minimize DR errors.

Formation	Turn Together (°)	Wheel (°)
Line Abreast	180 (day); 90 (night)	30
Column	180 (day); 90 (night)	180
Wedge	Do not use	30
Echelon	Variable (Note)	90

Note: Turns within an echelon are limited by the desire to keep the guide at the front of the formation. In view of this, an echelon formation turn may be of any degree, up to the point where the formation becomes a line abreast.

Figure 4-13. Maximum Limits for Turns Together and Wheels

4. Radar can generally detect large surface contacts such as an LSD at distances of 12 to 15 nm. Low-lying beach areas are difficult to detect beyond 6 to 8 nm.

5. LCAC load and speed, and wind speed and direction will have a significant effect on DR, advance, and transfer.

6. Strobe lights used to mark CPPs and CLZs may be difficult to see from seaward, necessitating the use of NVGs from ranges as close as 3 nm.

4.7 TURNAROUND AT THE BEACH AND RTF

When the LCAC wave approaches the surf line seaward of the CPP, the LWC reports to the CCT on the CLZ control net for direction through the CPP and into the CLZ via the ingress route. The LWC reports "feet dry" to the LCAC control team on the LCAC control net as the LCAC passes through the CPP. Depending on the width of the ingress route, the CCT may direct the movements of the LCAC wave or an individual LCAC into the CLZ.

Upon completion of offload/onload in the CLZ, the CCT uses the CLZ control net to direct the movement of the LCAC wave or individual craft out of the CLZ and along the egress route to the high water mark. Prior to entering the surf zone, the LWC must report to the LCAC control team on the LCAC control net and obtain permission to go "feet wet" and commence the return transit.

Control procedures for return to amphibious shipping are the same as those used in proceeding to the beach. The PCO normally passes operational control of outbound LCAC to support ships after the LCAC pass through the final CCP in the return transit lane. Support ships assume control of returning LCAC on the LCAC operations net.

RTF procedures should be employed if the ATF or advance force has remained OTH, since LCAC's rapid closure rate on radars can easily be mistaken as a threat to the force. RTF options include:

1. Using IFF (LCAC are equipped with the AN/APX-100 IFF transponder)

2. Designating a PIRAZ station

3. Using challenge and reply procedures

4. Radiating LCAC surface search radar for ES identification

5. Executing prearranged maneuvers while still OTH but within radar range of the force

6. Using IR flashing light for close range identification

7. Positive identification through installed AN/KSQ-1 equipment.

4.8 GENERAL UNLOADING

General unloading is the debarkation of LF units, supplies, and equipment as rapidly as conditions ashore permit. LCAC are best employed in the general unloading of ships further from the beach, while displacement landing craft are best employed in unloading ships closer to the beach. Appendix B provides observations and considerations for employment of assault craft mixes with various amphibious ship classes.

Control during general unloading is usually delegated to each ship, with the PCO coordinating the allocation of LCAC to LCAC-capable ships. Accordingly, ships will coordinate the ship-to-shore movement directly with the CCTs or beach party teams, as appropriate, over the BRAVO net.

CHAPTER 5

LCAC Vulnerability and Protection During Ship-to-Shore Movement

5.1 PURPOSE

This chapter discusses the vulnerability of LCAC to enemy threats, LCAC self-defense, and measures which can be employed to minimize disruption to LCAC operations in the AOA.

5.2 LCAC VULNERABILITY

LCAC is vulnerable to enemy detection and attack during ship-to-shore movement.

5.2.1 Vulnerability to Detection. LCAC is vulnerable to enemy detection by radar, visual, ES, IR, and acoustic means. General considerations for reducing LCAC vulnerability to detection include:

1. Sea spray generated by LCAC reduces both IR and radar signatures but makes craft more visible.

2. Operations in restricted EMCON reduce vulnerability to ES but may decrease navigational accuracy.

3. High seas, precipitation, and fog can mask LCAC but may increase transit time, increase the possibility of weather-related damage, and slow the build up of combat power ashore.

The following paragraphs provide specific considerations for reducing LCAC vulnerability to detection.

5.2.1.1 Radar Detection. Considerations for reducing LCAC vulnerability to radar detection include:

1. Choose LCAC control areas outside the coverage of known enemy radar sites.

2. Use weather when possible to reduce the effectiveness of enemy radar (keeping in mind the effects of reduced LCAC speed).

3. Deploy LCAC waves in formations which reduce their radar cross section.

4. Use offshore islands; oil platforms; and other stationary, unmanned objects to confuse enemy radar operators.

5.2.1.2 Visual Detection. Considerations for reducing LCAC vulnerability to visual detection include:

1. Conduct operations at night and away from population centers or heavy traffic areas.

2. Extinguish navigation lights.

3. Use precipitation, fog, islands, and terrain to mask movements.

5.2.1.3 ES Detection. Considerations for reducing LCAC vulnerability to ES detection include:

1. Minimize electronic emissions to those necessary for mission accomplishment.

2. Use the GPS alone, particularly in good visibility and light traffic, when available.

3. Use the surface search radar intermittently for collision avoidance and navigation.

4. When voice radio is required, use nets with the least counterdetection range at the lowest necessary power output.

5. Place IFF equipment in standby until activation is required during RTF.

5.2.1.4 IR Detection. Considerations for reducing LCAC vulnerability to IR detection include:

1. Maintain bow or stern aspect to the enemy when possible.

2. Use the masking effect of precipitation and fog.

3. Use reverse sea spray suppression techniques (see paragraph 5.3.3).

5.2.1.5 Acoustic Detection. Considerations for reducing LCAC vulnerability to acoustic detection include:

1. Conduct operations at night and away from population centers and heavy traffic areas.

2. When operating over land, avoid terrain features such as canyons which tend to amplify or reflect noise.

3. When operating over land, minimize the time on-cushion.

4. Use the masking effect of environmental background noise (heavy surf and wind).

5. When possible, avoid pointing the noisiest craft aspects (beam and stern) toward the enemy.

5.2.2 Vulnerability to Enemy Attack. LCAC are vulnerable to enemy attack with small arms/direct fire weapons; indirect fire weapons; CBR weapons; some types of mines; aircraft; patrol boats/ships; and beach obstacles.

5.2.2.1 Small Arms/Direct Fire Weapons. LCAC vulnerability to direct and indirect fire weapons lies in the susceptibility of propellers and lift fans to FOD and the possibility of critical equipment damage and personnel injury due to aluminum skin penetration. Critical areas of the craft are lightly armored and capable of withstanding 7.62 millimeter and smaller projectiles. However, small arms will penetrate the unarmored aluminum skin of the craft at all but the most extreme ranges.

LCAC is most likely to encounter fire from small arms/direct fire weapons when approaching the beach or transiting over land. Considerations for reducing LCAC vulnerability to small arms/direct fire weapons include:

1. Select CPPs and CLZs where the threat of small arms/direct fire weapons is minimal.

2. Use armored vehicles in initial waves to provide protection for embarked troops.

3. Launch AAVs from LCAC at sea when sea state permits (see paragraph 3.3.2).

4. Use NSFS/CAS/helicopter escort to eliminate the threat.

5. Present a bow aspect (least vulnerable) to the heaviest concentration of enemy fire.

6. If the threat is coming from a surface craft, use return fire from LCAC or embarked vehicle weapons to degrade the effectiveness of the enemy fire.

7. An LCAC configured for personnel transfer should not be used during the initial phase of an assault unless deemed absolutely necessary by the tactical commander.

5.2.2.2 Indirect Fire Weapons. Unlike small arms, indirect fire weapons such as artillery and mortars can threaten LCAC well out to sea. Considerations for reducing LCAC vulnerability to indirect fire weapons include:

1. Select landing sites where the threat of indirect fire weapons is minimal.

2. Use high speed maneuvering at sea including zigzags, weaves, and abrupt speed changes to disrupt enemy fire control solutions.

3. Extend the interval between craft operating in a group at sea.

4. Disperse over land to increase the size of the target area.

5. Minimize time on the beach.

6. Use NSFS/CAS to reduce the threat.

5.2.2.3 CBR Weapons. Chemical and biological weapons can be delivered against LCAC by indirect fire weapons or aircraft. While on-cushion at sea, LCAC can use its mobility to avoid chemical and biological weapons. While off-cushion, LCAC is extremely vulnerable. LCAC is vulnerable to radiological weapons at all times.

If a CBR attack occurs while at sea LCAC crew members and passengers should don masks, secure craft ventilation and hatches, and maneuver to avoid the cloud. If the attack occurs while off-cushion they should don masks, secure craft ventilation and hatches, and make preparations to get underway.

Note

Chapter 6 of NWP 22-3/FMFM 1-8 describes CBR countermeasures in general, including the use of MOPP and the development of a CBR defense plan. Volume III, Chapter 7 of the "Safe Engineering and Operations (SEAOPS) Manual for Landing Craft Air Cushion (LCAC)" describes CBR decontamination procedures for LCAC. LCAC does not have the capability to completely self-decontaminate, and must rely upon a support ship to complete the process.

5.2.2.4 Mines. LCAC's vulnerability to mines is primarily hull/skirt damage from mine explosion. Enemy antilanding doctrines can be expected to employ various types of mines in the landing area. Figure 5-1 is a table of the expected mine threats that could be encountered.

In general, LCAC is vulnerable to some types of mines in SW, VSW, SZ, and shore areas. On cushion, LCAC is less vulnerable to contact mines in the water or antitank mines ashore. LCAC vulnerability to influence mines in SW and VSW is dependent upon mine type, mine settings, and load carried by LCAC.

Avoidance and neutralization of the mine threat is the most reliable way to reduce LCAC vulnerability. Paragraph 1.2.1.3.9 discusses LCAC mission impact from various propulsion and skirt casualties.

5.2.2.5 Aircraft. LCAC is vulnerable to fixed- and rotary-wing aircraft armed with missiles, bombs, or guns. The most effective means of reducing its vulnerability is to evade at maximum speed and call for friendly ship or aircraft support to remove the threat.

5.2.2.6 Patrol Boats/Ships. LCAC is vulnerable to a patrol boat or ship armed with guns or missiles although LCAC usually has a speed advantage. Accordingly, LCAC should evade and remain outside the enemy's weapons range until friendly ship or aircraft support can remove the threat.

5.2.2.7 Beach Obstacles. LCAC is vulnerable to tank traps, concertina wire, wooden or steel stakes, and other obstacles while operating on the beach or inland. LCAC may incur significant skirt damage by impacting or running over such obstacles. Paragraph 1.2.1.3.1 discusses LCAC rough terrain capabilities and limits. LCAC vulnerability to beach obstacles can be lessened by reducing the obstacles or selecting CPPs, ingress and egress routes, and CLZs free of obstacles.

Mine Type	Landing Area Location			
	Shallow Water (SW)	Very Shallow Water (VSW)	Surf Zone (SZ)	Craft Landing Zone (CLZ)
Antipersonnel	No	No	Yes	Yes
Antitank	No	No	Yes	Yes
Antilanding	No	No	Yes	No
Bottom Sea	Yes	Yes	Yes	No
Moored Sea (Contact)	Yes	Yes	No	No

Figure 5-1. Expected Mine Threat by Location Within the Landing Area

5.3 LCAC SELF-DEFENSE

LCAC self-defense is a function of craft armament, weapons available on or with embarked vehicles and troops, and craft operational capabilities.

5.3.1 LCAC Armament. LCACs 1 through 33 may be armed with two portable M-60 machine guns. One gun station is atop the port passenger cabin at the observer's dome and the other is at the forward starboard line handling station. Figure 5-2 illustrates nominal firing arcs for LCACs 1 through 33 weapon stations. LCACs 34 through 84 may be equipped with three gun stations. Gun stations are at locations described above

with an additional station located at the forward port linehandling station. LCACs 34 through 84 are equipped with multiweapon stanchions and the MK 16 MOD 0 stand assemblies. These weapon stands can accommodate a variety of weapons that include: M60 7.6 mm machine gun; M2HB .50 cal machine gun; and the MK 19 MOD 3, 40 mm machine gun. Mission and availability will determine type of weapon used by the LCAC crew. Figure 5-3 illustrates nominal firing arcs for LCACs 34 through 84 weapon stations.

LCAC machine guns can counter small arms fire on the beach and inland. LCAC's bow aspect presents the maximum field of machine gun fire and the least vul-

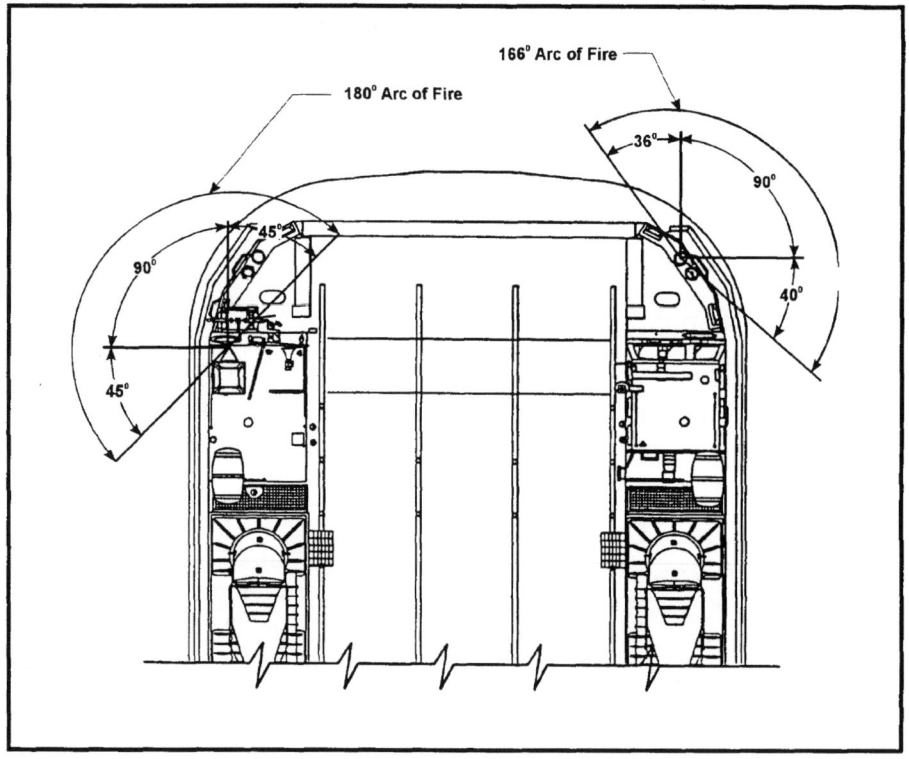

Figure 5-2. LCAC 1 Through 33 Firing Arcs

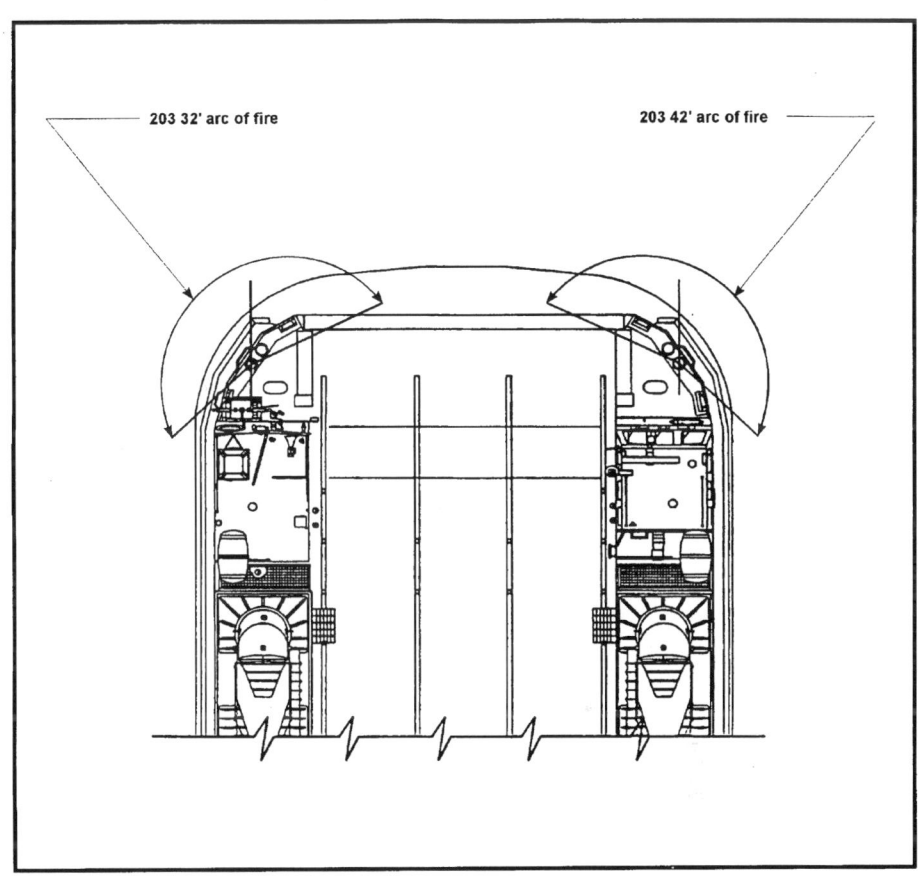

203 32' arc of fire

203 42' arc of fire

Figure 5-3. LCAC 34 Through 84 Firing Arcs

nerability to small arms fire. LCAC should be placed in close proximity to each other to provide mutual support and concentration of fire against enemy positions. LCAC machine guns cannot be utilized while the craft is underway due to significant safety hazards to personnel manning guns on deck.

5.3.2 Embarked Vehicle/Troop Weapons. Weapons integral to embarked vehicles or carried by embarked troops may offer additional LCAC self-defense under the right operational circumstances. Examples include the use of stinger missiles for antiair defense; mortars, machineguns, and rockets mounted on vehicles for defense against small arms/direct fire weapons; and 25 millimeter guns mounted on LAVs for

ORIGINAL

defense against a variety of targets including floating mines.

Some weapons may not be utilized while the craft is underway due to significant safety hazards to personnel on deck. Extreme caution must always be taken to restrict FOD, such as spent brass, shell casings, or missile tubes, resulting from weapons use. Additionally, correct firing arc cut-outs must be in place for embarked weapons to prevent damaging the craft with self-inflicted fire, especially during rough transits through surf-zones.

5.3.3 LCAC Operational Capabilities. In addition to the use of speed and maneuverability to evade enemy threats, LCAC may also employ spray suppression techniques to reduce its visual signature. Two spray suppression techniques are described in Volume I, Chapter 3 of SEAOPS. Spray suppression techniques may also be reversed to increase the amount of spray and thus decrease LCAC's radar and IR signatures.

5.4 PROTECTIVE SUPPORT MEASURES

Protective support measures employed to minimize disruption of LCAC operations include NSFS, CAS, AAW/ASUW support, and AH-1 Cobra helicopter escort.

5.4.1 Naval Surface Fire Support. NSFS can provide close support and counterfire against enemy direct and indirect fire weapons. The ability of NSFS ships to support LCAC depends on how far the NSFS ships are from the beach. During assault operations from OTH, it may be difficult to position NSFS ships close enough to the beach to support initial LCAC waves. Figure 5-4 lists the NSFS capabilities of the 5 inch/54 caliber gun.

Due to LCAC's substantial speed advantage over displacement landing craft, the lifting of supporting fire is even more time critical. Close coordination between the PCO and the CATF's SACC is critical to ensure the safety of the initial LCAC waves if NSFS support is available. Consideration should be given to placing NSFS spotters aboard the initial LCAC wave destined for each CLZ to request call fire.

5.4.2 Close Air Support. CAS can be provided by both fixed- and rotary-winged aircraft against enemy direct and indirect fire weapons. CAS may be critical to the success of LCAC assault operations if NSFS is not available.

5.4.3 AH-1 Cobra Helicopter Escort. The AH-1 Cobra helicopter can be used as an effective airborne escort for LCAC. AH-1 Cobra helicopters are effective against hostile small arms, direct fire weapons, indirect fire weapons, helicopters, and patrol boats.

5.4.4 AAW/ASUW Support. BG/ATF AAW and ASUW support can be provided against hostile aircraft, patrol boats, and ships. In providing AAW support, care should be taken in stationing CAP to avoid disclosure of the CPP and CLZ.

Max Range (yd)	Max Effective Range (yd)	Max Ordinate (ft)	Projectile Weight (lb)	Burst Radius	Rate of Fire RPMPG (Rapid/Sus)	Ammunition Available
23,500 (full) 13,350 (reduced)	21,500 (full) 12,000 (reduced)	49,600 (full) 19,800 (reduced)	70	40	30/20	HE/HC, ILLUM, WP, PD, MT, CVT, VT, DEL

Figure 5-4. 5 Inch/54 Caliber Gun NSFS Capabilities

CHAPTER 6

Sustainment of LF Operations Ashore

6.1 INTRODUCTION

The guiding principle for combat support and CSS operations in OMFTS is responsiveness. The speed, range, mobility, and lift capabilities of LCAC can greatly enhance the responsiveness and flexibility of combat support and CSS operations in support of the CLF's concept of operations through sustainment of LF operations ashore.

This chapter discusses the LFSP organization to the extent that it affects LCAC operations, and how LCAC supports the seabasing concept, bulk fuel/water transfer, and MEDEVAC.

6.2 LFSP OPERATIONS

The LFSP is the temporary LF organization, composed of Navy and LF elements, that ensures unity of effort, facilitates ship-to-shore movement, and provides initial combat support and CSS to the LF. The LF component of the LFSP is the shore party and the Navy component is the beach party. The LFSP is organized to facilitate the rapid buildup of combat power ashore by ensuring an organized and uniform flow of personnel, equipment, and supplies by surface and air means in support of the LF scheme of maneuver ashore. NWP 22-3/FMFM 1-8, "Ship-to-Shore Movement," appendix K describes the LFSP in detail. Although there is no standard organization for an LFSP, a basic sample organization is shown in figure 6-1.

LCAC supports LFSP operations by moving troops, equipment, and supplies into CLZs during the ship-to-shore movement. While LCAC remain under CATF operational control at all times, the employment of LCAC must be coordinated through the LFSP to ensure efficient and effective use of the craft for combat support and CSS.

The efficiency of LCAC operations in combat support and CSS operations once the scheduled waves are ashore depends on physical measures taken to improve the CLZ. CLZ improvements are the responsibility of the LFSP and may include measures to:

1. Clear land mines and obstacles

2. Install matting or other material to minimize wind-blown dust and sand and improve trafficability for vehicles debarking or embarking LCAC

3. Create berms to control dust and sand and to provide limited CLZ cover and concealment

4. Reduce natural obstacles to permit straight line access to various CLSs

5. Install fuel/water systems to facilitate the receipt of bulk fuel/water transferred ashore by LCAC.

The principal LCAC-related elements of the LFSP shore party and beach party are the CST and CCT, respectively. The CST, CCT, and command relationship between them are discussed in the following paragraphs.

6.2.1 Craft Landing Zone Support Team.
A CST is an LF organization composed of shore party personnel who perform support functions in the CLZ. A CST is assigned to each CLZ located beyond the confines of a numbered colored beach. In those cases where a CLZ falls within the confines of a numbered colored beach, a CST section is task organized to work with a corresponding CCT section. A CST unloads personnel, equipment, and supplies from LCAC and facilitates their movement out of the CLZ. The activities of the CST are normally confined only to the CLZ. The organization of a CST is described in the following paragraphs.

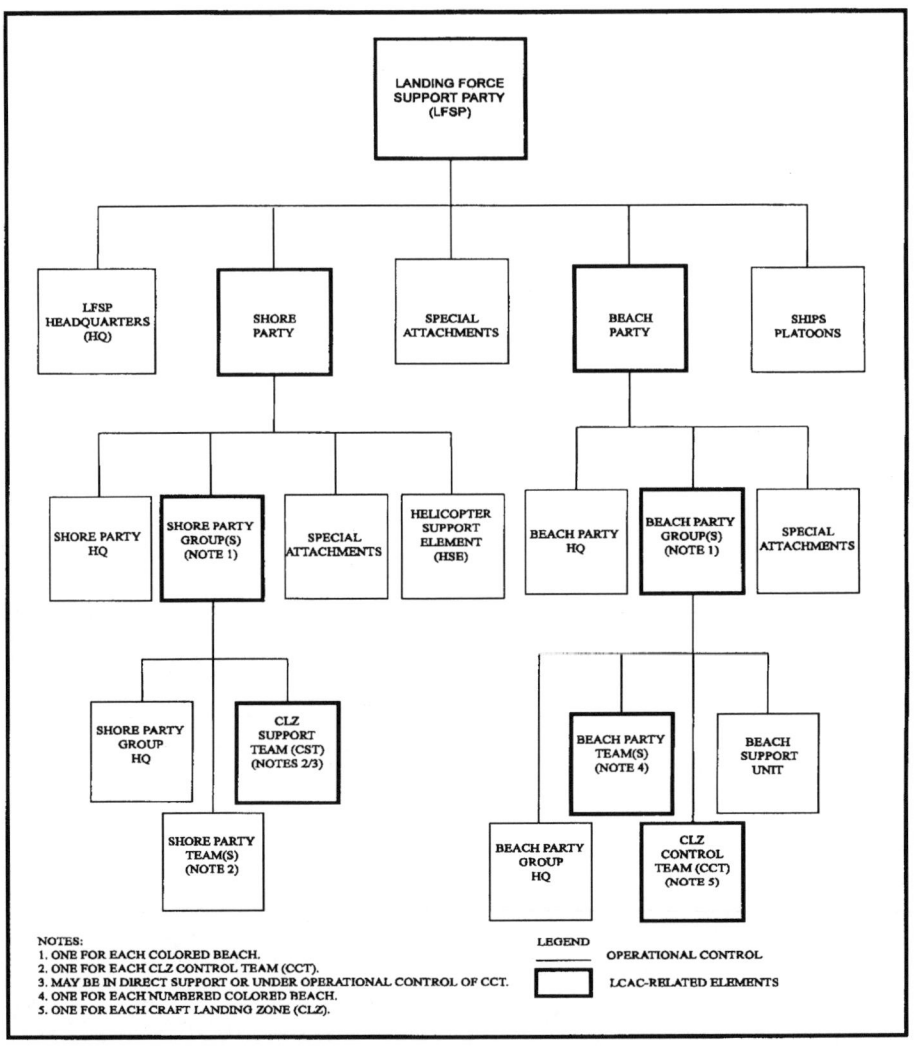

Figure 6-1. Basic LFSP Organization

ORIGINAL

6.2.1.1 CST Advance Party. The CST advance party lands as early as possible, usually with the initial LCAC wave. The CST advance party assists the CCT advance party in surveying the CLZ, ingress routes, and egress routes; and establishing LCAC ITG capabilities. Additionally, it establishes communications with the LFSP HQ and TACLOG group afloat. When the CST lands, the CST advance party is disestablished and members report to parent sections within the CST.

6.2.1.2 CST Command Section. The CST command section coordinates all activity associated with unloading/loading of LCAC and moving of personnel, equipment, and supplies from/into the CLZ.

6.2.1.3 CST Movement Control Section. The CST movement control section directs the flow of personnel, equipment, and supplies.

6.2.1.4 CST MHE Section. The CST MHE section provides and operates equipment used to unload/load LCAC and move equipment and supplies from/into the CLZ.

6.2.1.5 CST Maintenance Section. The CST maintenance section provides maintenance support for equipment (exclusive of electronics) and vehicles used by the CST and CCT, including inoperative vehicles/equipment in serials coming ashore in order to clear them from the LCAC/CLZ.

6.2.1.6 CST Motor Transport Section. The CST motor transport section provides the vehicles used by the CST.

6.2.2 CLZ Control Team. A CCT is a Navy organization composed of personnel from the NBG's ACU (air cushion)/BMU. A CCT is assigned to each CLZ located beyond the confines of a numbered colored beach. In those cases where a CLZ falls within the confines of a numbered colored beach, a CCT section is placed under the operational control of the beach party team responsible for that beach. A CCT controls LCAC from seaward of the CPP along an ingress route to the CLZ, within the CLZ during unloading/loading, and from the CLZ along an egress route to the SZ.

The CCT's primary mission is to provide command, control, and communications to facilitate the landing of troops, equipment, vehicles, and supplies in CLZs. The CCT:

1. Establishes the command post

2. Enters radio nets with the LCAC control team, LWCs, LCAC, and other waterborne ship-to-shore movement organizations, as required

3. Organizes the CLZ

4. Provides traffic control for LCAC from the CPP to the CLZ and return to the surf zone

5. Assists in evacuation of LF casualties/EPWs

6. Reports surf conditions and the general beach situation to the PCO, LCO, and LCAC-capable ships during general offload.

A basic CCT organization is depicted in figure 6-2 and described in the following paragraphs.

6.2.2.1 CCT Advance Party. The CCT advance party lands as early as possible, usually with the initial LCAC wave. Assisted by the CST advance party, the CCT advance party surveys the CLZ, ingress routes, and egress routes to determine their suitability for LCAC operations and submits reports to the PCO, as required. Additionally, it establishes communications with the control group afloat and LCAC ITG. When the CCT lands, the advance party is disestablished and members report to parent sections within the CCT.

6.2.2.2 CCT HQ. The CCT HQ provides command and control for all LCAC operations between the CPP and the CLZ, including operations within the CLZ.

6.2.2.3 CCT Terminal Guidance Section. The CCT terminal guidance section employs visual signals to direct LCAC through the CPP, along ingress routes, into and out of the CLZ, and along egress routes back to the SZ.

6.2.2.4 CCT Communications Section. The CCT communications section provides communications between the CCT, PCO, LCO, LWCs, LCAC, and LCAC-capable ships, and the beach party team.

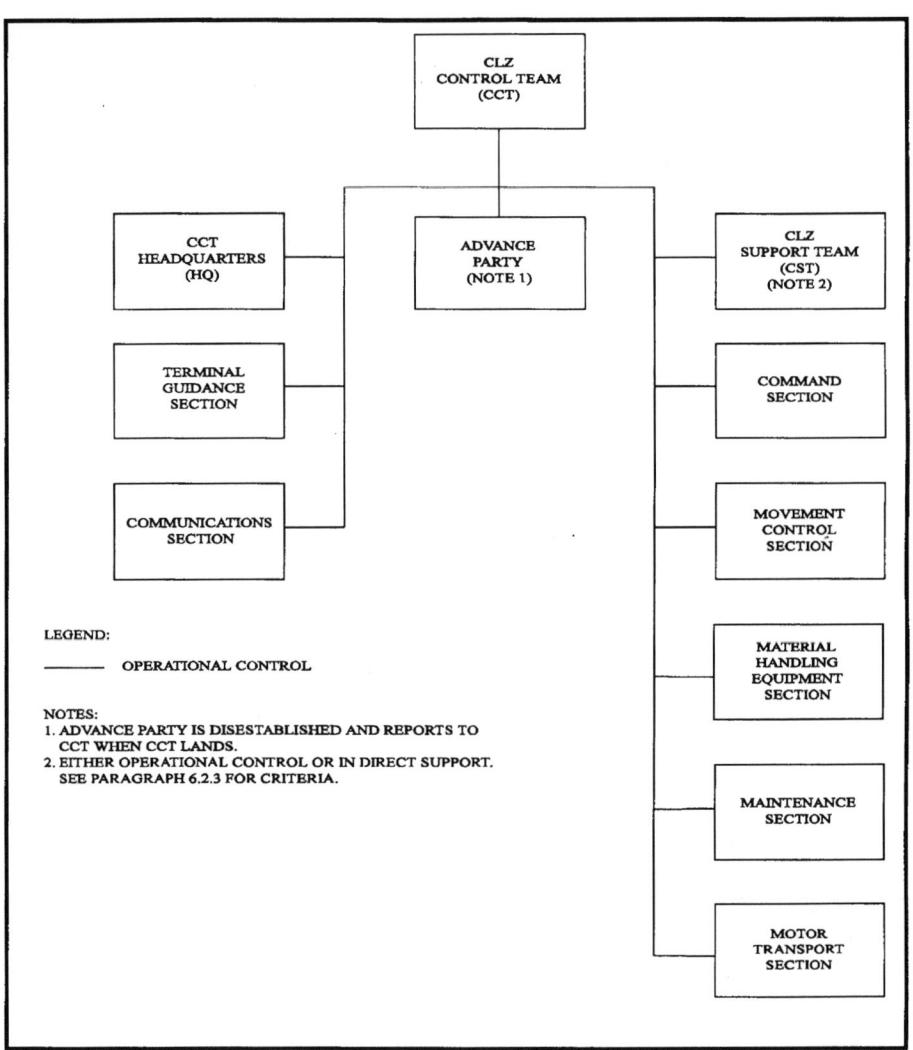

Figure 6-2. Basic CCT Organization

6.2.2.5 CLZ Support Team. The CST may be assigned as a subordinate to the CCT when operational control is relinquished to the CCT (see paragraph 6.2.3).

6.2.3 Command Relationship. The command relationship between the CCT, a Navy organization, and the CST, an LF organization (CCT section and CST section within the confines of a numbered colored beach), involves the CST either under the operational control or in direct support of the CCT. The type of command relationship usually depends on the distance of the CLZ from other shore party activities. The three possible CLZ locations which drive the command relationship depicted in figure 6-3 are:

1. CLZ is located within the confines of a numbered colored beach and is close to other shore party activities. LFSP commander specifies the command relationship which usually has the CST in direct support of the CCT.

2. CLZ is located outside the confines of a numbered colored beach but in close proximity to other shore party activities. LFSP commander specifies the command relationship which may have the CST either under operational control or in direct support of the CCT.

3. CLZ is located outside the confines of a numbered colored beach and is far from other shore party activities. LFSP commander specifies the command relationship which usually has the CST under operational control of the CCT.

6.3 SEABASING

Seabasing is a concept in which the majority of CSS is maintained aboard assault shipping and LF combat operations are sustained with minimum safety levels of supplies positioned ashore. Seabasing provides CATF and CLF maximum flexibility and security for combat support and CSS operations. It is generally employed when the ATF mission does not require establishing facilities ashore to perform supply, transportation, medical, intermediate level maintenance, automated data processing, and engineer support CSS operations. Since seabasing relies heavily on a capability to rapidly build-up supply levels at multiple locations ashore in response to a changing tactical situation, the speed, range, mobility, and lift capabilities of LCAC make it ideally suited for use in seabasing operations.

6.4 BULK FUEL/WATER TRANSFER

LCAC may be used to transfer fuel/water in bladders, pods, trailers, or trucks from assault shipping to CLZs or between CLZs when other bulk transfer systems are inoperative or where the distances are too great to lay transfer hoses.

6.5 MEDICAL EMERGENCY EVACUATION

LCAC may be used to provide rapid MEDEVAC of patients from the beach to assault shipping. Patients MEDEVACed by LCAC must be transferred in enclosed ambulances, rigid covered vehicles, or deck mounted shelters (see chapter 7) to protect them from the environment during the transit. Patients with motion sensitive wounds should be immobilized and cushioned as much as possible. Selection of the CRTS must be considered carefully, since all available CRTSs may not be LCAC-capable.

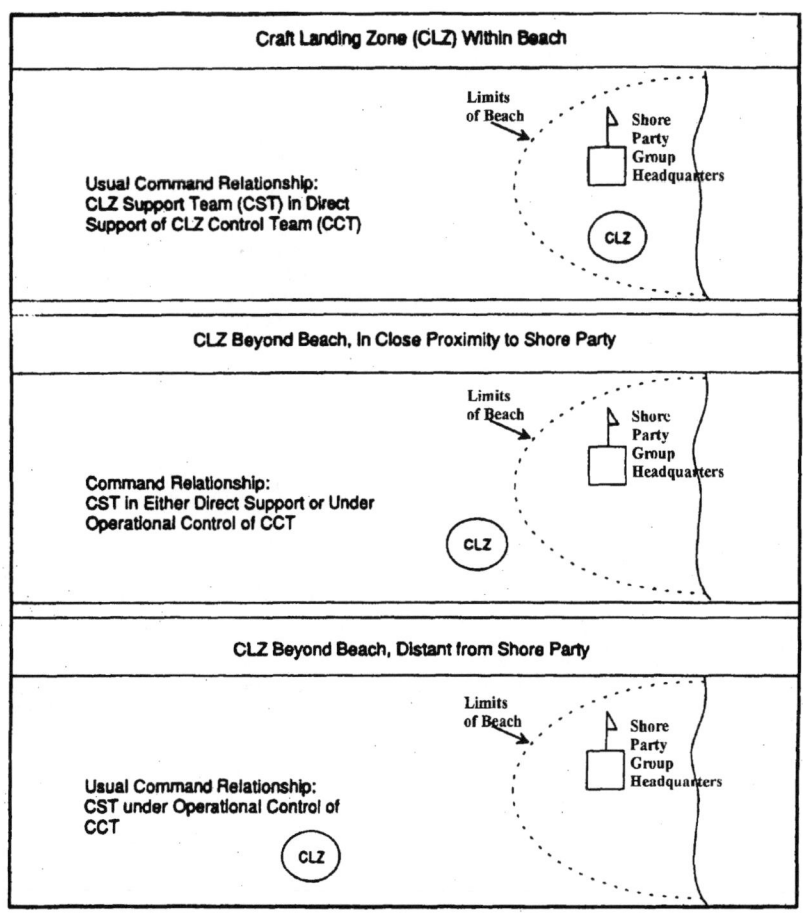

Figure 6-3. The Effect of CLZ Location on CCT and CST Command Relationship

CHAPTER 7

Other LCAC Operations

7.1 INTRODUCTION

Previous chapters of this NWP discussed LCAC's role in AMW, including preassault operations, amphibious raids, ship-to-shore movement, and sustainment of LF operations ashore. This chapter discusses how LCAC can be configured for the transfer of a greater number of personnel in support of AMW, as well as other operations, such as:

1. NEO

2. ATF choke point transit

3. MIO

4. ATF military OPDEC

5. AOA MCM

6. HA and disaster relief operations.

7.2 LCAC CONFIGURATION FOR PERSONNEL TRANSFER

LCAC was designed to carry 24 troops in its port and starboard cabins (see paragraph 1.2.1.1). LCAC's troop-carrying capability is meager compared with the LCU which can carry over 400 combat-equipped troops. LCAC, however, remains a viable means of transferring personnel, equipment, and supplies from OTH during waterborne ship-to-shore movement. Additionally, LCAC can be configured with temporary accommodations to increase its personnel transfer capacity. The following configurations can be employed to increase LCAC's personnel transfer capacity:

1. LF vehicles designed for troop transport can be deck-loaded aboard LCAC. The three vehicles in the Marine Corps inventory suitable for troop trans-

port in LCAC are the AAV, the LAV, and the HMMWV configured with a hard top as a cargo/troop carrier.

2. Portable structures can be installed on LCAC's deck to accommodate additional personnel. The MCESS includes a collapsible shelter which can be modified for use aboard LCAC as an interim measure until a designed shelter system is available. A PTM, a shelter designed for maximizing LCAC's troop-carrying capability, is currently under development by the Navy.

Figure 7-1 depicts LCAC's troop-carrying potential with various configurations. These configurations are discussed in the following paragraphs.

7.2.1 Vehicle Configurations for Personnel Transfer. The embarkation of AAVs and LAVs aboard LCAC to increase its personnel transfer capacity, and the advantages and disadvantages of vehicle configurations are discussed in the following paragraphs.

7.2.1.1 LCAC Configured with AAVs. The AAV is a full tracked amphibious vehicle designed to provide armored transportation for landing forces and their supporting equipment and supplies. The vehicle is constructed of welded aluminum armor plate to which additional applique armor is attached. The troop-carrying version of the AAV is the amphibious assault vehicle, personnel (AAVP-7).

The AAVP-7 holds a maximum of 25 troops in its compartment plus a crew of three and the troop commander forward. To accommodate full battle gear, the donning of chemical protective clothing in a potential CBR environment, and to avoid undesirable overcrowding during lengthy missions, a compartment capacity of 18 to 21 troops is used for planning purposes.

Configuration	Number of Troops			
LCAC only	24			
LCAC with vehicles	2 AAVs (Note 1)	3 AAVs (Note 1)	5 LAVs (Note 2)	12 HMMWVs (Note 3)
	60 to 66	78 to 87	44	72
LCAC with MCESS	2 shelters	4 shelters	5 shelters	6 shelters
2 rows of seats (Note 4)	64	104	124	144
3 rows of seats (Note 5)	84	144	174	204
LCAC with PTM	3 sections	6 sections		
	114	204		

Notes:
1. 18 to 21 troops per AAV plus 24 troops in LCAC cabins.
2. 4 troops per LAV plus 24 troops in LCAC cabins.
3. 4 troops per hard top-configured HMMWV plus 24 troops in LCAC cabins.
4. 20 troops per MCESS shelter plus 24 troops in LCAC cabins.
5. 30 troops per MCESS shelter plus 24 troops in LCAC cabins.
6. 30 troops per PTM section plus 24 troops in LCAC cabins. Capacity of PTMs is reduced when carrying combat-equipped troops to 24 per section.

Figure 7-1. LCAC Troop-Carrying Potential

An LCAC is capable of carrying two AAVPs with applique armor installed. An LCAC is capable of carrying three AAVPs without applique armor in an overload condition. Load planners must consider the balance between craft load and fuel to prevent exceeding LCAC maximum gross weight of 368,250 pounds.

7.2.1.2 LCAC Configured with LAVs. The LAV is a wheeled amphibious vehicle designed to provide armored, highly mobile transportation and additional firepower to landing forces. The troop carrying configured LAV, the LAV-25, carries a maximum of six in the personnel compartment plus a crew of three. For reasons similar to those of the AAVP, a compartment capacity of four troops is used for planning purposes. An LCAC, in an overload condition, can carry five LAVs. Including the capacity of its own personnel compartment, LCAC can carry up to 44 combat-equipped troops when five LAVs are embarked.

7.2.1.3 LCAC Configured With HMMWVs. The HMMWV is a four-wheeled truck that serves as the LFs primary light tactical vehicle. The HMMWV has several variants including a hard top cargo/troop carrier capable of carrying four troops plus a crew of two. The HMMWV is not armed.

An LCAC is capable of carrying 12 tactically loaded HMMWVs. Including the capacity of its own personnel compartment, an LCAC can carry up to 72 combat-equipped troops when 12 HMMWVs are embarked.

7.2.1.4 Vehicle Configuration Advantages. The advantages of vehicle configuration of LCAC for personnel transfer are:

1. Vehicles and troops can be loaded and offloaded quickly, helping to reduce LCAC cycle times.

2. AAVs and LAVs provide an additional degree of armor protection to embarked troops during transit to the CLZ.

3. Vehicles provide mobility for the embarked troops after they are delivered to the beach.

4. Vehicles provide additional firepower to reduce LCAC vulnerability to enemy attack (see paragraph 5.2.2.1).

7.2.1.5 Vehicle Configuration Disadvantages.
The disadvantages of vehicle configuration of LCAC for personnel transfer are:

1. Troop carrying capacity of LCAC with vehicles embarked is substantially less than that of displacement landing craft.

2. Vehicles cannot be configured for carrying large numbers of stretcher-borne MEDEVACs.

7.2.2 MCESS Configuration of LCAC.
Using MCESS shelters as a means of increasing LCAC personnel lift capability has been proven during several MAGTF deployments. MCESS encompasses a family of prefabricated, "knockdown" containers and buildings which are included in the Marine Corps FLS. However, MCESS shelters are not always carried as part of a deploying MAGTF loadout. Therefore, the requirement for shelters to configure LCAC for personnel transfer should be determined during embarkation planning.

A MCESS shelter is a collapsible box measuring 8 X 8 X 20 feet expanded and 1.75 X 8 X 20 feet collapsed. It comes with roof and floor assemblies, two side panels which run the length of the shelter, two end panels, and four post assemblies. One end panel contains a 79 X 39-inch door that can be swung open. The other end panel contains fittings for air circulating equipment and a 21 X 27-inch escape hatch. The panels are constructed of double-skinned aluminum sheets filled with honeycomb to provide rigidity. Figure 7-2 depicts a knockdown MCESS shelter and its major components.

The MCESS shelter has banks of flourescent lights permanently mounted in the roof and has its own power distribution system. However, in the absence of special modifications to facilitate connecting the shelter to the LCAC's power system, chemlights may be used for interior lighting.

The following should be considered when planning to use MCESS shelters aboard LCAC:

1. Space required to store the MCESS shelters when not in use

2. Limitations on craft use for transporting vehicles and supplies and in other mission roles until the MCESS shelters can be removed (mix of MCESS shelters and vehicles aboard the same LCAC is possible when only one or two shelters are installed)

3. Lifejackets and hearing protection must be provided for all personnel housed in the MCESS shelters.

7.2.2.1 MCESS Modifications.
Two modifications are required to prepare the MCESS shelter for use aboard LCAC. These modifications include:

1. Fitting the shelter with removable bench seats that run the length of each side. A third row of welded metal bench seats can also be installed along the centerline of the shelter to increase personnel capacity.

2. Outfitting the shelter with a U-shaped air scoop, one end of which is fitted into a ventilation port in the rear end panel of the shelter while the other end is positioned above the shelter, facing toward the LCAC's bow.

7.2.2.2 Assembling and Securing MCESS Shelters.
Depending on the support ship, MCESS shelters can be assembled either on the LCAC, or at another location and then moved aboard LCAC using available cranes. Fifteen personnel are required for manual setup after positioning the collapsed shelter. MCESS shelters are assembled and secured aboard LCAC as follows:

1. The collapsed shelter is positioned in a suitable work area in the well deck or aboard the LCAC using a well deck overhead crane or a boat crane aboard an LSD class ship.

2. The roof section of the shelter is lifted to accommodate placement of the four post assemblies. Tethered bolts are inserted into the posts to hold them in place. The side and end panels which are stowed inside the collapsed shelter are then mounted in place.

7-3

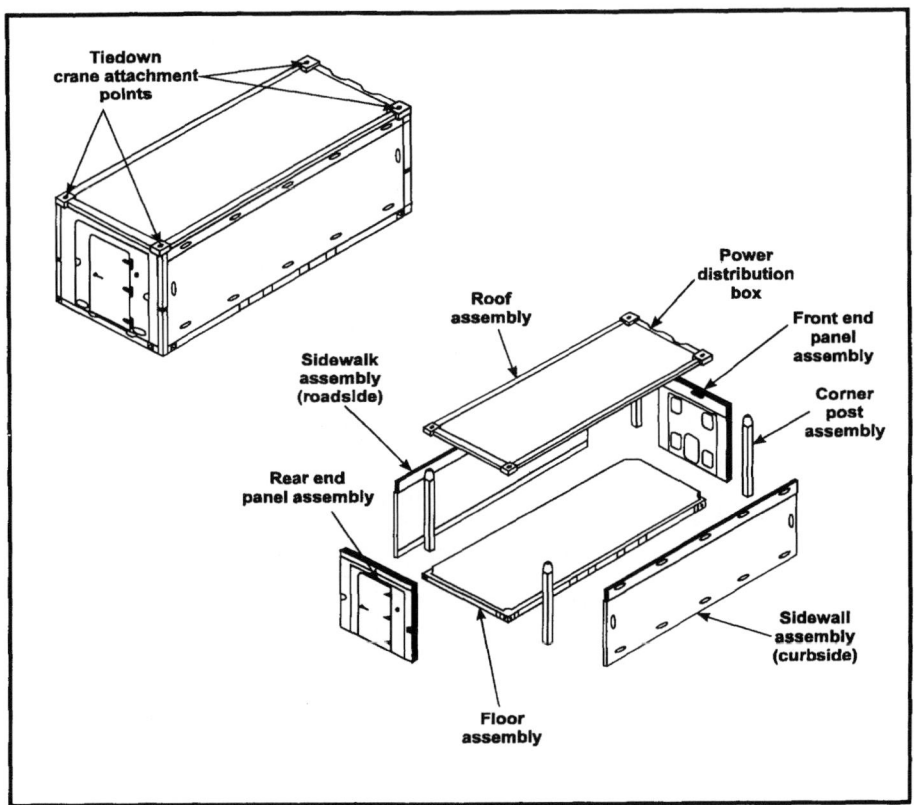

Figure 7-2. Knockdown MCESS Shelter and Major Components

3. The assembled MCESS shelter is secured to the LCAC's deck with gripes. Each shelter is secured by its upper corners, with two gripes per corner, for a total of eight gripes per container.

MCESS shelter assembly and securing time is a function of the number of shelters to be installed and the experience of the installation team. Evaluation has shown that an inexperienced team may require up to three hours per shelter. Highly experienced teams can install a shelter in as little as 30 minutes. Figure 7-3 depicts the MCESS shelter assembly process.

7.2.2.3 MCESS Configuration Options. The total troop carrying capacity depends on the configuration of the installed MCESS shelters. Up to six MCESS shelters can be installed on the deck of one LCAC. One of the tradeoffs in mission planning for shelter use is total troop capacity versus their ability to rapidly embark and debark the LCAC. Although the installation of four

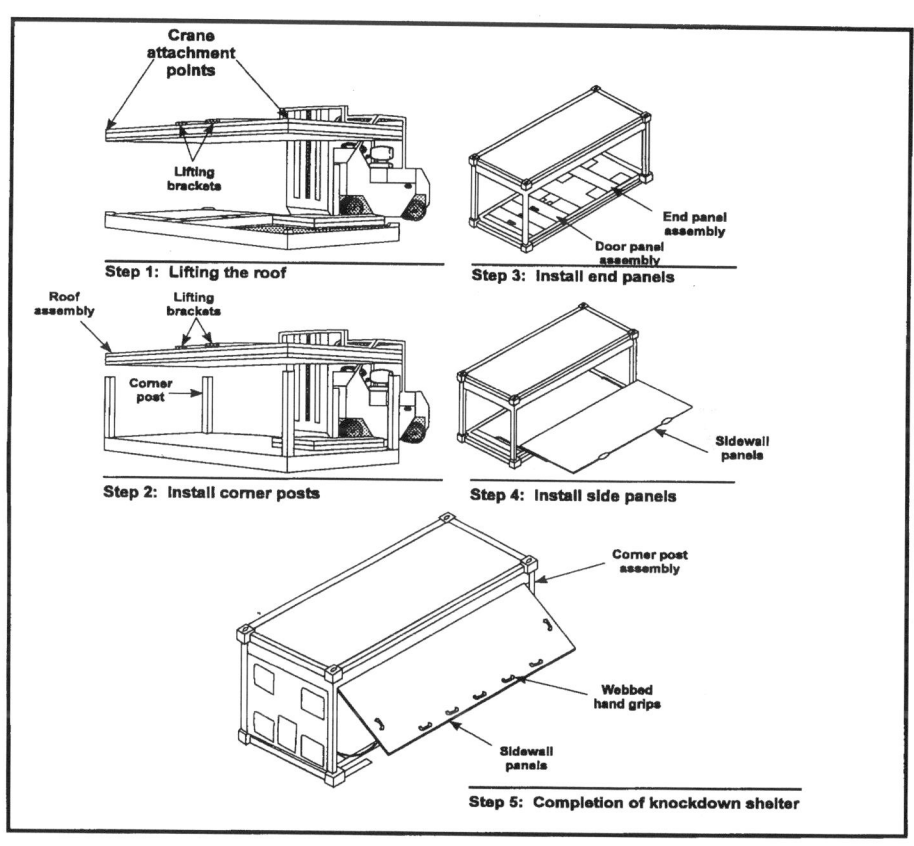

Figure 7-3. MCESS Shelter Assembly Process

or less shelters does not maximize the use of LCAC's deck space, it does permit easy access to all shelters. Figure 7-4 depicts the various MCESS shelter configurations for LCAC.

7.2.2.4 MCESS Capacity. The personnel capacity of each MCESS shelter is a function of the embarked troops' combat load and whether or not the center row of bench seats is installed. The maximum capacity for heavily combat-loaded troops is approximately 30 per shelter with 3 rows of benches installed and slightly more for civilian personnel carrying only a few small personal articles. Including the capacity of its own cabins, LCAC can carry up to 204 heavily combat-loaded troops with 6 MCESS shelters installed.

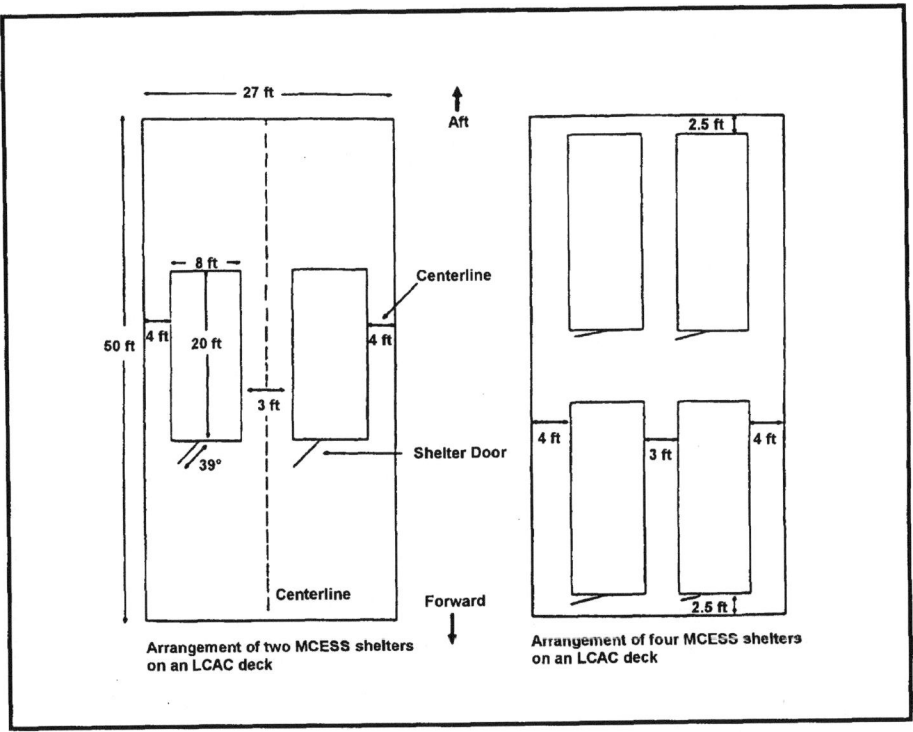

Figure 7-4. MCESS Shelter Configurations (Sheet 1 of 3)

7.2.2.5 MCESS Configuration Advantages.

The advantages of MCESS configuration of LCAC for personnel transfer are:

1. Provides significantly increased troop or evacuee carrying capacity

2. Uses existing equipment with only simple and inexpensive modifications

3. Takes advantage of LCAC's capabilities for rapid insertion/withdrawal of troops or evacuees from OTH, including amphibious raids (see paragraph 3.3.1)

4. Provides flexibility by mixing troops and vehicles in the same craft

5. Provides limited protection against open-deck hazards such as small-arms fire and explosion fragments

6. Provides possibility of configuring shelters for emergency MEDEVAC using additional MCESS components available in the Marine Corps FLS (see paragraph 6.5)

7-6

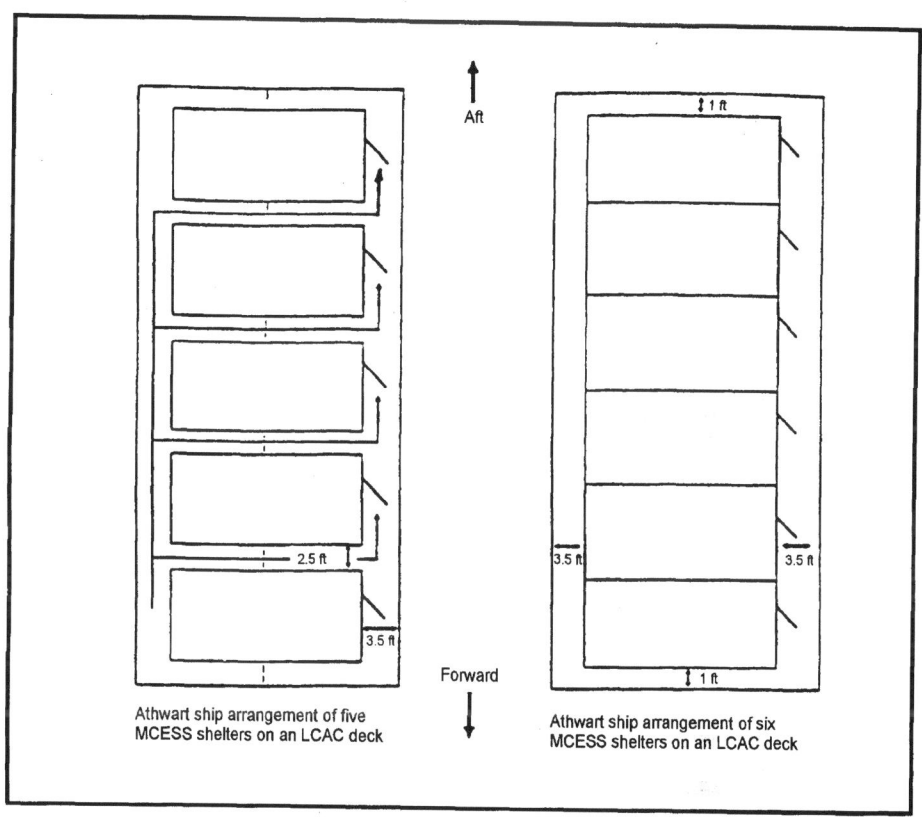

Figure 7-4. MCESS Shelter Configurations (Sheet 2 of 3)

7. Accommodates rapid removal as a single unit by bridge crane to allow loading of LCAC with vehicles or cargo.

7.2.2.6 MCESS Configuration Disadvantages.
The disadvantages of MCESS configuration of LCAC for personnel transfer are:

1. Limited number of modified shelters that may be forward-deployed

2. Time required to position, assemble, and secure shelters aboard LCAC and the attendant limitations on craft use while shelters are installed

3. Limited noise attenuation and the requirement for issuing hearing protection to personnel housed in the shelters

4. No water or sanitation facilities.

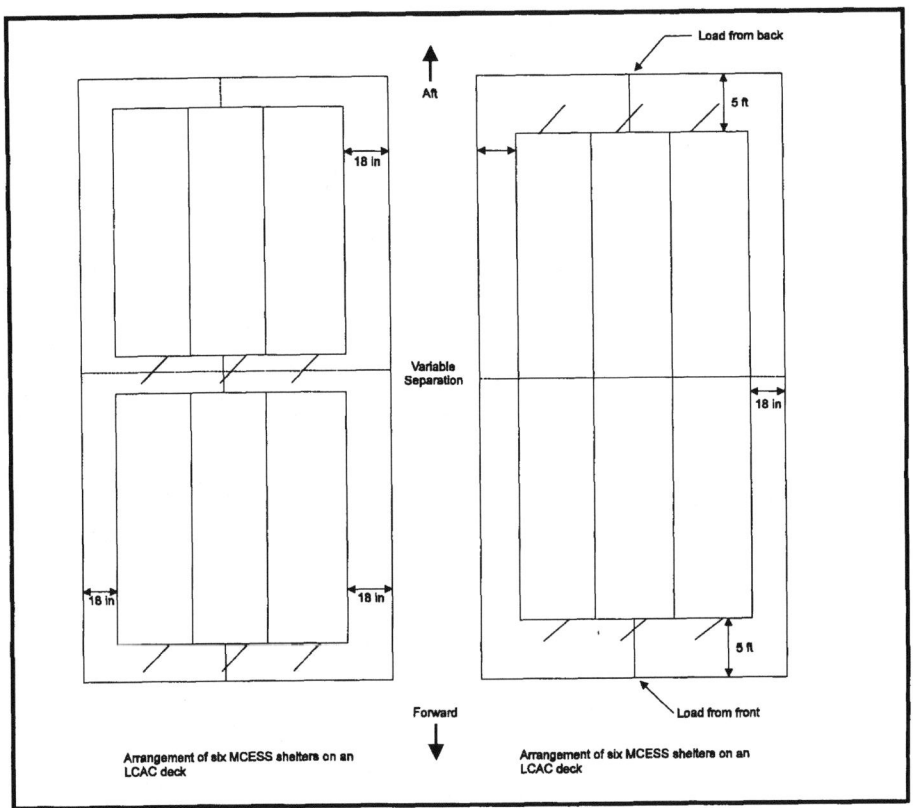

Figure 7-4. MCESS Shelter Configurations (Sheet 3 of 3)

7.2.3 PTM Configuration of LCAC. A PTM-configured LCAC substantially increases its personnel transfer capacity. The PTM-configured LCAC design mission roles include:

1. Transporting combat-ready troops from OTH during ship-to-shore movement

2. Transporting military or civilian casualties from shore to ship and shore to shore during MEDEVAC operations

3. Transporting civilian evacuees from shore to ship or shore to shore during a NEO.

An LCAC PTM structure is composed of up to six sections made up of individual panels which can be assembled in various configurations. Each section is made up of roof and floor panels and exterior and interior side panels to which end panels may be affixed. End panels are installed three abreast to provide multiple avenues of ingress and egress. Six doors are provided, three forward and three aft. Simple canvas-type, foldup seats with lap belts are installed with quick assemble brackets to the side panels. The foam core aluminum skin panels are interchangeable with the exception of the end panels. The entire six-section PTM can be stowed in one 8 X 20-foot ISO container. Figure 7-5 depicts an example of an assembled and secured six-section PTM with major components identified. Figures 7-6 and 7-7 provide a closeup view of the PTM section assembly and a PTM cross sectional view, respectively.

Note

Extended transit times (greater than 30 minutes) may degrade combat readiness of embarked troops. Personnel inside the PTM have no visual horizon and seasickness may occur. Environmental factors such as temperature and sea state will contribute to degradation of effectiveness, as well.

CAUTION

An LCAC configured with a PTM is intended to be used as a follow-on assault asset only and should not be used during the initial phase of an assault unless deemed absolutely necessary by the tactical commander.

7.2.3.1 PTM Design Features. Design features incorporated into the MCAC PTM include:

1. Can be erected manually without use of a crane or forklift by 12 trained installers in less than 6 hours.

2. Has fittings to accommodate up to 54 litters for MEDEVAC and is capable of mixed configurations with litters and seats installed simultaneously.

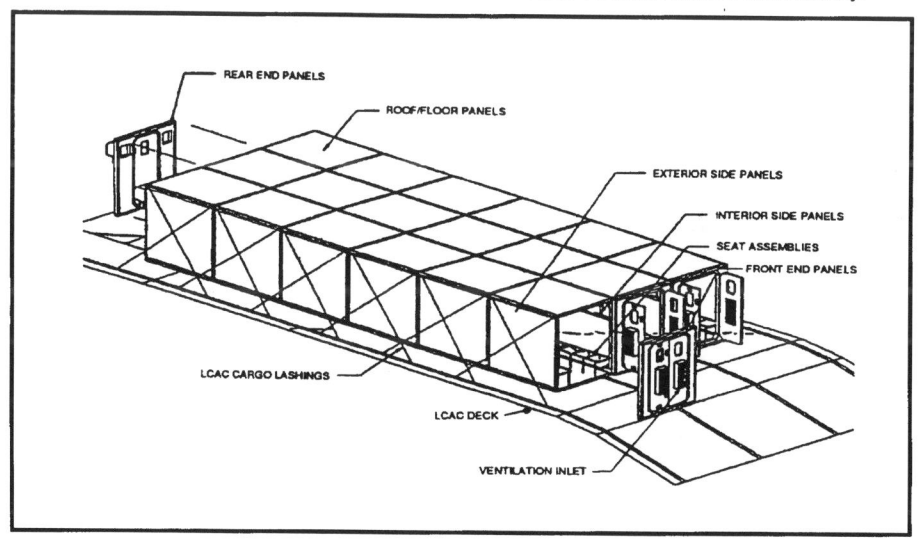

REAR END PANELS
ROOF/FLOOR PANELS
EXTERIOR SIDE PANELS
INTERIOR SIDE PANELS
SEAT ASSEMBLIES
FRONT END PANELS
LCAC CARGO LASHINGS
LCAC DECK
VENTILATION INLET

Figure 7-5. Six-Section PTM-Configured LCAC with Major Components

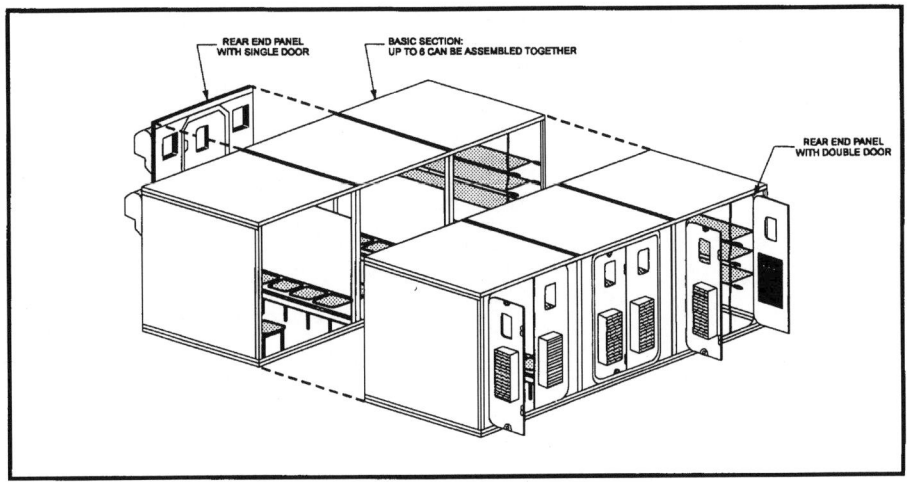

Figure 7-6. PTM-Configured LCAC Assembly

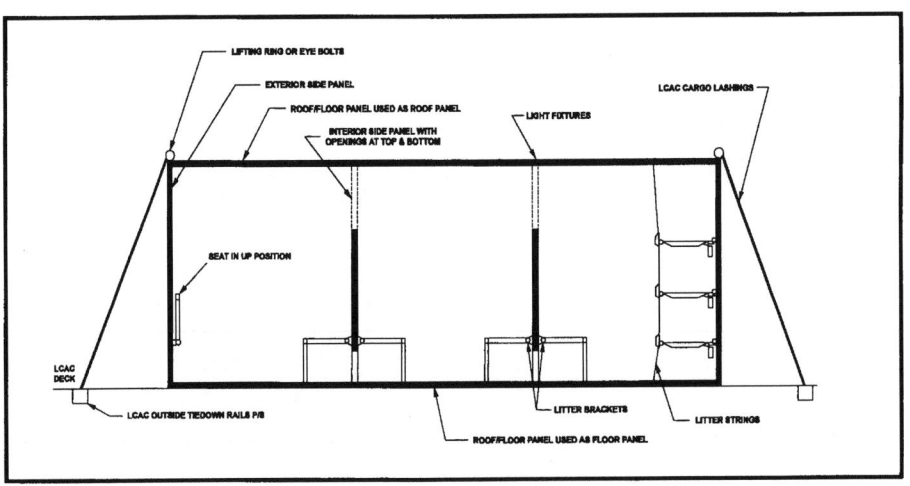

Figure 7-7. LCAC PTM Cross Sectional View

3. Provides forced ventilation and lighting, with battle lantern backup, drawing 400 Hz power from the LCAC through a special craft modification.

4. Has an LCAC IVCU connection with a MOMS voice radio backup.

5. Provides acoustic attenuation to less than 105 decibels. Double hearing protection is required for all passengers inside the PTM.

6. Provides 3.8 cubic feet of cargo space under each seat.

7. Can be transported by crane/forklift in assembled single section units.

8. Provides limited protection against airborne debris of relatively low velocity.

Note

Life jackets for troops transported in the LCAC PTM must be provided by the parent ship.

7.2.3.2 PTM-Configured LCAC Options. Figure 7-8 depicts the two PTM-configured LCAC options.

7.2.3.3 PTM Capacity. Each PTM section has the capacity for 30 personnel. Including the capacity of its own personnel compartment, LCAC can carry up to 204 personnel. Because of oversized gear and weapons carried by combat-loaded troops the capacity of the PTM shelter is approximately 24 troops per PTM section. Actual seating capacity will vary depending on amount of gear carried by passengers.

7.3 SUPPORT OF NEO

A NEO is an operation conducted to evacuate personnel from locations in a foreign (host) country. Normally, the personnel to be evacuated are U.S. ci-

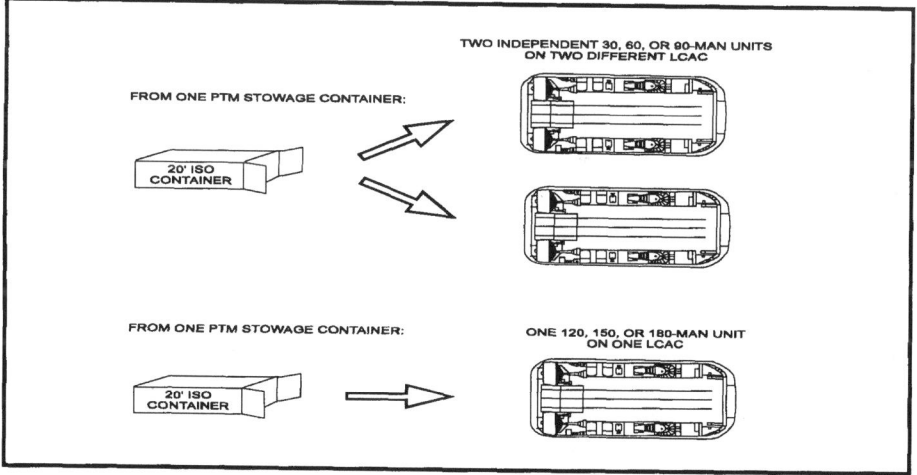

Figure 7-8. PTM-Configured LCAC

ORIGINAL

vilians whose lives are in danger. However, evacuation may also be required for:

1. U.S. military personnel

2. Host-country personnel

3. Third-country nationals.

An ATF is particularly well-suited to conduct a NEO when the location to be evacuated is accessible from the sea. A NEO is similar to an amphibious raid (see paragraph 3.3) since it involves a swift incursion into or temporary occupation of an objective followed by a planned withdrawal upon completion of the mission. A NEO differs from an amphibious raid in that the degree of force used is normally limited to that required to protect the evacuees and the evacuation force.

LCAC, with its unique capabilities, can be used in various roles in support of a NEO. LCAC roles and employment considerations in support of NEO operations are discussed in the following paragraphs.

7.3.1 LCAC NEO Roles. LCAC may be used in the NEO roles described in the following paragraphs.

7.3.1.1 Delivery of an Evacuation Force Ashore. An evacuation force must conduct a myriad of operational tasks in a dynamic political and threat environment during a NEO. LCAC provides the speed and range necessary to support the rapid insertion, sustainment, reinforcement, and withdrawal of a waterborne evacuation force from OTH in response to a quickly changing situation. OTH operations may be necessary for the protection of the ATF, as well as a political constraint of the NEO in order to minimize the operation's visibility. The craft's mobility can facilitate accessing many evacuation locations inaccessible to displacement landing craft. Finally, LCAC's lift capability can be instrumental in the transport of vehicles and equipment required for collecting and processing evacuees, particularly when evacuees are widely dispersed. The delivery of an evacuation force ashore by LCAC is subject to the ship-to-shore movement procedures discussed in chapter 4.

7.3.1.2 Shore-to-Ship or Shore-to-Shore Transfer of Evacuees. The focus of a NEO is the transfer of evacuees to a friendly or neutral location where their lives are no longer in danger. LCAC, configured with vehicles, MCESS shelters, or PTMs, can be used to transfer large numbers of evacuees from CLZs near evacuation sites to designated evacuation units of the ATF. PTM-configured LCAC can also be used to transfer evacuees to destinations in adjacent friendly or neutral countries within the craft's range. The capability for rapid waterborne evacuation of large numbers of evacuees is advantageous if the NEO environment is uncertain or should turn hostile. Similarly, PTM-configured LCAC can readily be adapted for emergency MEDEVAC should the need arise.

7.3.2 LCAC NEO Employment Considerations. Considerations for employment of LCAC in support of NEO operations include:

1. Makes shallow rivers and dry riverbeds available as potential ingress/egress routes to evacuation sites

2. Increases the number of options available to CATF and CLF for insertion/withdrawal of an evacuation force and extraction of evacuees

3. Facilitates expeditious completion of the NEO through the use of LCAC's speed and mobility

4. Requires consideration of LCAC's susceptibility to small-arms fire when in uncertain or hostile NEO environments

5. Requires consideration of LCAC's noise signature when a low profile or the element of surprise is required

6. Allows for a rapid reinforcement and dramatic increase in combat power.

7.4 SUPPORT OF ATF CHOKE-POINT TRANSIT

During the movement phase of an amphibious operation the ATF may be required to transit through choke points en route or while operating within the AOA. Choke points are ocean areas where the susceptibility of the ATF to enemy attack is greater due to a lack of sea maneuvering room caused by geographic or hydrographic restrictions.

LCAC, with its speed, range, and endurance, may be used to support ATF choke-point transits. LCAC may be used to fulfill a scouting role, extend the force's radar coverage, or conduct military OPDEC.

7.4.1 LCAC in a Scouting Role.
LCAC can be launched on a scouting mission at extended range from the choke point and proceed ahead of the ATF at high speed to detect, report, and monitor enemy activity in the vicinity of the choke point. Communications connectivity with the ATF can be maintained using the procedures for LCAC OTH control described in paragraph 4.2.3.2. Consideration should be given to launching LCAC without vehicles and equipment embarked to increase the launch range and extend the mission time. LCAC is less vulnerable to enemy AAW systems which might otherwise hazard aircraft used in a scouting role.

7.4.2 LCAC Extension of ATF Radar Coverage.
LCAC can be launched and positioned along enemy threat axes beyond the limits of ATF search radar coverage as the force approaches and passes through a choke point. LCAC's radar may be able to detect small craft, low/slow flying aircraft which might pose a threat to the ATF, and the periscopes or snorkels of hostile submarines. The possibility of LCAC counterdetection by hostile submarines is considerably less than that of other ATF escorts.

7.4.3 LCAC in Military OPDEC.
Paragraph 7.6.3 describes the use of LCAC in military OPDEC for support of an ATF chokepoint transit.

7.5 SUPPORT OF MIO

Ships of the ATF may be tasked to support a MIO which involves the interception, visiting, boarding, searching, and potential seizing of merchant shipping. LCAC, with its speed, endurance, and lift capabilities, can provide flexibility in boarding vessels over a large area. The following factors make LCAC a viable asset in supporting a MIO:

1. Capability to overtake slower merchant vessels

2. Ability to act as a force multiplier by supporting multiple boardings over a large area

3. Capability of lifting, launching, and recovering CRRC, as discussed in paragraph 3.2.1.1, which are

excellent platforms for the final approach and boarding of merchant vessels

4. Ability to accommodate up to two 11-man boarding parties in its personnel cabins

5. Capability of installed radio suite which can support voice communications with both a mother ship and target ships over an installed bridge-to-bridge VHF FM radio

6. Availability of limited but sufficient self-defense M-60 machine guns which can be augmented with other portable weapon systems

7. Capability to work in tandem with another boarding vessel to provide dual axis boarding of merchant vessels if required.

7.6 SUPPORT OF ATF MILITARY OPDEC

ATF military OPDEC involves the use of feints, amphibious demonstrations, or specially configured EA platforms to mislead enemy forces at sea and ashore as to the ATF's actual mission. LCAC, with its speed, range, mobility, and lift capabilities, is a viable platform for each of the foregoing military OPDEC uses.

LCAC's role in feints and amphibious demonstrations is identical to the craft's role in ship-to-shore movement as discussed in Chapter 4. A deception van-configured LCAC, can also carry and employ various autonomously supportable EA vans in support of military OPDEC. The two types of EA vans which can be loaded aboard an LCAC and their employment considerations are discussed in the following paragraphs.

7.6.1 CADS Van.
LCAC can be loaded with a CADS van which is an air/ground transportable system that has its own power source. Several CADS-van variants are available through C^2WGRULANT or C^2WGRUPAC.

CADS vans have a variety of capabilities which may be used to support ATF military OPDEC including HF, VHF, and UHF voice communications. CADS-van characteristics are described in NWP 3-58.1, "Navy Operational Deception and Counterdetection (U)."

7.6.2 SSQ-74 Van. LCAC can be loaded with an SSQ-74 van which is also available through C^{2}WGRU-LANT or C^{2}WGRUPAC. SSQ-74 vans have a wide range of capabilities which may be used to support ATF military OPDEC, including HF and UHF voice communications. SSQ-74 van characteristics are described in NWP 3-58.1.

7.6.3 Deception Van-Configured LCAC Employment Considerations. Considerations for employment of deception van-configured LCAC include:

1. Can be employed against open-ocean, chokepoint, or nearshore surface, subsurface, and air threats

2. Can be employed to deceive the ground threat to the LF

3. Can be employed at OTH distances from ATF transit groups to provide electronic emissions to confuse enemy ASUW targeting

4. Can be employed in conjunction with feints and amphibious demonstrations to cause enemy redeployment of ground forces away from planned landing beaches

5. Requires preloading vans in LCAC because of size and weight

6. Can provide tactical advantages by redistributing enemy forces.

7.7 SUPPORT OF AOA MCM

LCAC's role in mine warfare is discussed in paragraph 3.2.2. MCM-configured LCAC, can be used for minesweeping, minehunting, and SZ lane breaching. These roles and their employment considerations are discussed in the following paragraphs.

7.7.1 Mechanical Minesweeping. Testing indicates that MCM-configured LCAC is a viable platform for deploying, towing, and recovering Mk 103 mechanical minesweeping equipment.

LCAC used in mechanical minesweeping will likely be able to operate in moderate seas at moderate speeds. The average time it takes LCAC to stream and

recover Mk 103 gear appears to compare favorably with the time to stream and recover the same gear from other LCM platforms.

7.7.2 Acoustic and Magnetic Minesweeping. Testing indicates that MCM-configured LCAC is a viable platform for deploying, towing, and recovering a Mk 106 device composed of Mk 104 acoustic and Mk 105 magnetic minesweeping equipment.

7.7.3 SZ Lane Breaching. Research indicates that MCM-configured LCAC is a viable platform for firing M58 linear demolition charges to help establish breach lanes through the SZ.

7.7.4 MCM-Configured LCAC Employment Considerations. Considerations for employing MCM-configured LCAC include:

1. May require partial cushion operations to minimize spray effects during streaming and recovery operations.

2. Will require deck installation of a high-capacity winch to support deployment, towing, and recovery of minesweeping and minehunting gear.

3. Will complicate handling of craft when towing gear.

4. May employ MOMS voice communications to link operators in LCAC's cabin with personnel manning deck rigs.

5. Will add a new safety concern involving tow tension that increases greatly with increased tow speed, higher sea state, and turns.

6. Will not cause mutual interference among various types of MCM equipment.

7. Can tow MCM equipment in all LCAC operational sea states. Sea state limitations are driven by crew safety concerns when deploying and recovering equipment. Tow speed of the MCM-configured LCAC is limited by the maximum tow speed of the MCM equipment.

7.8 SUPPORT OF HA AND DISASTER RELIEF OPERATIONS

HA and disaster relief operations are conducted to mitigate the results of natural or manmade disasters, conflicts, or other endemic conditions. Their goal is to reduce human pain and suffering, disease, hunger, hardship, and privation that might present a serious threat to life or result in a great loss of property. HA and disaster relief operations conducted by U.S. forces are limited in scope and duration. The assistance provided supplements or complements the primary efforts of the host nation.

An ATF is particularly well-suited to conduct HA and disaster relief operations where assistance is required in areas accessible from the sea. HA and disaster relief operations frequently occur concurrently with other military operations, many of which are MEU SOC in nature. The general principles of support for HA and disaster relief operations are responsiveness, simplicity, economy, flexibility, sustainability, and security.

LCAC, with its unique capabilities, is an ideal platform for use in both concurrent MEU SOC operations and in achieving HA and disaster relief general support goals. MEU SOC missions which may involve LCAC are listed in paragraph 1.2.2.5. LCAC's role in the general support of HA and disaster relief operations, and in conducting those operations at sea and ashore are discussed in the following paragraphs.

7.8.1 LCAC's General Support Role. LCAC can support HA and disaster relief as follows:

1. Responsiveness. LCAC, with its speed, range, and mobility, can be used to reduce the ATF closure time to the troubled area by proceeding ahead of the ATF.

2. Simplicity. LCAC lends itself to simplified planning by being able to access shorelines that might otherwise be inaccessible to displacement craft.

3. Economy. LCAC allows CATF and CLF to maintain a large reserve of assets for unforeseen emergencies and surge those assets quickly to stabilize critical situations.

4. Flexibility. LCAC can be readily adapted to a variety of roles in support of rapidly changing needs in the troubled area.

5. Sustainability. LCAC can contribute to the sustainability of the operation by continuing to support seabasing as discussed in paragraph 6.3.

6. Security. LCAC can be used to support security force insertion and movement. LCAC's support of seabasing also contributes to security of the operation by facilitating centralized supply functions.

7.8.2 LCAC's Role in HA and Disaster Operations at Sea and Ashore. LCAC can be used in HA and disaster relief operations at sea and ashore as described in the following paragraphs.

7.8.2.1 At Sea. HA operations at sea include the interception of vessels containing migrants or refugees. LCAC's role in supporting migrant/refugee interception is similar to that discussed in paragraph 7.5 for a MIO, principally for the identification of vessels needing assistance and the delivery of survey crews to those vessels in need of assistance.

7.8.2.2 Ashore. LCAC can be employed in a wide variety of roles for HA and disaster relief operations ashore including hurricane aftermaths, floods, droughts, famines, and epidemics. LCAC's principal roles include the transportation of seabased cargo and equipment, MEDEVAC (see paragraph 6.5), and the transportation of security forces.

7.8.3 LCAC HA and Disaster Operations Support Considerations. Historically HA operations have involved the transport of large quantities of bulk cargo and foodstuffs. Cargo provided by relief agencies may be palletized or loose. Palletized cargo is preferred because of ease in handling. Nonpalletized cargo can substantially increase time required for LCAC onload and offload.

All cargo should be protected from sea spray by placing tarps both under and over cargo to help in maintaining packaging and content integrity. Covering the tarps with cargo nets will further reduce FOD hazards.

The time required to load unpalletized bulk items manually will decrease the number of sorties per day and overall volume of relief supplies. The following may assist in increasing overall LCAC cycle rate:

1. Use large preloaded morning sorties

2. Use small loads to take advantage of daytime operating hours

3. Preload LCAC in the evening after the day's last cycle

4. Conduct advanced and daily liaison with civilian relief agencies

5. Use nylon aircraft tiedowns to expedite loading and unloading.

When selecting CLZs, consider the following factors in addition to those discussed in paragraphs 2.5.2.3 and 2.5.2.4:

1. Storm related topography changes.

2. Abnormal tidal range.

3. Degraded beach trafficability.

4. CLZ proximity to roads and warehouses.

5. CLZ suitability for staging and moving large quantities of cargo.

6. Ingress/egress route obstructions.

7. CLZ and surrounding area security. Coordinate with local police or military for crowd control in and around the CLZ for safety and security.

8. Advance RECON of possible CLZs by beachmasters and LCAC detachment OIC.

9. Nearshore LCAC support ship operations to include:

(a) More LCAC cycles per crew day

(b) Reduced LCAC fuel consumption

(c) Better control ship monitoring of weather and sea state in area of LCAC operation.

10. Advance and continuous coordination between the ATF and relief agency director. The communications plan should support liaison between key control agencies.

11. Supply of dunnage, banding material, pallets, and material handling equipment adequate to support projected cargo transfer on support ships and at beach site.

CHAPTER 8

LCAC Operations in Extreme Environmental Conditions

8.1 INTRODUCTION

Previous chapters discussed a variety of LCAC operations under normal environmental conditions. This chapter discusses LCAC operations in extreme environmental conditions. Extreme environmental conditions include cold weather, high heat, high airborne particle levels, and heavy weather.

8.2 OPERATIONS IN COLD WEATHER

Cold weather affects LCAC performance, personnel, and well deck operations. Figure 8-1 shows some of the effects of cold weather.

An LCAC cold-weather kit has been developed to reduce the effects of cold weather. The LCAC cold-weather kit consists of components permanently installed in LCAC and removable components that are installed only when cold weather is anticipated. This paragraph discusses the LCAC cold-weather kit and the effects cold weather has on LCAC performance, personnel, and well deck operations.

8.2.1 LCAC Cold-Weather Kit. The special equipment and fluids that make up the LCAC cold-weather kit provide:

1. Fuel and component heating and a means to preheat main engine and APU inlet air

Ambient Temperature (°F)	Effect
48	F-76 waxing begins
32	JP-5 waxing begins Icing occurs in main engine and APU inlet filtration systems (reduced combustion airflow/clogged filters) Icing occurs on shroud edge surfaces (risk of propeller tip damage) Icing occurs on cabin module windshields (reduced visibility) Icing occurs on propeller FOD screens (reduced propulsion airflow/missile hazard) Craft and cargo icing begin (increased craft weight/fall hazard) Icing occurs on lift fan FOD screens and internals (missile hazard) Icing occurs in main engine and windshield water wash systems (water wash not available; salt buildup on gas turbine blades/reduced visibility)
25	P-250 utility pump oil thickens
10	APU difficult to start with F-76 (no craft power available)

Figure 8-1. Effects of Cold Weather on LCAC Operations

2. Main engine inlet combustion air heating

3. A means of defogging and removing ice from command module windshields

4. A means to heat the leading edges of propeller shrouds

5. A means to prevent main engine and APU blow-in doors from freezing to door seals

6. Alcohol for use in the main engine and windshield water wash systems. No change of MIL-L-23699 oil is required.

8.2.1.1 Cold-Weather Kit Permanent Components.

The permanently installed cold-weather kit components include:

1. Electrically powered main fuel tank, fuel coalescer, and APU fuel heaters

2. Window heaters

3. Main engine and APU blow-in door strip heaters

4. Cold-weather equipment remote controls

5. Cabin module heating

6. Propeller shroud anti-icing system that uses APU bleed air to heat the leading edge of the shroud

7. Electrical, hydraulic, and mechanical systems that interface with removable cold-weather kit components.

LCAC main engine and APU fuel heaters allow the use of either NDF (NATO number F76) or JP-5 (NATO number F44) fuel. At temperatures of 48 ^{o}F and below, fuel heaters must be activated to sustain NDF at acceptable temperature. For JP-5, fuel heaters must be activated only at temperatures of 32 ^{o}F and below. The NDF fuel heater is the only cold-weather kit component used when the ambient temperature is above freezing. For operations below 32 ^{o}F, it is mandatory to use JP-5 fuel because of its low soot contamination of inlet barrier filters.

8.2.1.2 Cold-Weather Kit Removable Components.

When the cold-weather kit removable components are in place, LCAC equipment can be operated to design specifications in temperatures down to minus 30 ^{o}F. Removable components of the cold-weather kit include:

1. Ducts that recirculate main engine exhaust gasses to heat engine inlet air

2. Sacrificial window panels with heating elements

3. Antifreeze (methyl alcohol and distilled water) for the main engine, APU, and windshield water wash system tank

4. 5W30 weight oil to replace the engine oil in the P-250 utility pump at temperatures below 25 ^{o}F

5. Silicon grease to treat door and hatch gaskets, including main engine and APU blow-in door seals, to keep them from freezing and sticking.

The two most significant parameters of optimum gas turbine engine performance in cold weather are inlet air temperature and air flow resistance through the main engine inlet. A pair of exhaust feedback tubes controlled by two manually set flaps take hot exhaust gas from each main engine stack and pass it through remotely controllable flapper (butterfly) valves in two transverse tubes leading to the main engine inlet ducts. The main engine inlet air temperature must be carefully monitored and the flow of hot gasses regulated by the flapper valve to maintain inlet air temperature in the 40 to 50 ^{o}F range. Lower inlet air temperatures in a wet marine environment are conducive to ice formation and subsequent blockage of the main engine filtration system.

The lower portion of each main engine inlet duct has a manually operated inlet door that can be opened to bypass the recirculation duct when operating in warmer conditions and in the well deck.

8.2.2 Effects on LCAC Performance.

The effects of cold weather on LCAC performance vary with temperature and the installation and use of the cold-weather kit. Volume I, Chapter 3 of the "Safe Engineering and Operations (SEAOPS) Manual for Landing Craft Air Cushion (LCAC) Operations" addresses the effects of cold weather on LCAC systems, recommended system operating procedures in cold weather, and guidance for when the cold-weather kit removable components are not installed. The principal considerations for operating LCAC with and without the cold-weather kit removable components installed are discussed in the following paragraphs.

8.2.2.1 Cold-Weather Kit Removable Components Not Installed.

When LCAC equipment operates at freezing temperatures without the cold-weather kit removable components installed, the main engine air inlet screens may experience rapid icing and clogging from frozen sea spray. With longer engine operating periods, the inlet hookvanes and other portions of the engine filtration system may also develop an ice buildup. Inlet screen icing and filter blockage is more pronounced at temperatures just below freezing (between 20 and 32 °F) when the ice is mostly slush. Complete blockage of the inlet system can occur in heavy rain and spray conditions, leading to the loss of one or more engines. Over water, spray suppression techniques should be employed to reduce the rate of blockage until the craft can return to the support ship's well deck to have the cold-weather kit removable components installed. In an emergency the inlet leaf screens can be removed which will reduce air blockage and allow craft to return to base.

8.2.2.2 Cold-Weather Kit Removable Components Installed.

Normal LCAC operations are not affected by the permanently installed components of the cold-weather kit. Craft capability degradations due to installation of the removable components of the cold-weather kit are discussed in the following paragraphs.

8.2.2.2.1 Exhaust Gas Recirculation Disadvantages.

Using exhaust gas for heating main engine inlet air may result in the ingestion of exhaust soot. Soot ingestion can lead to rapid fouling of the engine filtration system, increased air flow resistance in the engine inlet and exhaust ducting, and loss of turbine power and efficiency. The soot ingestion problem will be compounded if the craft is burning NDF instead of the cleaner burning JP-5. SEAOPS Volume I, requires JP-5 to be used in environments of 32 °F or lower.

8.2.2.2.2 Use of Bypass Doors During Well Deck Operations.

With the removable recirculation ducts installed, there is a significant increase in the engine inlet-air temperature during well deck operations, and a corresponding decrease in engine efficiency, even with the recirculation duct butterfly valves fully closed. Because the well deck overhead tends to inhibit circulation of hot exhaust gasses, the added exhaust heat can raise the inlet-air temperature substantially, dependent on the craft position in the well deck. Opening the manually operated bypass doors in the lower section of the engine inlet ducts admits cooler combustion air.

The most critical time for the inlet duct bypass doors to be open is during LCAC well deck entry. During well deck departure, the ambient temperature outside the well deck will determine the position of the bypass doors. The bypass doors will normally be closed when the ambient temperature is below freezing, facilitating recirculation of exhaust gasses as required to maintain the inlet-air temperature within the appropriate range.

8.2.2.2.3 Cargo Positioning Constraints on the Craft's Deck.

The vertical ducts of the main engine exhaust gas recirculation component extend approximately 12 inches into the cargo area from the engine compartments. Room must be left to open or close the manual bypass doors in the vertical portion of the duct.

8.2.2.2.4 Restricted Access to Engine Compartment Hatches.

Although the horizontal and vertical ducts of the recirculation component can be unlatched and rotated to provide access to top hatches and side access panels of the engine compartments, full rotation of the vertical ducts and access to the engine compartments from the deck may not be possible under certain cargo loads.

8.2.2.2.5 Main Engine Firefighting Limitations.

Since the vertical ducts of the recirculation component block access to the fire view and halon injection ports on the main engine access panels, firefighting may be limited initially to use of the fire view ports in the top hatches of the engine compartments. These ports allow a visual confirmation of compartment status and can be broken to admit Halon from a portable extinguisher if the installed Halon system fails to extinguish an engine fire.

8.2.2.2.6 Main Engine Inlet Pressure Drop and Loss of Engine Efficiency.

Depending on engine power requirements, the normal inlet-air pressure drop across the filtration system can vary from minus 3 to minus 8 inches of water. Installation of the recirculation component will raise the inlet-air pressure loss an additional 1 inch with the bypass doors open and about 3 to 4 inches with the bypass doors closed. The increased inlet-air pressure drop results in a loss of engine efficiency.

8.2.2.2.7 Light Craft Weight for Mission Planning.
The cold-weather kit weight is included in the light craft weight, therefore, no additions are necessary for MPP computations.

8.2.2.3 Craft and Cargo Icing.
In addition to the effects of engine inlet screen icing and filter blockage and the precautions necessary for keeping LCAC equipment on line as discussed in paragraph 8.2.2.2, operations in cold weather can also result in icing of the craft and cargo. The effects of craft and cargo icing are discussed in the following paragraphs.

8.2.2.3.1 Ice Overload.
Freezing spray could overload LCAC with ice and, in an extreme situation, force the craft off cushion. Ice overload will generally be indicated by changes of LCAC trim and mushy handling characteristics. Craft operations on cushion at slow speeds should be avoided to minimize cushion-generated icing. The application of icephobic or other low adhesion coatings to exposed LCAC vertical surfaces has been used successfully to reduce ice adhesion.

Note

For ice overload to occur, craft must be exposed or operating in extreme conditions for an extended period of time. Usually, the range and fuel capacity will limit the possibility of ice overload. SEAOPS instructions require ice removal after each mission.

8.2.2.3.2 Reduced Visibility.
Installed washers, wipers, and heaters are generally effective in preventing the icing and fogging of LCAC command module windshields.

8.2.2.3.3 Reduced Deck Traction.
Ice-covered decks may be extremely difficult for personnel and wheeled vehicles to negotiate and are potentially hazardous. The application of nonskid deck coatings to all cargo deck and ramp areas used by personnel and vehicles is an effective means of improving traction. The use of deicing devices such as steam "jennys" and granular compounds including sand have also been used successfully to improve traction.

8.2.2.3.4 Cargo Tiedown Icing.
The icing of cargo tiedowns may increase their release time significantly. Accumulated ice can be removed by kicking the cargo tiedowns or, in more severe icing conditions, striking the cargo tiedowns with mallets or broom handles.

8.2.2.3.5 Vehicle Icing.
Icing which inhibits vehicle offload can be minimized by loading vehicles aboard LCAC with their radiators and engine inlets facing aft. This technique has the added benefit of reducing vehicle windshield icing. Putting grease on vehicle door and hatch seals can prevent ice adhesion.

8.2.2.4 Considerations for Operating Over Ice.
LCAC operations conducted over sea ice may be required in a cold weather environment and are subject to special considerations. When operating over sea ice, the banks and ditches encountered by LCAC on land will be replaced by ice ridges and leads. Figure 8-2 depicts sea ice topographical features and craft parameters that must be considered when crossing each. LCAC ice-to-water transition is similar to land-to-water transition discussed in paragraph 1.2.1.3.7.

Operating over sea ice is similar to operating over concrete, except ice creates less friction. Small amounts of propulsive force cause craft movement, and the distances required for stopping and to complete maneuvers are greater. All LCAC over-ice maneuvers should be planned in advance and executed with care. Additional considerations for operating LCAC over ice are discussed in the following paragraphs.

8.2.2.4.1 Crossing Ice Ridges.
LCAC should not cross ice ridges with a height greater than 70 percent of the height of the cushion. This equates to a maximum ridge height of 3.5 feet. The inability of the cushion to rapidly recover when crossing higher ridges in quick succession may result in hard-structure impacts, and will add appreciably to skirt bag and finger damage.

8.2.2.4.2 Speed Considerations.
When operating over sea ice, LCAC speed is determined by ice surface conditions. For flat and low rubble ice of 2 feet

TOPOGRAPHICAL FEATURE	ICE PRESENTATION	CRAFT PARAMETERS
PRESSURE RIDGE		• SKIRT HEIGHT • OPERATING SPEED
PRESSURE RIDGE		• SKIRT HEIGHT • CRAFT LENGTH • OPERATING SPEED
LEAD		• DEPTH TO SKIRT HEIGHT • WIDTH TO CRAFT LENGTH • APPROACH SPEED
FLAT ICE RUBBLE		• SKIRT DURABILITY • OPERATING SPEED • SPEED AND HEIGHT
WATERFACE TRANSITION		• CRAFT CUSHION HEIGHT
BEACH RUBBLE		• CRAFT CUSHION HEIGHT

Figure 8-2. Ice Topographical Features

or less, hump speed can be maintained. In more dense and higher rubble of 2 feet or more, skirt drag and wear will be encountered and speed should be 10 to 15 knots. LCAC speed must be used selectively to clear obstacles. Limiting factors associated with increasing speed to cross various impediments include:

1. Decrease in control of craft over ice surfaces

2. Increased risk of hard-structure impact with taller obstacles

3. Increased likelihood of skirt damage in ice rubble of 2 feet or higher

4. Insufficient time for the cushion to be replenished between obstacles, resulting in hard-structure impact when crossing obstacles in quick succession

5. Reduced reaction time in approaching or trying to avoid obstacles.

8.2.2.4.3 Operating in Sea Ice Rubble. Special precautions must be taken when operating LCAC in sea ice rubble. Sea ice rubble is composed of rafted pancake and ice cake floes creating numerous ice obstacles of varying height and density. The hardness and sharpness of the ice are a function of age, when it was broken, and ambient conditions causing it to melt or harden. Sea ice rubble can be found in all ice flow conditions. Due to potential skirt bag, finger, and underhull structural damage, recommended speed limitation of 10 to 20 knots for LCAC operating in sea ice rubble height greater than 1.5 feet. Operating in these conditions requires the addition of hull fuel tank protection plates.

Note

Snow cover can obscure rubble. The first indication may be when LCAC cushion air blows the snow off the broken ice.

8.2.2.4.4 Turning Maneuvers. Due to the lower frictional resistance encountered when operating over smooth sea ice, LCAC's advance and transfer (and hence turning radius) are substantially greater than during operations over open water.

8.2.2.4.5 Ice Breaking. LCAC can be used effectively as an icebreaker. At speeds less than 12 knots, craft cushion pressure depresses the water surface below the sea ice sheet. As the craft advances, the unsupported ice beneath the cushion breaks of its own weight. This technique is effective with ice up to 12 inches thick. LCAC high speed icebreaking (12 to 20 knots) is more effective due to the combined effect of bow wave compression and cushion pressure. A loaded craft is more effective at breaking ice.

8.2.2.4.6 Safe Navigation. LCAC safe navigation over sea ice is subject to a variety of factors including:

1. Reduced visibility due to snow clouds formed by escaping cushion air when fresh snow is on the ice.

2. Operations restricted to the use of instruments (compass courses and timed runs) if geographic or other reference points such as radar beacons are not marking the track. Use of GPS is required.

3. Potential for crew vertigo and disorientation due to a lack of suitable visual references in a flat field of white.

4. Need for prior helicopter reconnaissance to identify obstacles and map safe craft routes through difficult ice topography.

8.2.3 Effects on Personnel Embarked in LCAC. Cold weather affects LCAC crew members' and passengers' safety and comfort.

8.2.3.1 Personnel Safety. During LCAC operations in temperatures below 32 °F, icing of the craft becomes a problem as discussed in paragraph 8.2.2.3. The possibility of falling is increased, and extreme care should be exercised in moving about the craft's cargo deck. Safety lines should be rigged, as appropriate, and personnel should work in pairs if cargo deck operations cannot be avoided.

Another personnel safety concern is missile hazards caused by ice being shaken off propeller FOD screens. In freezing weather, rain and sea spray quickly freeze to FOD screens, restricting air intake and posing FOD hazard to the propellers. Ice can normally be shaken free from the FOD screens by varying/reversing the propeller pitch. This creates a missile hazard.

If operations in temperatures below freezing are anticipated, the craftmaster or higher authority may direct the removal of propeller FOD screens. FOD screen removal shall only be accomplished when the main engines are shut down. Typical LCAC propeller FOD screen removal can be accomplished in 4 hours. FOD screens around the lift fans should not be removed, however. Lift fan FOD screens should be deiced as required to maintain sufficient air flow for craft lift.

8.2.3.2 Personnel Comfort. Personnel comfort in cold weather is a function of the clothing worn and the climate control system for the command and personnel cabin modules. The climate control system consists of electrical resistance heaters in the module air conditioning units. These heaters can barely keep the modules warm on very cold days. A supplemental heater is under design for use on LCAC in extremely cold temperature environments, and craft alterations are being made to increase installed heater output. Nonetheless, the wearing of appropriate cold weather and extreme cold weather clothing is recommended.

8.2.4 Effects on LCAC Well Deck Operations. The effects of cold weather on LCAC well deck operations include increased possibility of injury to well deck personnel from LCAC-generated ice missile hazards and additional LCAC maintenance and support concerns.

8.2.4.1 Missile Hazards. LCAC lift fan FOD screens are subject to the same accumulation of ice as propeller FOD screens. During well deck entry, pieces of ice may be dislodged from the fan FOD screens, drawn into the lift fans, expelled through the bow thruster, and present high-speed missile hazard to all well deck personnel including the ramp marshall guiding the LCAC into the well deck. Therefore, consideration should be given to unassisted LCAC well deck entries during operations in cold weather.

8.2.4.2 Maintenance and Support Concerns. Cold-weather maintenance and support concerns are discussed in the following paragraphs.

8.2.4.2.1 Well Deck Temperature. In cold weather LCAC maintenance times can increase as much as 50 percent due to the cold temperatures, bulky clothing, and well deck icing. Without the warming effect of the hot exhaust gasses from LCAC operating under their own power, well deck temperatures may be only a few degrees above the outside temperature.

Testing has shown that use of portable 350,000 BTU fuel heaters may raise well deck temperatures 20 to 30 °F above the ambient temperature, creating a satisfactory working environment for maintenance personnel. The need for portable fuel heaters for cold-weather well deck operations should be considered during embarkation planning.

8.2.4.2.2 Fuel Type. As discussed in paragraph 8.2.2.2.1, the burning of JP-5 rather than NDF in LCAC engines results in cleaner emissions and places less of a burden on engine inlet filters when operating with the cold-weather kit. The burning of JP-5 also reduces pollution levels in the well deck. SEAOPS Volume I, requires JP-5 to be used in environments of 32 °F or lower.

8.2.4.2.3 Electrical Power Demand. LCAC cold-weather operations can place substantially greater demands on shipboard 400 Hz electrical power service when craft are operating off well deck power. Each LCAC may require nearly 30 kilowatts of power beyond normal housekeeping requirements for fuel tank and cabin module heating.

8.3 OPERATIONS IN HIGH-HEAT/HIGH-AIR-BORNE PARTICLE ENVIRONMENTS

LCAC operations in high-heat/high-airborne particle environments can affect LCAC performance, personnel, and well deck operations. A high-heat environment is an environment in which the ambient temperature is high enough to limit LCAC MCP operation for a particular craft weight. A high-airborne particle environment is an environment in which the levels of suspended particles of sand, dust, salt, water, ash, or other contaminants may be ingested into LCAC engines with combustion air. High-heat/high-airborne particle environments affect LCAC performance, personnel, and well deck operations.

8.3.1 Effects on LCAC Performance. The primary effects of high-heat/high-airborne particle environments on LCAC performance are increased rates of gas turbine engine wear, inlet-air filtration system clog-

ging, engine fuel consumption, and limitations on total craft weight.

8.3.1.1 Engine Wear. High ambient temperatures result in higher temperature combustion air entering LCAC's engines and, subsequently, hotter burning gasses entering the engines' power turbines. To reduce turbine wear, the temperature of the burning gasses must not rise above a specified level determined by the engine manufacturer.

Operating LCAC gas turbine engines at or below the MCP for the given ambient temperature and craft weight ensures that the manufacturer-specified turbine inlet-air temperature is not exceeded. If LCAC must operate in extremely high-heat environments with full cargo loads, engine MCP may be routinely exceeded, and engine life will be significantly shortened due to wear.

8.3.1.2 Engine Inlet-Air Filtration System Clogging. As in inlet screen icing and filter blockage which can occur in cold-weather operations (see paragraph 8.2.2.1), the accumulation of airborne particles in the gas turbine engine air filtration system may lead to complete blockage of inlet air and loss of one or more engines. At a minimum, frequent filter changes will be required to minimize loss of engine efficiency due to increased main engine inlet-air pressure drop.

8.3.1.3 Increased Engine Fuel Consumption. High ambient air temperatures reduce the power produced for a given LCAC main engine speed. In order to maintain the power necessary to achieve the craft speed required for a particular mission, the speed of the main engines must be increased. Since the fuel burn-rate depends on the speed of the main engines, operations in extremely high ambient temperatures will result in significant increases in LCAC fuel consumption, and reduced mission durations and time between refuelings.

8.3.1.4 Limitations on Total Craft Weight. During operations in high-heat environments, limitations may be placed on total craft weight to ensure craft are operated at or below engine MCP in a given sea state. Figure 8-3 provides a close approximation of the total craft weight allowable in sea states 1, 2, and 3 over a temperature range from 0 to 100 °F. For routine operations in temperatures exceeding 100 °F in sea state 2 or

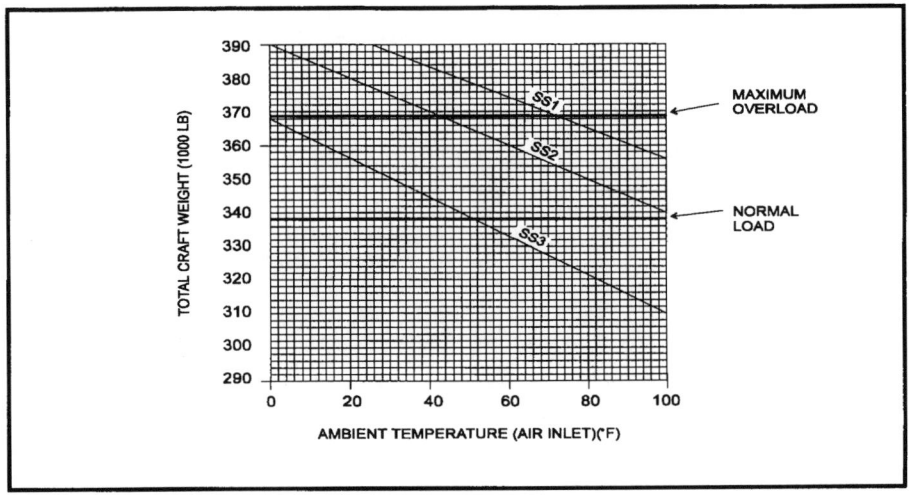

Figure 8-3. LCAC Load as a Function of Ambient Temperature

greater, the total craft weight is limited to less than a normal load (total craft weight of 338,250 pounds).

8.3.2 Effect on Personnel Embarked in LCAC.
The principal effect on personnel of LCAC operations in a high-heat environment is heat stress. Since personnel embarked in LCAC are usually housed in the craft's air-conditioned cabin modules or in portable shelters with their own ventilation systems, heat stress is generally not a greater factor in LCAC than in other operations in the same environment.

8.3.3 Effects on LCAC Well Deck Operations.
The principal effect of a high ambient temperature on LCAC well deck operations is excessive main engine inlet-air temperature. This effect, discussed in paragraph 8.3.1.1, is exacerbated by the added heat from LCAC exhaust gasses while operating within the confines of a well deck. Accordingly, the length of time between engine start and LCAC departure from the well and between LCAC well deck entry and engine shutdown should be kept as short as possible to minimize gas turbine wear and potential damage to the engine.

8.4 OPERATIONS IN HEAVY WEATHER

LCAC heavy-weather operations are defined as operations conducted in sea state 4 and above. Heavy-weather operations subject LCAC to severe damage from wave impact on rotating lift fans or propellers. Figure 8-4 depicts wave heights and sea states in relation to LCAC and figure 8-5 provides guidance for estimating sea states. General guidance for minimizing the hazards of wave impact in sea state 2 and above include:

1. Observe all safe operating procedures detailed in SEAOPS to minimize risk to the craft or machinery

2. Maintain on-cushion operations as long as possible

3. Minimize the time in turns

4. Execute turns into the sea and time turns to avoid the largest wave in a prevailing sea, whenever possible

ORIGINAL

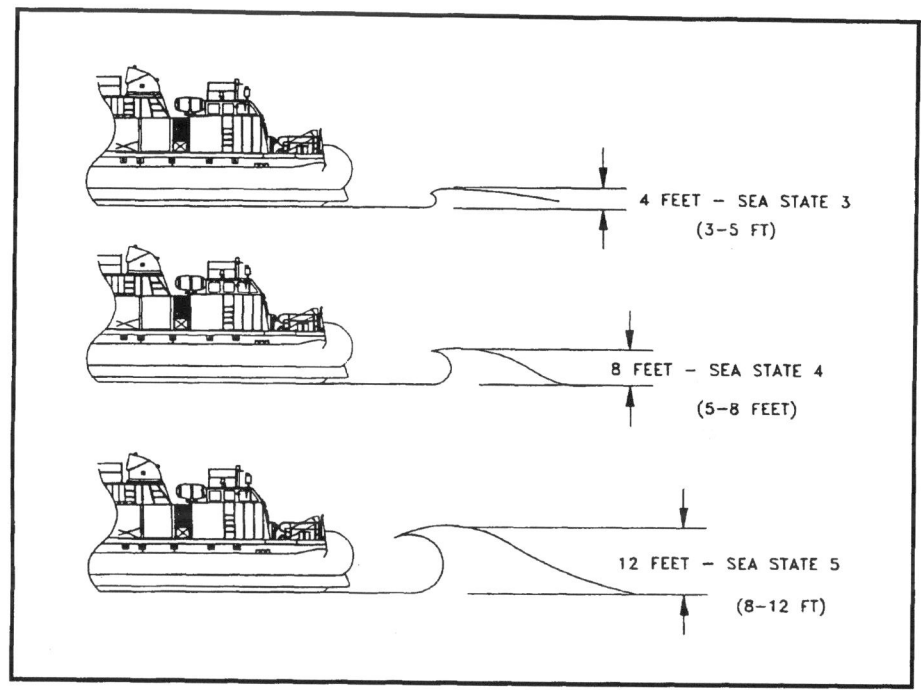

FEET — SEA STATE 3
(3–5 FT)

8 FEET — SEA STATE 4
(5–8 FEET)

12 FEET — SEA STATE 5
(8–12 FT)

Figure 8-4. Wave Height Compared to LCAC

5. Avoid prolonged subhump operation in beam or quartering seas, whenever possible.

In addition to the general guidance for sea state 2 and higher operation, heavy-weather guidance (SS4) for LCAC operations conducted over water and land are discussed in the following paragraphs.

8.4.1 LCAC Heavy-Weather Operations Conducted Over Water. Guidance for LCAC heavy-weather operations conducted over water in sea states 4 and 5 are discussed in the following paragraphs.

8.4.1.1 Operations Conducted in Sea State 4. LCAC operations conducted in sea state 4, which includes significant wave heights of 5 to 8 feet, greatly

restricts the maximum allowable craft speed over water (see figure 1-6). Due to the restricted craft speeds and the hazard to rotating equipment from high-wave impact, routine LCAC operations in sea state 4 are not recommended. Procedures for operating LCAC in sea state 4 which can not be avoided include:

1. Reduce craft speed, but remain on full cushion.

2. Check the security of cargo.

3. If the mission permits, seek shelter or return to base (ship, port).

4. Initiate all turns using bow thrusters vice rudders.

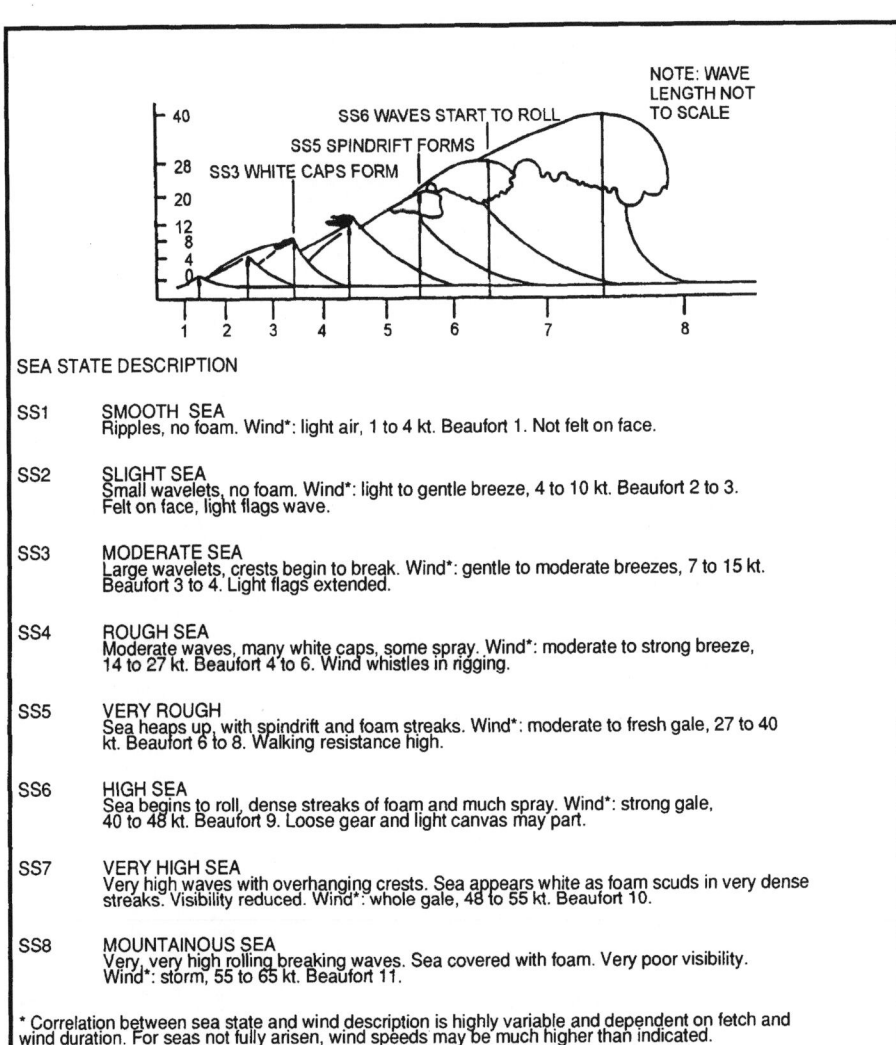

SEA STATE DESCRIPTION

SS1   SMOOTH SEA
Ripples, no foam. Wind*: light air, 1 to 4 kt. Beaufort 1. Not felt on face.

SS2   SLIGHT SEA
Small wavelets, no foam. Wind*: light to gentle breeze, 4 to 10 kt. Beaufort 2 to 3.
Felt on face, light flags wave.

SS3   MODERATE SEA
Large wavelets, crests begin to break. Wind*: gentle to moderate breezes, 7 to 15 kt.
Beaufort 3 to 4. Light flags extended.

SS4   ROUGH SEA
Moderate waves, many white caps, some spray. Wind*: moderate to strong breeze,
14 to 27 kt. Beaufort 4 to 6. Wind whistles in rigging.

SS5   VERY ROUGH
Sea heaps up, with spindrift and foam streaks. Wind*: moderate to fresh gale, 27 to 40
kt. Beaufort 6 to 8. Walking resistance high.

SS6   HIGH SEA
Sea begins to roll, dense streaks of foam and much spray. Wind*: strong gale,
40 to 48 kt. Beaufort 9. Loose gear and light canvas may part.

SS7   VERY HIGH SEA
Very high waves with overhanging crests. Sea appears white as foam scuds in very dense
streaks. Visibility reduced. Wind*: whole gale, 48 to 55 kt. Beaufort 10.

SS8   MOUNTAINOUS SEA
Very, very high rolling breaking waves. Sea covered with foam. Very poor visibility.
Wind*: storm, 55 to 65 kt. Beaufort 11.

* Correlation between sea state and wind description is highly variable and dependent on fetch and
wind duration. For seas not fully arisen, wind speeds may be much higher than indicated.

Figure 8-5. Estimating Sea States

5. Adjust craft heading and speed to avoid quartering or following seas and to prevent taking green water through the propellers.

6. Maintain craft trim.

8.4.1.2 Operations Conducted in Sea State 5 and Higher. LCAC operations in sea state 5 and higher, which includes significant waves above 8 feet, should be avoided. Sea state 5 conditions exceed LCAC's structural limitations for maneuvering at any speed over the water. If the craft must maneuver in sea state 5 or above, structural/rotating machinery damage is likely. Mandated procedures if the sea conditions should deteriorate to sea sea state 5 or higher during planned LCAC operations include:

1. Maintain craft speed to maneuver and remain on full cushion.

2. Seek shelter from the wind and sea such as a lee or a harbour.

3. Attempt to bring the craft ashore if conditions permit.

4. Initiate all craft turns using bow thrusters vice rudders.

5. Keep the craft's bow up into the wind and sea and avoid a quartering sea.

6. Attempt to stay ahead of or in phase with the waves when required to run before the sea.

7. When hullborne operations become necessary, attempt to run upwind and upcurrent. To conserve fuel in this situation, two engine operation should be considered.

8.4.2 LCAC Heavy-Weather Operations Conducted Over Land. Relative wind velocity is the primary consideration for LCAC heavy-weather operations conducted over land. Guidance for operating LCAC in heavy weather over land includes:

1. Maneuver the craft's bow into the wind, when possible.

2. Reduce craft speed as visibility decreases.

3. Be alert to counter gusting winds.

4. Seek shelter.

5. Avoid terrain features that could attract lightning.

Other LCAC Operational and Administrative Considerations

A.1 PURPOSE

This appendix provides additional operational and administrative considerations germane to the deployment and employment of LCAC. Considerations include components and characteristics; maintenance, repair, and docking; salvage, towing, and disabled craft launch and recovery operations; mooring and anchoring; and administrative support and craft manning.

A.2 COMPONENTS AND CHARACTERISTICS

The following paragraphs provide basic information on LCAC components and characteristics. Volume I, Chapter 1 of the "Safe Engineering and Operations (SEAOPS) Manual for Landing Craft Air Cushion (LCAC)" provides in-depth descriptions of all LCAC systems.

A.2.1 LCAC Hull System. The LCAC hull system consists of the hull and an attached skirt system. The primary components of the hull system include a flotation box; bow and stern ramps; and a superstructure that includes the control compartment, passenger compartment, main engine and APU compartments, lift fan compartment, and propeller shrouds. The skirt system is discussed in paragraph A.2.2. Figure A-1 depicts LCAC hull system components.

A.2.2 LCAC Skirt System. The LCAC skirt system contains the air cushion beneath the craft. The skirt's flexibility enables the craft to remain on cushion in rough seas and over land. The system includes the peripheral skirt, a spray suppressor, a longitudinal stability seal, and two lateral stability seals.

The peripheral skirt is constructed of 12 segments, each with outer and inner bags, connected at breakdown joints for ease of maintenance and repair. Open fingers are suspended below the outer bag along the sides and around the bow; the stern is fitted with planing cone fingers. The stability seals divide the cushion into three chambers, restricting the movement of cushion air. The spray suppressor reduces the spray generated by the air cushion by creating a catchment area with the outer bag and fingers. Figure A-2 depicts LCAC skirt system components.

A.2.3 LCAC Cold Weather Kit. Chapter 8 describes the installation and function of the LCAC cold weather kit. Figure A-3 depicts the location of cold weather kit permanent and removable components.

A.2.4 LCAC Operational Characteristics. Figure A-4 provides a summary of LCAC's operational characteristics, including critical craft dimensions, design information, speed capabilities, operational range, and tactical operating capabilities.

A.3 MAINTENANCE, REPAIR, AND DOCKING

The following paragraphs provide information on LCAC maintenance, repair, and docking.

A.3.1 LCAC Maintenance and Repair. Routine LCAC preventive maintenance is governed by the PMS and craft premission and postmission procedures. Key LCAC preventive maintenance procedures include visual inspections, craft water washes for corrosion control, and inspections when main engines accumulate 60 hours of operation in excess of MCP. Anticipated corrective maintenance includes frequent bag and skirt repairs due to damage from LCAC open-ocean operations.

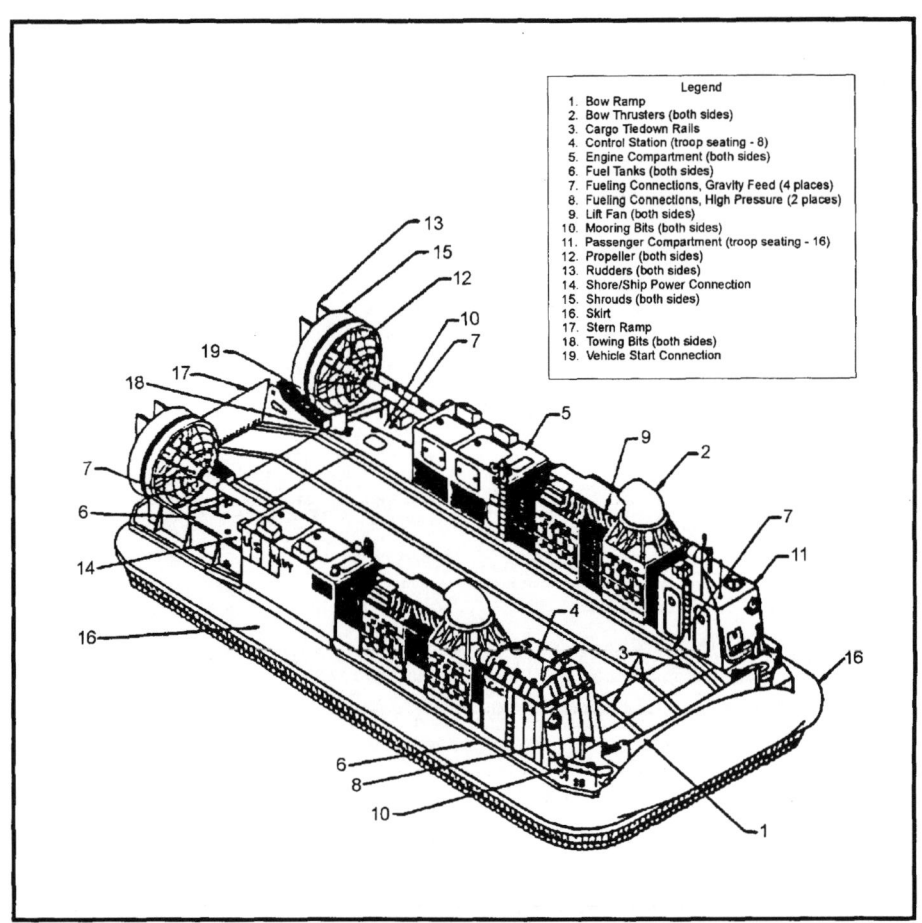

Legend
1. Bow Ramp
2. Bow Thrusters (both sides)
3. Cargo Tiedown Rails
4. Control Station (troop seating - 8)
5. Engine Compartment (both sides)
6. Fuel Tanks (both sides)
7. Fueling Connections, Gravity Feed (4 places)
8. Fueling Connections, High Pressure (2 places)
9. Lift Fan (both sides)
10. Mooring Bits (both sides)
11. Passenger Compartment (troop seating - 16)
12. Propeller (both sides)
13. Rudders (both sides)
14. Shore/Ship Power Connection
15. Shrouds (both sides)
16. Skirt
17. Stern Ramp
18. Towing Bits (both sides)
19. Vehicle Start Connection

Figure A-1. LCAC Primary Features

Premission and postmission procedures, craft water wash, and repair considerations are discussed in the following paragraphs.

A.3.1.1 Premission Procedures. Premission procedures are performed before each LCAC mission.

Volume I, Appendix A of SEAOPS contains a premission checklist, including a systems alignment verification. The premission checklist is used during an LCAC walk-around inspection by the craftmaster and his crew immediately before starting craft engines. Inspection discrepancies must be corrected prior to craft operation

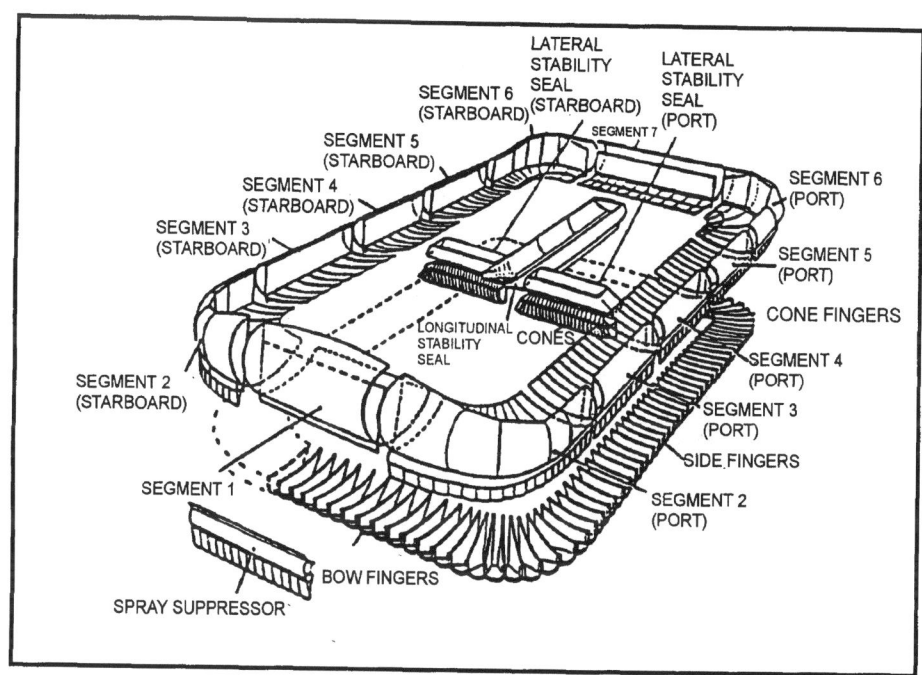

Figure A-2. 3-Dimensional LCAC Skirt Component Drawing

or be listed as outstanding maintenance requirements, depending on safety factors and the mission impact involved (see paragraph A.3.1.4). Typical premission procedures require 30 to 45 minutes to accomplish.

A.3.1.2 Postmission Procedures. Postmission procedures are performed after the last LCAC mission of the day. Postmission procedures include a thorough craft inspection, including maintenance and servicing, and a craft washdown. Volume I, Appendix B of SEAOPS contains a postmission checklist. Typical post-mission procedures, including craft washdown, require 1 to 1.5 hours to accomplish. Volume I, Appendix B of SEAOPS also provides a thru-mission checklist. A thru-mission checklist is used when one mission follows another by 72 hours or less and only minor maintenance is possible between missions. Typical thru-mission checks require 30 minutes. Inspection discrepancies

uncovered during the postmission or thru-mission inspection are handled the same as discrepancies found during the premission inspection.

A.3.1.3 Craft Water Wash. The purpose of the LCAC postmission water wash is to prevent craft corrosion by removing salt water, salt deposits, dirt, and debris. Craft water wash consists of an external craft water wash and a periodic water wash of internal parts of the engines.

Volume I, Appendix B of SEAOPS contains an external LCAC water wash checklist. LCAC water wash in the well deck of a support ship shall be accomplished as soon as possible after the craft's last mission of the day. The on-cushion portion of the checklist is omitted for water wash in a well deck.

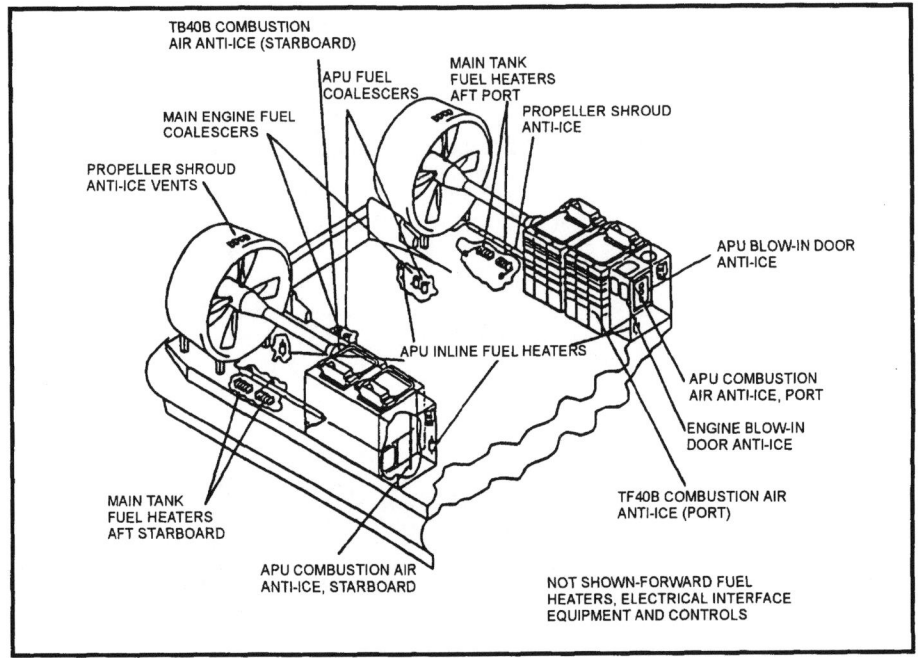

Figure A-3. LCAC Cold Weather Kit Component Location

LCAC engine internals shall be detergent washed every 25 hours of operation and when a repaired engine module is reinstalled. Craft main engine and APU engine internal water wash may be performed at any time during external craft water wash and shall be conducted in accordance with appropriate manuals and PMS documentation.

A.3.1.4 Repair Considerations. The following safety concerns and mission impacts determine how quickly degraded or damaged LCAC components must be repaired:

1. Degraded or damaged LCAC components that jeopardize personnel, craft, or cargo safety must be repaired before craft operations are continued.

2. If safety is not a factor, mission impact must be considered. If a craft has all systems/subsystems fully operational and has no outstanding maintenance actions, it is classified as FMC. If a craft has one or more systems/subsystems inoperable or a maintenance action pending, but is still capable of performing its intended mission, it is classified as MC. If a craft has any mission-critical systems/subsystems down or maintenance actions pending that must be completed to adequately perform its mission, then it is classified as NMC. LCAC classified NMC may not be operated until appropriate repairs are made/pending maintenance is completed.

3. LCAC damage incurred during any incident in which total property damage is 10,000 dollars or more, or in which a lost workday or personnel injury occurs, is a reportable mishap under SEAOPS

Critical Craft Dimensions	
Length (Hard Structure)	81 ft
Length (Maximum On Cushion)	87 ft 11 in
Width (Hard Structure)	46 ft 9 in
Width (Maximum On Cushion)	47 ft
Height (Off Cushion)	19 ft 2 in
Height (Maximum On Cushion Mast Down)	23 ft 10 in
Height (Above Light Weight Waterline)	17 ft 2.5 in
Cargo Deck Area	1,809 ft^2
Cargo Space Dimensions	67 ft x 27 ft
Width of Forward Ramp	28 ft 4 in
Width of Stern Ramp	14 ft 10 in
Ramp Angles	14°
Ramp Operations:	
Close Bow	15 sec
Close Stern	13 sec
Open Bow and Stern	20 sec
Draft Off Cushion:	
Light Condition (Hard Structure)	1 ft 6 in
(Landing Structure)	2 ft 2 in
Design Condition (Hard Structure)	2 ft 2 in
(Landing Structure)	2 ft 7 in
Operating Crew Size	5
Maximum Allowable Weight of Craft	368,250 lb (temperature and sea state dependent)
LCAC Design Information	
Propulsors	Two shroud propellers and two bow thrusters
Lift Fans	Four double-entry, 63-in diameter centrifugal type
Controls	Rudders, bow thrusters, and controllable propellers
Skirt System	Pitch bag and finger with three stability trunks
Propulsion System	Four Textron-Lycoming TF408 gas turbine engines
Propellers	Two four-bladed, variable reversible pitch, 11.7-ft diameter propellers
Speed Capabilities	
Full Load:	
Sea State 1	50 kt
Sea State 2	40+ kt
Sea State 3	35 kt
Hullborne in Water	5 kt
Overland	25 kt
Operational Range	
4 hr Under Design Load Conditions	150 nm
Tactical Operating Capabilities	
Can operate independent of underwater beach gradient, underwater obstacles, and tides	
Can facilitate rapid buildup of forces ashore	
Can enhance deception and tactical surprise	
Has roll-on and roll-off deck and ramps	
Capable of limited over-the-side cargo handling (restricted to wave heights under 1 foot)	
Less vulnerable to underwater mines than displacement hull landing craft	

Figure A-4. LCAC Operational Characteristics

(see SEAOPS, Volume I, Chapter 2 for LCAC mishap investigating and reporting procedures).

A.3.2 LCAC Docking. LCAC must be positioned on aluminum docking blocks to allow skirt and hull maintenance and inspections. Figure A-5 depicts a well deck docking block and a typical docking block tiedown

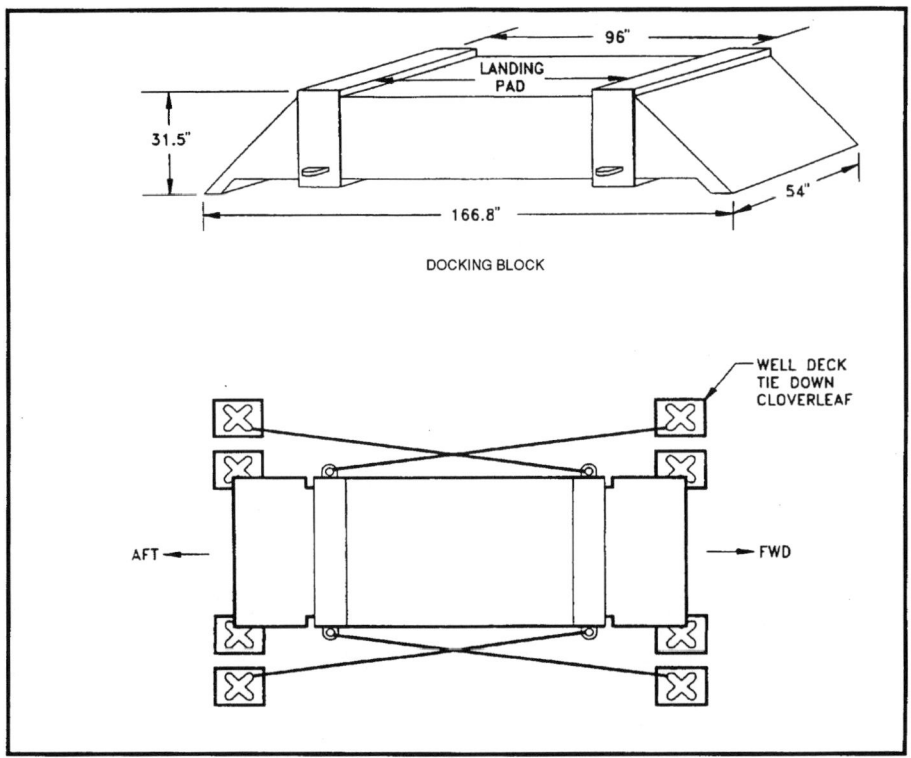

Figure A-5. LCAC Docking Block and a Typical Tiedown Configuration

arrangement. Four docking blocks are required to support an LCAC, and alignment of the craft on the blocks must be precise. Volume I, Chapter 3 of SEAOPS describes LCAC docking procedures.

Docking blocks may be disassembled when not in use, minimizing storage space requirements and allowing for easier transportation. Well deck docking blocks are provided to ships by the LCAC detachment and are transported and secured in the well deck by the ship's crew. The availability and prepositioning of LCAC docking blocks within the ATF should be discussed during embarkation planning. The use of

docking blocks in well decks has been validated for LHD 1, LSD 49, LSD 41, and LSD 36 class ships.

A.4 SALVAGE, TOWING, AND DISABLED CRAFT LAUNCH AND RECOVERY OPERATIONS

The following paragraphs provide information on LCAC salvage, towing, and disabled craft launch and recovery operations.

A.4.1 LCAC Salvage Operations. LCAC salvage operations during an amphibious operation are conducted under the existing ATF salvage organization.

A.4.1.1 Seaward of the Surf Zone. Salvage operations of a disabled LCAC seaward of the surf zone is coordinated by the PCO. Typically, an LCAC that is unable to go on-cushion is still able to provide its own propulsion in the displacement mode and can return to an LCAC support ship for repairs. If an LCAC is unable to provide its own propulsion, it can be towed by another LCAC (see paragraph A.4.2).

A.4.1.2 Inland of the Surf Zone. Beachmasters from the LFSP assist LCAC that have lost mobility inside the surf zone. Normally, a bulldozer with a tow line is used in this type of situation. For a disabled LCAC requiring assistance beyond the maintenance capability of the craft's crew or on board supply support, beachmasters coordinate the required assistance with the PCO. The PCO then assembles the required organizational level repair expertise/supply support and arranges their transportation to the beach.

LCAC salvage operations conducted inland of the high water mark on the beach are coordinated by the beachmasters with the shore party component of the LFSP. Craft salvage inland of the high water mark is analogous to the salvage of a disabled helicopter ashore.

A.4.2 LCAC Towing Procedures. LCAC is capable of towing or being towed hullborne or on-cushion in the water, but may only be towed on-cushion over land. A towing bridle carried aboard the craft is used for towing the LCAC or to tow another craft or vessel. An LCAC towing operation is potentially hazardous to both crewmembers and the craft, and safety during the operation is a paramount consideration. Volume I, Chapter 3 of SEAOPS describes the safety actions that shall be implemented and the procedures that shall be followed during LCAC towing operations.

A.4.3 Disabled LCAC Launch and Recovery. A disabled LCAC is a craft that is seriously impaired in its ability to maneuver into or out of a well deck and requires assistance from the ship or another craft. For disabled LCAC launch and recovery in the hullborne mode, the ship should have at least 5 feet of water at the sill.

A.4.3.1 Launching a Disabled LCAC. A disabled LCAC in the well deck may be towed by another craft, or by the ship's boat handling winches, capstans, or other line handling equipment.

A.4.3.2 Recovering a Disabled LCAC. Ship maneuvering may be required to recover a disabled LCAC. If the craft can generate a cushion, it probably is capable of limited maneuvering with its bow thrusters, and may be capable of propelling itself into a dry well. When the craft cannot propel itself on-cushion into a dry well, the ship must create a wet well for recovery. A hullborne LCAC can either be driven under its own power or be towed into the well deck with the ship's boat handling winches, capstans, or other inhaul devices in accordance with the ship's wet well deck emergency procedures. Figure A-6 depicts the basic sequence for emergency recovery of a hullborne LCAC into the well deck.

A.5 MOORING AND ANCHORING

LCAC is usually moored and secured for sea in the well deck of a support ship. LCAC can also moor to a ship, pier, or buoy and is capable of anchoring in 200 feet of water with a three to one scope. Volume I, Chapter 3 of SEAOPS provides detailed LCAC mooring and anchoring procedures.

A.5.1 LCAC Well Deck Mooring. LCAC is moored and secured for sea in a support ship well deck with a system of tiedowns that include 13 lateral restraints on each side of the craft and 4 restraints both fore and aft. All restraints are provided by the support ship. The restraints should not be crossed when installed in order to provide maximum holding power. LCAC provides wire pendants to connect to the fore and aft restraints. Figure A-7 depicts an LCAC tiedown in a support ship well deck. Shoring shall not be used to brace or secure the craft.

A.5.2 LCAC Mooring to a Ship. When mooring to a ship, LCAC moors bow-on at the designated loading station. The ship must either be in port or at anchor with waves less than 1 foot. Mooring lines and fenders are provided by the ship. Figure A-8 depicts the basic sequence for LCAC mooring to a ship. Fleet experience has shown that, unless there is an operational requirement, LCAC mooring to a ship should be avoided due to potential craft damage from the movement of both ship and craft.

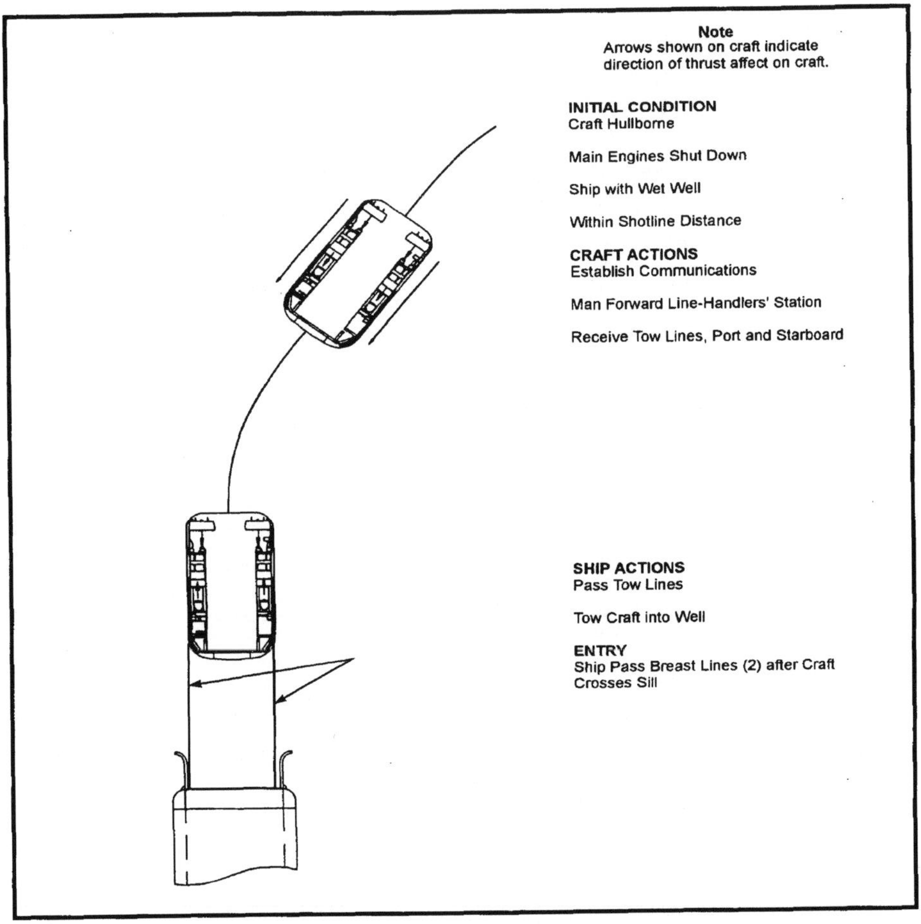

Note
Arrows shown on craft indicate
direction of thrust affect on craft.

INITIAL CONDITION
Craft Hullborne

Main Engines Shut Down

Ship with Wet Well

Within Shotline Distance

CRAFT ACTIONS
Establish Communications

Man Forward Line-Handlers' Station

Receive Tow Lines, Port and Starboard

SHIP ACTIONS
Pass Tow Lines

Tow Craft into Well

ENTRY
Ship Pass Breast Lines (2) after Craft
Crosses Sill

Figure A-6. LCAC Emergency Well Deck Recovery

CAUTION

LCAC shall not be moored alongside other craft or ships when wave height exceeds 1 foot.

A.5.3 LCAC Mooring to a Pier. LCAC can moor side-to or bow-on to a pier. Figure A-9 depicts the basic sequence for LCAC mooring side-to to a pier. LCAC mooring bow-on to a pier is similar to mooring to a ship. LCAC's portable fenders are used if wave heights do

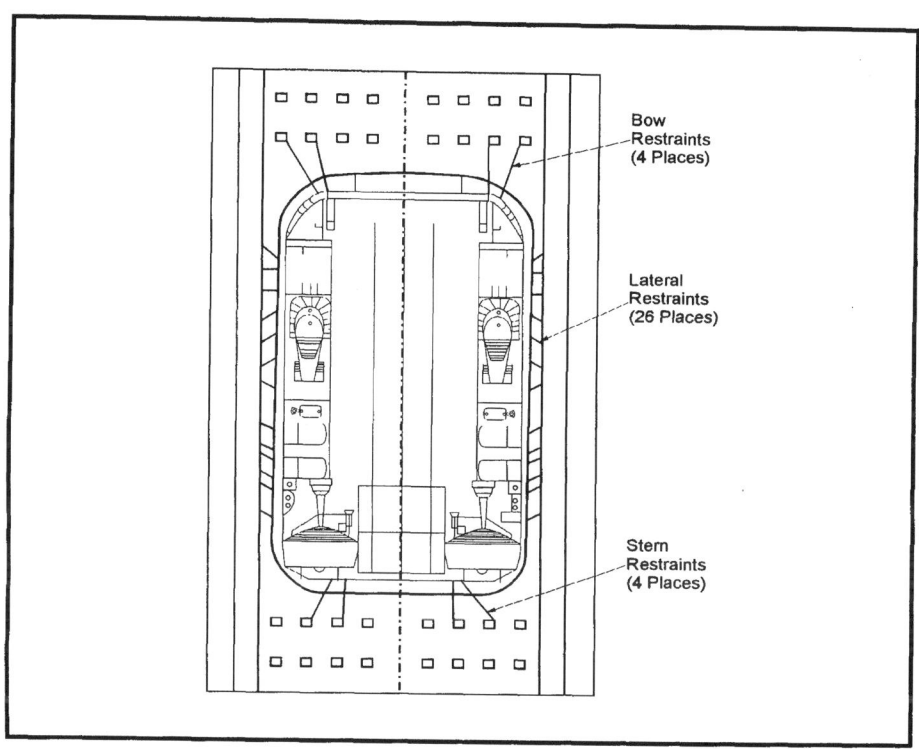

Bow
Restraints
(4 Places)

Lateral
Restraints
(26 Places)

Stern
Restraints
(4 Places)

Figure A-7. LCAC Tiedown in Well Deck

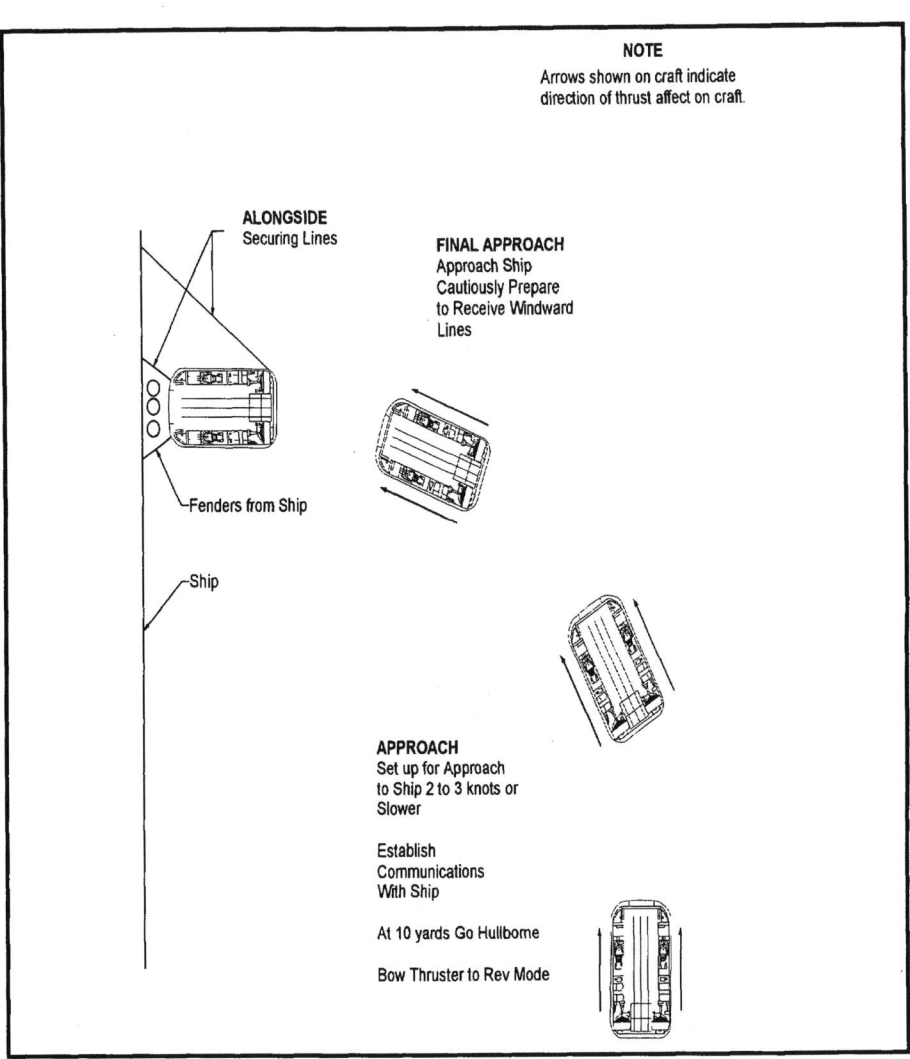

ALONGSIDE
Securing Lines

FINAL APPROACH
Approach Ship
Cautiously Prepare
to Receive Windward
Lines

Fenders from Ship

Ship

APPROACH
Set up for Approach
to Ship 2 to 3 knots or
Slower

Establish
Communications
With Ship

At 10 yards Go Hullbome

Bow Thruster to Rev Mode

Figure A-8. LCAC Mooring to a Ship

not exceed 1 foot. When wave heights exceed 1 foot, larger fenders are required.

A.5.4 LCAC Mooring to a Buoy. LCAC can moor to a buoy by either its bow or stern, but not both. LCAC should make a direct approach to the buoy into the wind/current, if possible. In restricted waters where there may be a requirement to maneuver to avoid other vessels, the craftmaster should attempt to keep the wind forward of the beam while closing the buoy. Figure A-10 depicts the basic sequence for LCAC mooring to a buoy.

A.5.5 LCAC Anchoring. LCAC is equipped with a 65-pound Danforth anchor, 600 feet of 4-inch double-braided nylon line, and a davit to handle the line with anchor attached. The weight of the anchor, the likelihood of a wet deck, and the small area of the port linehandler's station require that personnel exercise extreme care when anchoring, particularly in sea state 3 and above.

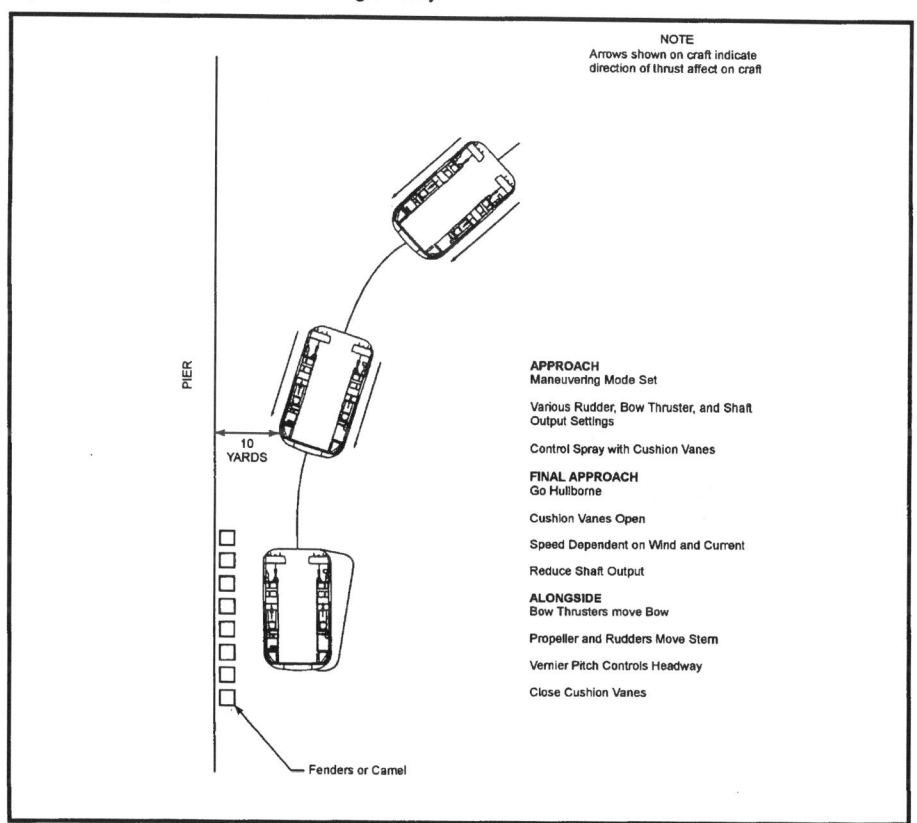

Figure A-9. LCAC Mooring to a Pier

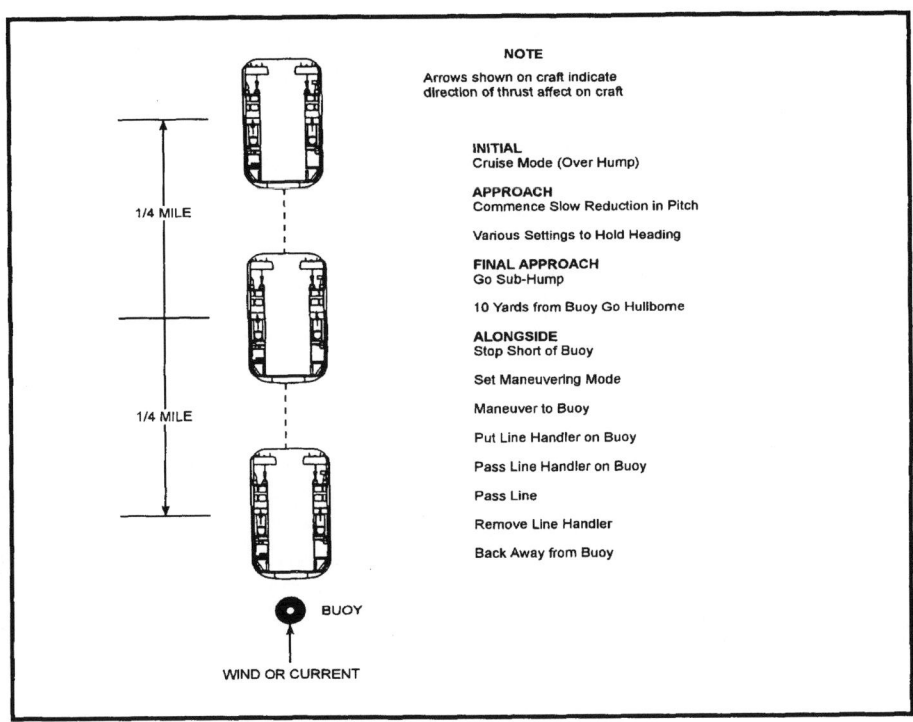

NOTE

Arrows shown on craft indicate
direction of thrust affect on craft

INITIAL
Cruise Mode (Over Hump)

APPROACH
Commence Slow Reduction in Pitch

Various Settings to Hold Heading

FINAL APPROACH
Go Sub-Hump

10 Yards from Buoy Go Hullborne

ALONGSIDE
Stop Short of Buoy

Set Maneuvering Mode

Maneuver to Buoy

Put Line Handler on Buoy

Pass Line Handler on Buoy

Pass Line

Remove Line Handler

Back Away from Buoy

1/4 MILE

1/4 MILE

BUOY

WIND OR CURRENT

Figure A-10. LCAC Mooring to a Buoy

treme care when anchoring, particularly in sea state 3 and above.

A.6 ADMINISTRATIVE SUPPORT AND CRAFT MANNING

The following paragraphs provide information on the administrative organization that supports deployed LCAC and how the craft are manned.

A.6.1 LCAC Administrative Support. Paragraph 4.2 describes the organization that exercises operational control of LCAC during ship-to-shore movement. Until LCAC are underway and the control organization as-

sumes control, the commanding officer of the host support ship retains control of the craft. LCAC supply, maintenance, personnel, and general administrative support is provided by Commander, Naval Beach Group through a shore-based ACU (air cushion) and a deployed LCAC detachment. Figure A-11 contrasts the LCAC operational and administrative chains of command while deployed.

A.6.1.1 ACU. The ACU (air cushion) is a shore-based command responsible for the organization, equipment, training, and support of deployed LCAC. The ACU is divided into two major elements: shore support and sea duty. The shore support element includes repair

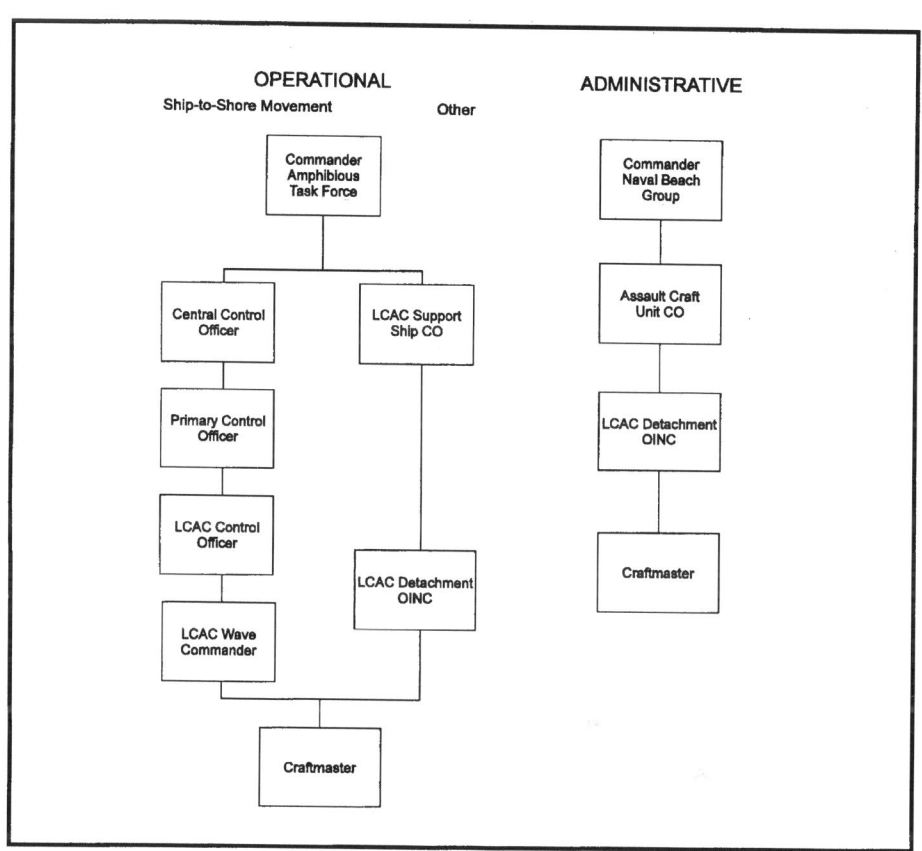

Figure A-11. LCAC Operational and Administrative Chains of Command While Deployed

and maintenance, supply, operations and training, and administrative support. The sea duty element is organized into deployable detachments which are each headed by an OIC.

A.6.1.2 LCAC Detachment. An LCAC detachment is composed of craft, crews, and support equipment and personnel. It is task organized to satisfy the LCAC requirements of the ATF and provide a high level of self-sufficiency while deployed. An LCAC detachment embarks and deploys aboard one or more LCAC-capable amphibious ships. The detachment OIC reports to the commanding officer of the ship in which he is embarked for operational matters and to the ACU (air cushion) commanding officer for supply support and administrative matters.

The LCAC detachment is supported by a PUK containing the majority of equipment and material essential for craft preventive and corrective maintenance. As discussed in paragraph 1.2.1.2, the use of MILVANs may be necessary to accommodate detachment work and storage space aboard ships.

Since the LCAC detachment is part of the NSE of the ATF, the berthing space for detachment personnel and the stowage area for MILVANs and other support equipment aboard ATF shipping comes from that assigned to the LF, and must be considered in embarkation planning.

A.6.2 LCAC Manning. LCAC are manned by a Navy enlisted crew that includes:

1. A craftmaster who is in charge of the craft and who mans the LCAC's control cabin (starboard module) and controls the propellers, rudders, and bow thrusters. The craftmaster is detailed as OIC of the craft. All passengers embarked in an LCAC are subject to the orders of the craftmaster, regardless of their military rank or rate.

2. A craft engineer who is assistant in charge and who mans the control cabin and monitors and controls propulsion and auxiliary systems.

3. A navigator who mans the control cabin and operates radar and external communications systems.

4. A loadmaster who mans the passenger cabin (port module) and is responsible for craft loading.

5. A deck engineer who mans the passenger cabin and assists other crew members with their duties.

Volume I, Chapter 2 of SEAOPS describes the duties and responsibilities of each crew member. Additional crew members may be assigned based on the nature of the LCAC mission and up to 24 passengers may be embarked in the cabins as discussed in paragraph 1.2.1.1.

ATF Surface Offload Considerations

B.1 PURPOSE

This appendix provides information useful in allocating ATF landing craft to the offload of the LF. Information contained in this annex includes craft allocation considerations and objectives, the advantages of using one type of assault landing craft over another type, and ship class-related offload considerations.

B.2 LANDING CRAFT ALLOCATION CONSIDERATIONS AND OBJECTIVES

As discussed in chapter 1, LCAC are the key surface assets for the rapid buildup of LF combat power ashore. The ATF landing craft mix may include LCAC only or a combination of LCAC and LCU. The allocation of landing craft for the LF offload is subject to the surface offload considerations and efficient offload objectives discussed in the following paragraphs.

B.2.1 Surface Offload Considerations.
Considerations for determining the best landing craft allocation for LF surface offload include craft mix, ATF composition, makeup of LF serials, standoff distance, tactical situation ashore, and weather.

B.2.1.1 Craft Mix.
Both LCAC and LCU offer distinct advantages that can influence the manner in which the surface assault is conducted. Since ATF surface ship-to-shore movement assets are generally in short supply, every craft must be employed where its advantages can best be utilized. Paragraph B.3 discusses the advantages of LCAC and LCU.

B.2.1.2 ATF Composition.
As discussed in chapter 1, newer amphibious ship classes were designed to operate with LCAC. Older amphibious ship classes were originally designed to operate with LCU and may have since been modified to operate with LCAC. In general, LSD 41/49/36 and LHD 1 class ships can better transport and support LCAC in their well decks, and LPD 4 and LHA 1 class ships can better transport and support LCU in their well decks.

B.2.1.3 LF Serials.
The offload sequence, type, and location of LF serials must be considered when allocating landing craft for offload. In general, serials composed of personnel, cargo, and the heaviest vehicles are more suited to LCU and serials composed of lighter vehicles are better suited to LCAC.

B.2.1.4 Standoff Distance.
The standoff distance from the beach at which the offload is conducted must be considered in craft allocation. LCAC's speed advantage can be exploited at greater standoff distances and LCU's lift capacity can be exploited at shorter standoff distances.

B.2.1.5 Tactical Situation Ashore.
The tactical situation ashore influences the type of ATF unloading operations and, therefore, the type of landing craft used. The two types of ATF unloading operations are initial unloading and general unloading.

Since the initial ATF unloading period is tactical, craft used during this period must provide for rapid vehicle deployment from the craft on the beach. Tactical loading is accomplished at the expense of efficient space utilization aboard the craft.

Since the general ATF unloading period is primarily logistical, craft used during this period must make more efficient use of craft deck space and increase the size of loads delivered to the beach. Unlike LCU, LCAC can offload at either end and its offload is less affected by administrative loading.

B.2.1.6 Weather.
Weather must be considered in landing craft allocation since craft heavy weather-handling characteristics at sea and in the well deck vary by

craft type. LCAC handles better than LCU in heavy weather and operates with a dry well deck, thus avoiding the adverse effects experienced by LCU in heavy seas during wet well deck operations. LCU, unlike LCAC, are not susceptible to propeller damage due to wave impact in heavy weather.

B.2.2 Efficient Surface Offload Objectives.
The two objectives of an efficient surface offload are constant well deck usage and minimized landing craft cycle time. These objectives and selected features that affect well deck usage and cycle time are discussed in the following paragraphs.

B.2.2.1 Well Deck Usage.
Amphibious ships with multispot well decks for LCAC can load two LCAC simultaneously in the well deck by lowering both ramps of the forward craft and driving vehicles through to the after craft. Studies have shown, however, that sequential loading of two LCAC (one in the well deck at a time) can be accomplished in a shorter period of time when refueling is not involved. Sequential offloading of LCAC is recommended except in cases where two craft arrive at the well deck together and one craft requires refueling.

B.2.2.2 Craft Cycle Time.
The appropriate number of landing craft that should be allocated to offload a particular amphibious ship is a function of craft cycle time. Too many craft assigned to offload a ship invariably result in craft loitering around the ship until the well deck is clear. Ideally, a craft returning from the beach for a subsequent load should have little or no loiter time prior too entering the well deck. Figure B-1 depicts the recommended number of LCAC to be assigned to a single ship at various standoff distances to minimize loiter and cycle time and efficiently offload the ship. Figure B-1 assumes sequential loading.

B.2.2.3 Direction of Vehicle Loading.
Driving vehicles forward is preferred to backing them onto LCAC during craft loading in the well deck. Backing vehicles onto LCAC takes longer and offers no tactical advantage at the beach, since LCAC's ramps facilitate offload at either end of the craft.

B.2.2.4 Griping Times.
Vehicle and cargo griping is required for the safety of the landing craft and its load. Griping should commence when the first vehicle is loaded and continue throughout the craft loading process. The extent of griping should be limited to that necessary for the prevailing sea state en route the beach. Dedicated griping teams should be employed. LCAC load griping is discussed in appendix C.

B.2.2.5 Partial Craft Loading.
At shorter standoff distances, partial loading of landing craft may result in a faster rate of force transfer ashore. Partial loading of craft substantially reduces craft time in the well deck and, coupled with quicker transits to and from the beach, results in fast cycle times. The fast cycle times may permit enough additional craft sorties to compensate for the partial loads and increase the overall transfer rate of forces ashore. Conversely, for longer standoff distances, partial loading always results in a lower force transfer rate and has no tactical value. Partial craft loading is a consideration during the ATF general unloading period only.

B.3 LCAC VERSUS LCU ADVANTAGES

The advantages of LCAC over LCU and vice versa are discussed in the following paragraphs.

B.3.1 LCAC Advantages Over LCU.
The principal advantages LCAC have over LCU are speed, access to more of the world's coastline, an overland capability, and a dry well deck capability.

B.3.1.1 Speed Advantage.
Under ideal conditions, LCAC have a more than four to one speed advantage over LCU. LCAC's maximum operational speed is 50 knots and LCU's is 11 knots. Figure B-2 compares

Number of LCAC	Range of Ship Standoff Distance for which LCAC are Efficiently Utilized (nm)
2	0 to 10
3	10 to 25
4	25 to 35

Figure B-1. Number of LCAC for Single Ship Offload

Standoff Distances (nm)	Average Transit Speeds (kt) (Notes 1 and 2)	
	LCAC	LCU
2	20	7
5	30	11
10	40	11
25	40	11

Notes:
1. Average transit speed is lower than maximum speed because the craft always moves at a slower speed when near the ship or beach.
2. As standoff distances increase, craft average speed approaches maximum speed.

Figure B-2. Average Landing Craft Speeds (LCAC and LCU)

average LCAC and LCU transit speeds for a variety of standoff distances.

LCAC's speed advantage is a significant factor in reducing craft cycle times. A cycle time is the sum of the times required for craft offload on the beach, transit from the beach to the ship, loading in the well deck, and transit back to the beach. Well deck times for LCAC and LCU are comparable for most amphibious ship classes, with LCAC averaging 30 minutes (including periodic fueling) for a full load and LCU averaging 35 minutes (not including refueling). Well deck times for LCAC include 5 minutes for entering and 5 minutes for exiting the well deck; LCU well deck entry/exit times are longer due to ship ballasting/deballasting requirements. Similarly, beach times for the two types of craft are comparable, with LCAC averaging 15 minutes and LCU averaging 10 minutes.

Figure B-3 compares average LCAC and LCU cycle times for various standoff distances.

B.3.1.2 Coastline Access. LCAC can access at least twice as much of the world's coastline as LCU due to its independence from tides and most hydrographic constraints. However, hydrographic constraints in some coastal areas could limit LCAC but not LCU offload.

B.3.1.3 Overland Capability. LCAC's overland capability is unique among assault landing craft. The craft's ability to operate over land can influence the LF scheme of maneuver ashore by facilitating the delivery of forces inland beyond the high water mark.

B.3.1.4 Dry Well Deck Capability. LCAC normally operate from a dry well deck. Dry well deck operations eliminate line handling and ballasting/debal-

Standoff Distances (nm)	Average Cycle Times (min) (Note)	
	LCAC	LCU
2	55	80
5	65	100
10	75	155
25	120	320

Note: Average cycle times are rounded to the nearest 5 minutes.

Figure B-3. Average Landing Craft Cycle Times (LCAC and LCU)

lasting delays experienced during wet well deck operations. LCU must operate with wet well decks unless sterngate marriages are conducted.

B.3.2 LCU Advantages Over LCAC. The principal advantages LCU have over LCAC are cargo deck area, cargo lift capacity, troop lift capacity, and the ability to sustain operations without frequent refueling.

B.3.2.1 Cargo Deck Area. LCU's cargo deck area exceeds that of LCAC by nearly 30 percent. LCU has 2,300 square feet of usable cargo deck area while LCAC has 1,809 square feet of usable area. LCU can transport the same force ashore in approximately 30 percent fewer craft sorties than LCAC. However, LCU's irregular cargo deck shape affects square-limited loads, in which case its advantage over LCAC is somewhat less than 30 percent.

B.3.2.2 Cargo Lift Capacity. LCU's cargo lift capacity is at least two and one-half times greater than the cargo lift capacity of LCAC. LCU can lift 180 short tons of vehicles and other cargo while LCAC can only lift 75 short tons at maximum overload and 60 short tons at normal load under ideal conditions. LCAC's lift capacity is further restricted by structural, hump transition, launch sea conditions, surf zone, and fuel management limitations discussed in paragraph 1.2.1.3. LCU's lift capacity is not constrained by sea state except when cargo safety is involved.

LCU's superior cargo lift capacity generally makes it a better candidate for transporting heavier combat vehicles including MBTs. LCU can carry two M1A1 MBTs (three in an overload condition) and LCAC can only carry one M1A1 MBT. Figure B-4 provides a comparison of LCAC and LCU carrying capacity for MBTs, LAVs, and HMMWVs. Figure B-5 identifies the most efficient craft type for transporting MBTs, LAVs, and HMMWVs over various standoff distances.

B.3.2.3 Troop Lift Capacity. Compared with LCU's troop lift capacity, the troop lift capacity of LCAC is negligible. LCU can carry 400 troops in its well, while LCAC, unless augmented for personnel transfer, can only carry 24 troops in the passenger compartments. Augmentation of LCAC with MCESS shelters or PTMs is discussed in chapter 7.

B.3.2.4 Refueling. LCU has a relatively large fuel capacity and a correspondingly small fuel consumption rate compared to the fuel capacity and consumption rate of LCAC. LCAC must refuel on the average of once every four hours or every 100 nm when operating over longer standoff distances, while LCU can operate 40 hours before refueling. Figure B-6 provides LCAC refueling frequencies for various standoff distances. The refueling time for LCAC and LCU is approximately 15 minutes.

B.4 LHA 1 CLASS SHIP SURFACE OFFLOAD CONSIDERATIONS

The LHA 1 Class ship was designed to operate with LCU. LHA 1, unlike any other amphibious ship class, has split well decks that facilitate loading two LCU simultaneously. As discussed in chapter 1, the LHA 1 Class can be modified to accommodate one LCAC in the well deck aft of the split portion of the deck. The

Type of Vehicle	Landing Craft Carrying Capacity	
	LCU	LCAC
Main Battle Tank M1A1	2	1
Light Armored Vehicle (LAV)	9	4 (Note)
Amphibious Assault Vehicle (AAV)		2
High Mobility Multipurpose, Wheeled Vehicle	12	13
Note: A fifth LAV fits on the LCAC and falls within its maximum overload of 75 tons, but exceeds the LCAC's normal 60-ton weight limit.		

Figure B-4. Carrying Capacity for Landing Craft

Vehicle Types	Standoff Distances (nm)	Most Efficient Craft
MBT	2 5 10 15	LCU LCU LCU LCAC
Light Armored Vehicle (LAV) (Note)	2 5 10 15	LCU LCU LCAC LCAC
High Mobility Multipurpose, Wheeled Vehicle (HMMWV)	2 5 10 15	LCAC LCAC LCAC LCAC
Note: LCU can deliver more LAVs to the beach than LCAC at 2 and 5 nm and about the same at 10 nm.		

Figure B-5. Landing Craft Efficiency in Transporting Vehicles

Standoff Distance (nm)	Refueling Frequency
2 5 10 20 30	Every 6th sortie Every 5th sortie Every 4th sortie Every other sortie Every sortie

Figure B-6. LCAC Refueling Frequency

unique configuration of the LHA 1 results in additional LF offload considerations when ships of that class are assigned to an ATF.

B.4.1 LCAC Well Deck Time. The average time for LCAC in an LHA 1 Class well deck is 40 minutes to embark a full load. This is due to to the unique configuration cited above and is longer than the well deck times for other LCAC-capable ships (30 minute average).

B.4.2 LHA 1 Class Ship Offload by LCAC. LHA 1 can transport four preloaded LCU in its well deck. Assuming that these preloads are delivered to the beach during offload by the LCU, a fully loaded LHA 1 Class ship has approximately 11 remaining LCAC-equivalent loads for offload. Figure B-7 provides estimates of the amount of time it takes two, three, and four LCAC to

offload the remainder of LHA 1 for standoff distances ranging from 0 to 50 plus nm.

B.4.3 LHA 1 Class Ship Offload by LCU. Including the preloaded vehicles/cargo in four LCU, there are a total of 13 LCU-equivalent loads aboard a fully loaded LHA 1 ship class. Figure B-8 provides estimates of the amount of time it takes two or four LCU to offload the entire LHA 1 ship class for standoff distances ranging from 0 to 50 plus nm. This figure includes the offload nomograph for a two-LCAC offload (with LCU delivering their own preloads) from figure B-7 for comparison purposes. It should be noted that inside approximately 4 nm, two LCU can offload an LHA 1 Class ship faster than two LCAC.

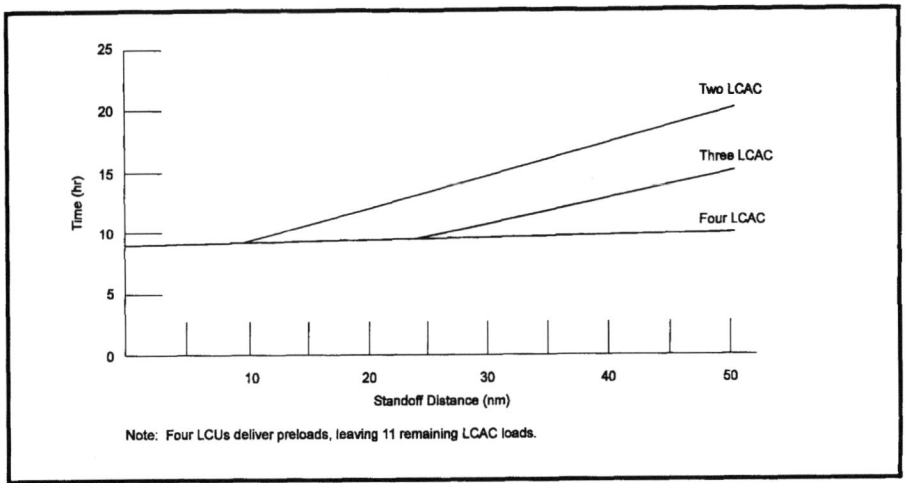

Figure B-7. Estimated Time to Offload an LHA by LCAC (LCU Deliver LCU Preloads)

B.4.4 LHA 1 Offload by LCAC or LCU. Including the preloaded vehicles/cargo in the four LCU, there are a total of 19 LCAC-equivalent loads aboard a fully loaded LHA 1 Class ship. Figure B-9 provides estimates of the amount of time it will take four LCAC or four LCU to offload the entire LHA 1 ship class, including the LCU preloads, for standoff distances ranging from 0 to 50 plus nm

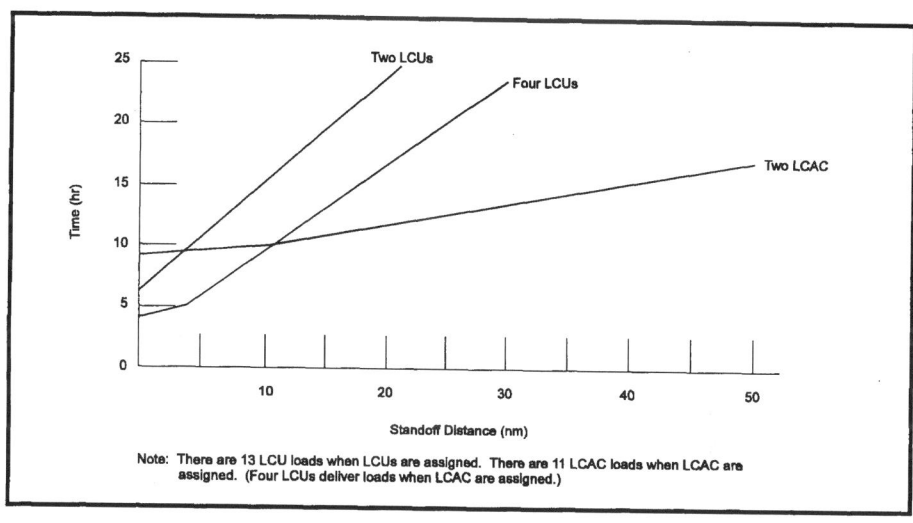

Figure B-8. Estimated Time to Offload an LHA by LCU or LCAC
(LCU Deliver LCU Preloads When LCAC Assigned)

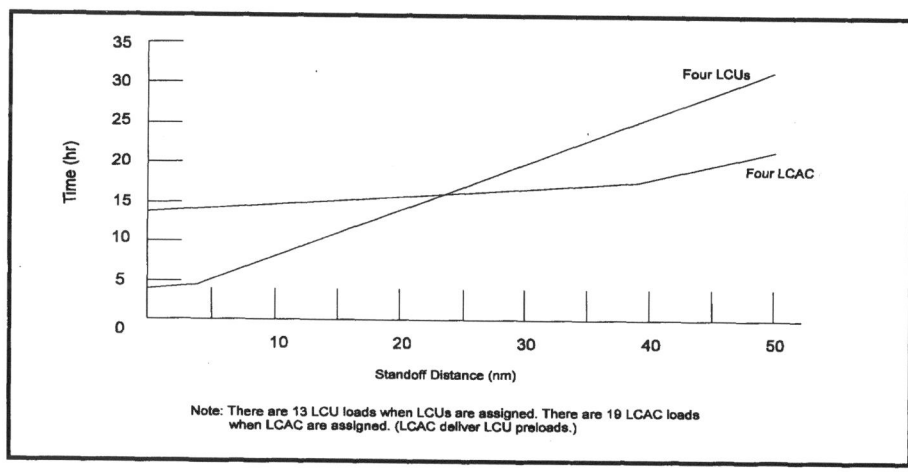

Figure B-9. Estimated Time to Offload an LHA by LCU or LCAC
(LCAC Deliver LCU Preloads When LCAC Assigned)

B-7 (Reverse Blank)   **ORIGINAL**

LCAC Loading and Unloading Operations

C.1 PURPOSE

This appendix discusses LCAC loading characteristics and considerations, locations and means suitable for LCAC loading/unloading, and LCAC standard loads.

C.2 LCAC LOADING CHARACTERISTICS AND CONSIDERATIONS

LCAC loading characteristics and considerations are discussed in the following paragraphs.

C.2.1 Loading Characteristics. LCAC's loading characteristics are a function of the size and load-bearing capacity of the craft's cargo deck and ramps.

C.2.1.1 Cargo Deck. The usable LCAC cargo deck space measures 1,809 square feet and accommodates all current combat and combat support equipment in the Marine Corps inventory. Four tiedown rails containing tiedown sockets every 12 to 15 inches run the length of the cargo deck and are spaced 99 inches apart. Deck areas near the center tiedown rails and the cargo deck forward of frame 11 are strengthened to support the M1A1 MBT; the AAVP-7; or a loaded RTCH. The maximum allowable cargo deck "footprint" loading is 80 pounds per square inch (approximately 11,500 pounds per square foot) without dunnage. Figure C-1 provides an LCAC deck load diagram.

The cargo deck contains yellow-painted deck markings to aid in cargo positioning. The deck markings identify the athwartship and longitudinal positions of LCAC's design CG; distances from the center of the craft in 10-foot intervals; and areas of the cargo deck that should be kept clear to allow flow of combustion air to the engines and access to command, passenger, and engine modules. Figure C-2 shows an LCAC cargo deck grid with tiedown rails and deck markings.

C.2.1.2 Ramps. LCAC's two ramps provide flexibility for loading and unloading cargo. Bow and stern ramps provide access to and from LCAC's cargo deck and can be used for the through-loading of vehicles to other craft. The ramps can accommodate any equipment that can be loaded on the cargo deck. The bow and stern ramp-opening widths are 28 feet 4 inches and 14 feet 10 inches, respectively.

For through-loading vehicles, the stern ramp of the forward LCAC may be lowered onto the lowered bow ramp of the LCAC behind it. This arrangement allows the wider bow ramp to evenly distribute the combined weight of the vehicle. However, the angle formed by the two ramps may be difficult for some vehicles or vehicle combinations to negotiate. In this case, the bow ramp of the after LCAC may be placed on the stern ramp of the forward craft or sufficient dunnage may be used to raise both ramps to reduce the angle.

C.2.2 Loading Considerations. LCAC has a strictly defined loaded-weight limit of 368,250 pounds. For many craft loads, the weight limit is reached with only a portion of the cargo deck space being utilized. LCAC mission planners determine the allowable mission cargo load weight for the conditions expected and possible weather variances using the MPP discussed in paragraph 2.7. The craft loadmaster then loads the craft to suit the specific mission requirements.

The LCAC loadmaster directs the safe movement, spotting, and tiedown of cargo aboard the craft in accordance with the "Safe Engineering and Operations (SEAOPS) Manual for Landing Craft Air Cushion (LCAC)," Volume IV, Part 1 (LCAC Loadmaster Manual). The LCAC loadmaster is particularly concerned with the impact of loads on the craft's CG, not exceeding the maximum-allowable cargo deck "footprint" weight limit, and safety during and after the

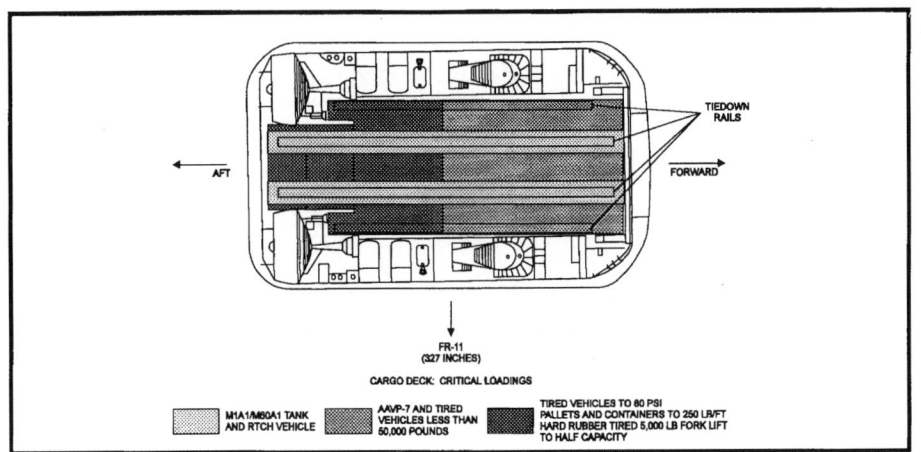

Figure C-1. LCAC Deck Load Diagram

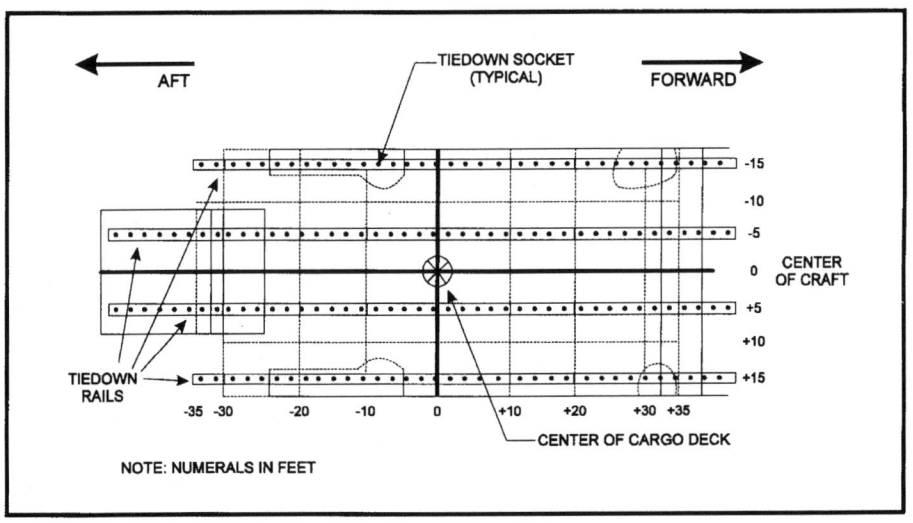

Figure C-2. LCAC Cargo Deck Grid

loading operation. LCAC loading considerations are discussed in the following paragraphs.

C.2.2.1 Cargo Movement and Spotting.

An assigned LF embarkation team, under the supervision of the craft loadmaster, assists in loading and tieing down cargo on an LCAC. Since the weight and balance of the craft are critical, the loadmaster must consider the weight and CG of each piece of cargo, compute its cargo deck spot, and direct the embarkation team to position it within 3 inches of the computed spot. Since LCAC has limited capability to trim itself, correctly spotting loads is critical in attaining proper craft trim. Figure C-3 provides the square footage and weight of common Marine Corps vehicles and equipment that may be loaded on LCAC. Figure C-4 provides the weight and square footage of various containers that may be loaded on LCAC.

Note

The weights in short tons of selected USMC vehicles and equipment vary considerably among various source documents. Those weights listed in figure C-3 are drawn from the LCAC Loadmaster Manual which is considered the authoritative source.

Guidance for cargo movement and spotting aboard LCAC include:

1. Deflation of tire pressures to 80 pounds per square inch on vehicles with pneumatic tires prior to craft embarkation

2. Movement and tiedown of all pneumatic-tired vehicles with tire pressures of 80 pounds per square inch or less anywhere on deck

3. Movement and tiedown of M1A1 or M60A1 MBTs or RTCH on center rails only

4. Movement and tiedown of vehicles with a gross weight of over 86,000 pounds on center rails only

5. Movement of AAVs anywhere on deck forward of frame 11 and on center rails aft of frame 11, and tiedown on any pair of rails

6. Tiedown of all types of ISO 20-foot containers that are fully loaded to 40,000 pounds anywhere on tiedown rails if dunnage is used

7. Movement and tiedown of hard rubber-tired 6,000-pound forklifts that are loaded to half capacity anywhere on deck

8. Tiedown of pallets anywhere on deck without dunnage as long as the weight limitations and maximum allowable "footprint" loading is not exceeded

9. Special load planning for over-sized equipment such as the RTCH or the 30-ton DROT crane

10. Providing for a straight load/off-load path for large vehicles such as MBTs and AAVs

11. Preventing damage to the deck by using dunnage with tracked vehicles

12. Providing adequate space (no less than 12 inches) between cargo and inboard engine module bulkheads for satisfactory engine air flow

13. Limiting preloaded cargo in well decks to 60 short tons (120,000 pounds) to avoid last minute cargo off-load when marginal weather is encountered

14. Loading heavier cargo forward for long-range operations to compensate for expected fuel consumption.

C.2.2.2 Backing Vehicles Versus Driving Vehicles Forward.

Experience has shown that LCAC vehicle loading averages less than 1 minute per vehicle when vehicles are driven forward onto the craft. Approximately 3 minutes are needed for each vehicle backed aboard LCAC. Figure C-5 estimates the time it takes to load LCAC by either driving vehicles forward or backing them onto the craft.

C.2.2.3 Cargo Restraint (Griping).

LCAC operations are not permitted unless on board cargo is properly restrained. Cargo is restrained to prevent movement in any direction, and the force required to prevent movement is expressed in units of force of gravity, or Gs. Restraint criteria for cargo is three dimensional and varies based on whether missions are peacetime/training

USMC Vehicles and Equipment				
Class	Item	Description (Note 1)	Square Footage (ft²)	Weight (S Tons) (Note 2)
Tracked Vehicles	M1A1	Main Battle Tank	356	70.0
	AAVP-7	Amphibious Assault Vehicle (with Applique Armor) + 18 Troops	270	27.6
	AAVP-7	Amphibious Assault Vehicle (without Applique Armor) + 18 Troops	260	26.6
	M88A1	Tank Retriever	323	53.9
	AVLB	Bridge	340	18.6
	D7G	Medium Tractor (Bulldozer)	226	26.9
Wheeled Vehicles	LAV-25	Light Armored Vehicle 25-mm Gun (Note 3)	173	12.0
	LAV-MEWESS	Light Armored Vehicle EW Variant	178	14.9
	M998	High Mobility, Multimission Wheeled Vehicle (HMMWV) (Cargo/Troops)	106	3.9
	M1045	HMMWV (Weapons)	112	3.2
	M1043	HMMWV (Ammunition)	112	3.2
	M817	5-Ton Dump Truck	236	11.1
	M923	5-Ton Cargo Truck (M198 Prime Mover) + 19 Man Gun Crew	216	15.9
	M923	5-Ton Cargo Truck (Cargo)	216	15.9
	M931	5-Ton Semi-Tractor	210	10.2
	M936	5-Ton Wrecker Truck	284	18.3
	Mk 48/Mk 14	Logistic Vehicle System (LVS) (Note 4)	332	32.7
	Mk 48/Mk 16	LVS, 5th Wheel	288	20.8
	FAV	Fast Attack Vehicle	65	25.0
Towed Artillery	M101A2	105-mm Howitzer	144	2.5
	M198	155-mm Howitzer	382	7.9
Trailers and Semi-Trailers	M105A2	Cargo Trailer, 1-1/2 Ton, 2-Wheel	96	2.9 (1.3 EW)
	M149	Water Trailer, 400-Gallon Tank	91	3.0 (1.3 EW)
	M353	Cargo Trailer	123	3.0 (1.3 EW)
	M870	Semi-Trailer, Low-Bed, 40-Ton	437	49.3 (9.4 EW)
	M970	Semi-Trailer, Refueler, 5,000-Gallon	245	24.6 (8.1 EW)
Material Handling Equipment	MC-4000	Rough Terrain Forklift	144	4.1
	MC-6000	Rough Terrain Forklift	152	9.8
	72-31M	Rough Terrain Forklift	167	12.1
	DROT 2500	30-Ton Rough Terrain Crane	440	36.1
Radar	TPQ36/V475	Radar	103	3.7

Notes:
1. Includes vehicle and equipment crews in addition to those listed.
2. Empty weight (EW) indicated in parenthesis.
3. LAV-M (mortar variant) and LAV-6 (logistics variant) have different weights than LAV-25.
4. Mk 40/Mk 15 (wrecker) and Mk 48/Mk 17 (cargo hauler) have different weights and square footages than Mk 48/Mk 14.

Figure C-3. Weight and Square Footage of USMC Vehicles and Equipment

or combat. LF vehicle operators, under the supervision of the LCAC loadmaster, are responsible for tieing down their vehicles and associated equipment to the cargo deck with gripes provided by the craft's crew. The number of gripes and tiedown arrangement required are a function of equipment weight and the nature of the mission.

Volume IV, Parts 1 and 2 of SEAOPS (LCAC Loadmaster Manual and Vehicle Loading Pocket Handbook, respectively) provides vehicle characteristics, CG, and tiedown arrangements (for operations in sea states 3 or less) for Marine Corps equipment normally transported on LCAC. The SEAOPS loadmaster manual discusses the procedures for tieing down palletized cargo, containers, and rubber small craft to LCAC's deck.

Container Type	Length (ft)	Width (ft)	Height (ft)	Maximum Gross Weight (lb)
International Standards Organization (ISO) Type 1CC	20	8	8.5	44,806
ISO Type 1C	20	8	8	44,806
Marine Corps Shelter System (MCESS) Variations	20	8	8	15,000

Figure C-4. Dimensions and Weights of LCAC-Compatible Containers

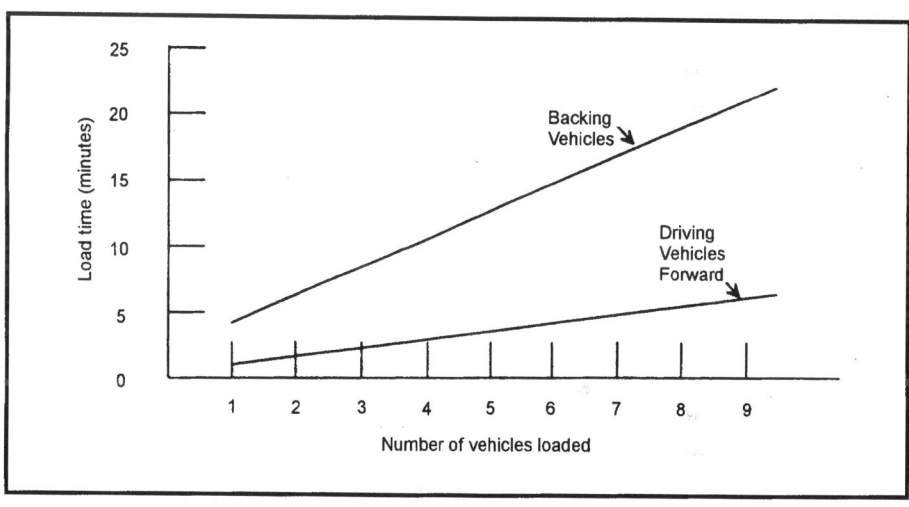

Figure C-5. Estimating Times for Backing Versus Driving Vehicles Forward onto LCAC

As discussed in paragraph 2.6.5.2, LCAC cycle times can be reduced by simultaneous loading and griping of equipment. Figure C-6 compares the combined loading and griping times for a typical (six vehicle) LCAC load using various loading and griping sequences.

C.2.2.4 Cargo Protection. Vehicles and other LF equipment are subject to salt water corrosion and pallet-ized cargo is subject to water intrusion/packaging deterioration when embarked on LCAC.

Covers for use during long embarkation periods are available for selected pieces of equipment including LAVs and M198 howitzers. These covers are compatible with LCAC as long as they are tied down in accordance with procedures contained in the SEAOPS Loadmaster Manual. The covers may become FOD

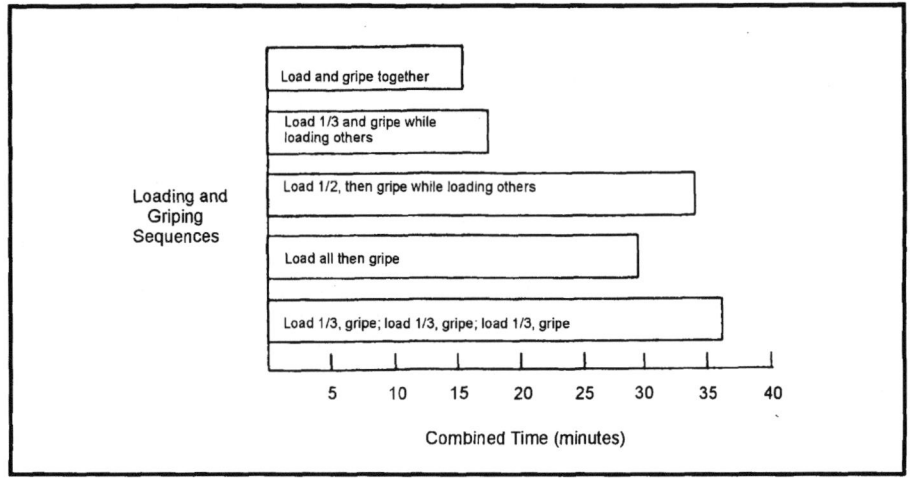

Figure C-6. Combined Times for Various LCAC Loading and Griping Sequences

hazards to the craft's propellers if not tied down properly.

The cardboard packaging of palletized cargo may disintegrate when soaked with salt water and become an additional FOD hazard. The use of plastic wrap or other water-shedding material should be considered for palletized cargo embarked on LCAC.

C.2.2.5 Safety. Shifting loads and FOD hazards are the principal safety concerns after loading LCAC. Prior to departure from the beach or clearing the well deck of an LCAC-capable ship, the craft loadmaster shall conduct a thorough inspection of palletized cargo, containers, vehicles, and other equipment for proper tiedown to prevent load shifts and FOD hazards. The LCAC loadmaster shall report the results of this inspection to the craftmaster.

General safety guidance for LCAC loading and unloading includes:

1. Cargo loading/unloading is prohibited within 50 feet of refueling operations. To reduce craft turnaround time during missions, craft cargo can be spotted on deck prior to commencement of refueling and griped in place while refueling.

2. All types of cargo shall be checked for FOD hazards prior to and after loading on the craft.

3. Crane loads shall be controlled by the craft loadmaster or other LCAC crew members, as assigned.

4. Only one vehicle shall be loaded/unloaded at a time.

5. Personnel working on the cargo deck when loading with the craft's main engines turning shall be reduced to a minimum.

C.2.2.6 Cargo Restraint on LCAC While in Well Decks. During periods of heavy weather when an LCAC is secured within the well deck, cargo on the LCAC deck may be subjected to G-forces equivalent to those experienced during sea state 7. As part of heavy weather precautions, both LCAC and their cargo may require additional griping to prevent movement while in the well deck.

C.3 LCAC LOADING/UNLOADING LOCATIONS AND MEANS

Locations for the loading and unloading of LCAC and the means available at each location to load/unload the craft are discussed in the following paragraphs.

C.3.1 In Well Decks. Depending on the size of the well deck, one or more LCAC may be loaded or unloaded simultaneously. Multiple LCAC loading or unloading is possible when through-loading discussed in paragraph C.2.1.2 is employed. Vehicles are normally driven on or off via the ramps with associated trailers/howitzers in trail. Palletized cargo may be carried on or off with forklifts via the ramps. Palletized cargo or containers may also be lifted on or off the craft by overhead monorail cargo handling systems and bridge cranes, when available.

C.3.2 Alongside Ships. Since LCAC does not have a sterngate marriage capability like the landing craft, utility (LCU), nonwell deck loading/unloading must be accomplished alongside a ship using the ship's deck cranes. Paragraph A.5.2 discusses the manner in which LCAC moors bow-to the side of a ship to avoid damage to its propeller ducts. Craft engines must be shut down while loading/unloading alongside due to the number of personnel on the cargo deck. During LCAC loading alongside a ship, cargo spotting requirements slow the pace of the evolution considerably. LCAC alongside loading/unloading should not be attempted in sea states greater than 1.

C.3.3 At Causeways and RO/RO Facilities. LCAC can load/unload all types of cargo at pontoon causeways and RRDFs via its ramps. Some RRDFs have been modified to allow LCAC to maneuver onto the RO/RO platform, providing more stability during the loading/unloading process.

C.3.4 In Beach/Inland Areas. LCAC can load/unload all types of cargo on the beach and in CLZs inland via its ramps. The craft's ramps must be lowered onto even and firm ground to equally distribute the weight of the ramps and the equipment traversing them.

C.3.5 At Sea. LCAC can load/unload CRRC (as well as other rubber small craft) at sea as discussed in paragraph 3.2.1.1.2. LCAC can unload AAVs at sea as discussed in paragraph 3.3.2. The transfer at sea of personnel from LCAC to another craft is possible but requires precise hullborne maneuvering of both craft. Other cargo can not be transferred from one craft to another at sea.

C.4 LCAC STANDARD LOADS

As discussed in paragraph 2.6.2, an LCAC standard load is used in developing notional landing plans and is defined as a combination of troops, vehicles, and other cargo that can be carried by LCAC. LCAC standard load equivalents are variations of LCAC standard loads. The use of standard loads in landing plan development can ensure the maximum utilization of LCAC's lift capacity in both the initial and general unloading phases of the ship-to-shore movement. Figure C-7 identifies typical LCAC standard loads and standard load equivalents, and provides plan views of LCAC cargo decks and all vehicles included in each load. Each load must be balanced in accordance with procedures found in the LCAC Loadmaster Manual to ensure optimum craft performance.

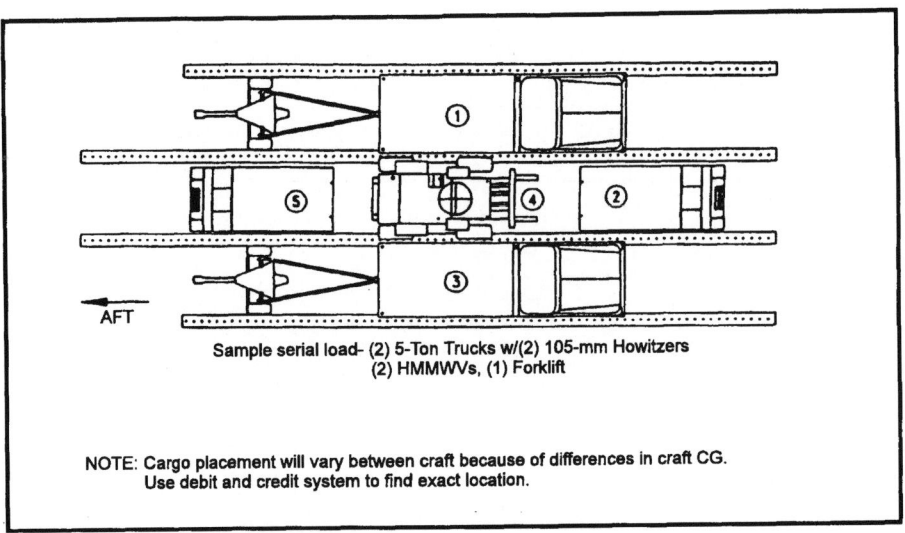

Sample serial load- (2) 5-Ton Trucks w/(2) 105-mm Howitzers
(2) HMMWVs, (1) Forklift

NOTE: Cargo placement will vary between craft because of differences in craft CG.
Use debit and credit system to find exact location.

Figure C-7. LCAC Standard Loads and Standard Load Equivalents (Sheet 1 of 4)

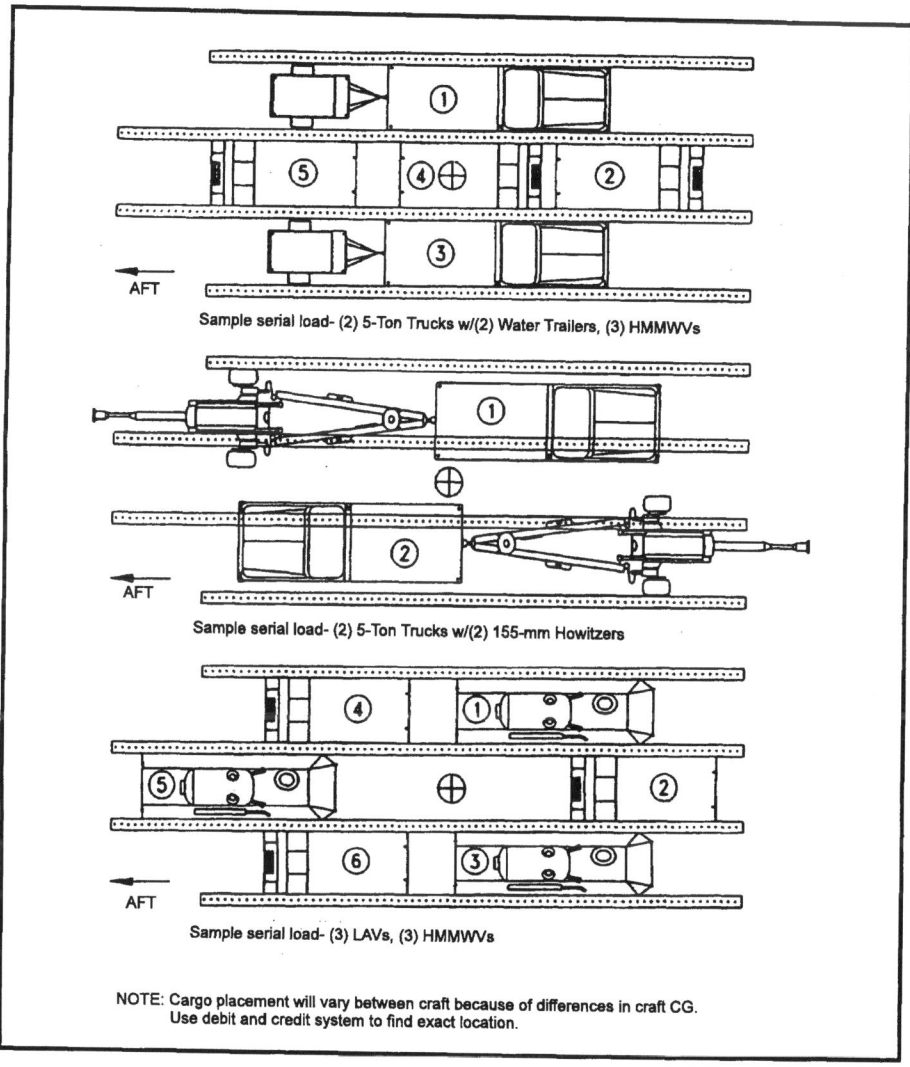

Sample serial load- (2) 5-Ton Trucks w/(2) Water Trailers, (3) HMMWVs

Sample serial load- (2) 5-Ton Trucks w/(2) 155-mm Howitzers

Sample serial load- (3) LAVs, (3) HMMWVs

NOTE: Cargo placement will vary between craft because of differences in craft CG.
Use debit and credit system to find exact location.

Figure C-7. LCAC Standard Loads and Standard Load Equivalents (Sheet 2 of 4)

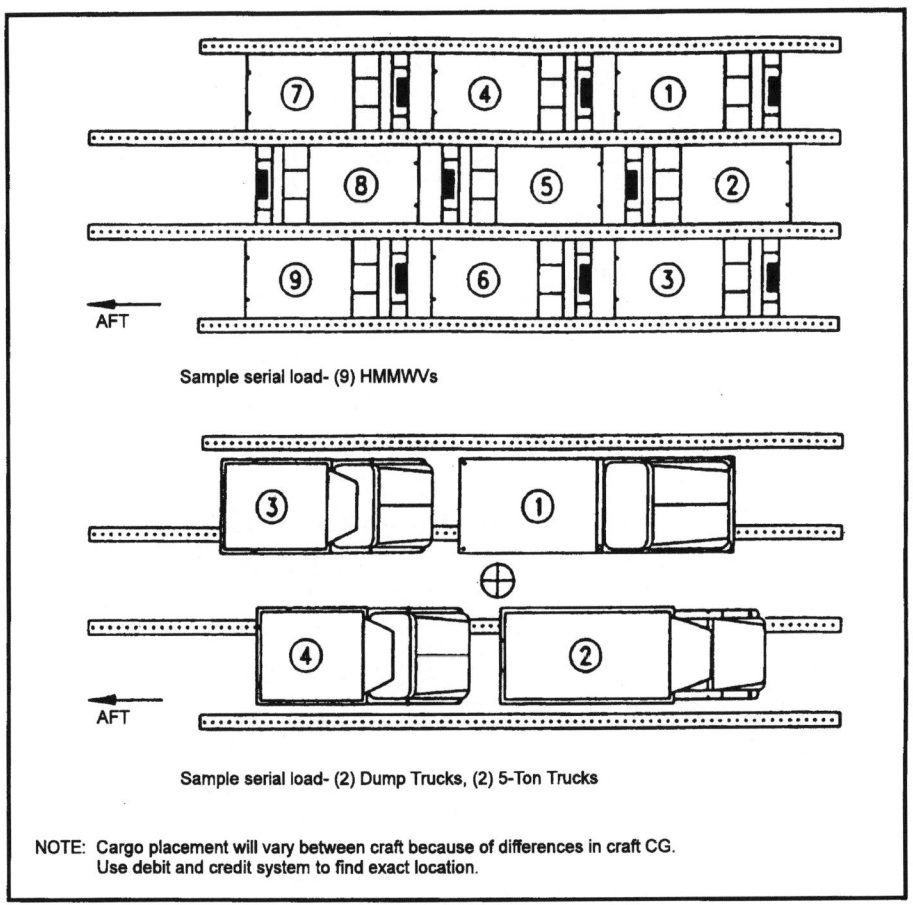

Sample serial load- (9) HMMWVs

Sample serial load- (2) Dump Trucks, (2) 5-Ton Trucks

NOTE: Cargo placement will vary between craft because of differences in craft CG.
Use debit and credit system to find exact location.

Figure C-7. LCAC Standard Loads and Standard Load Equivalents (Sheet 3 of 4)

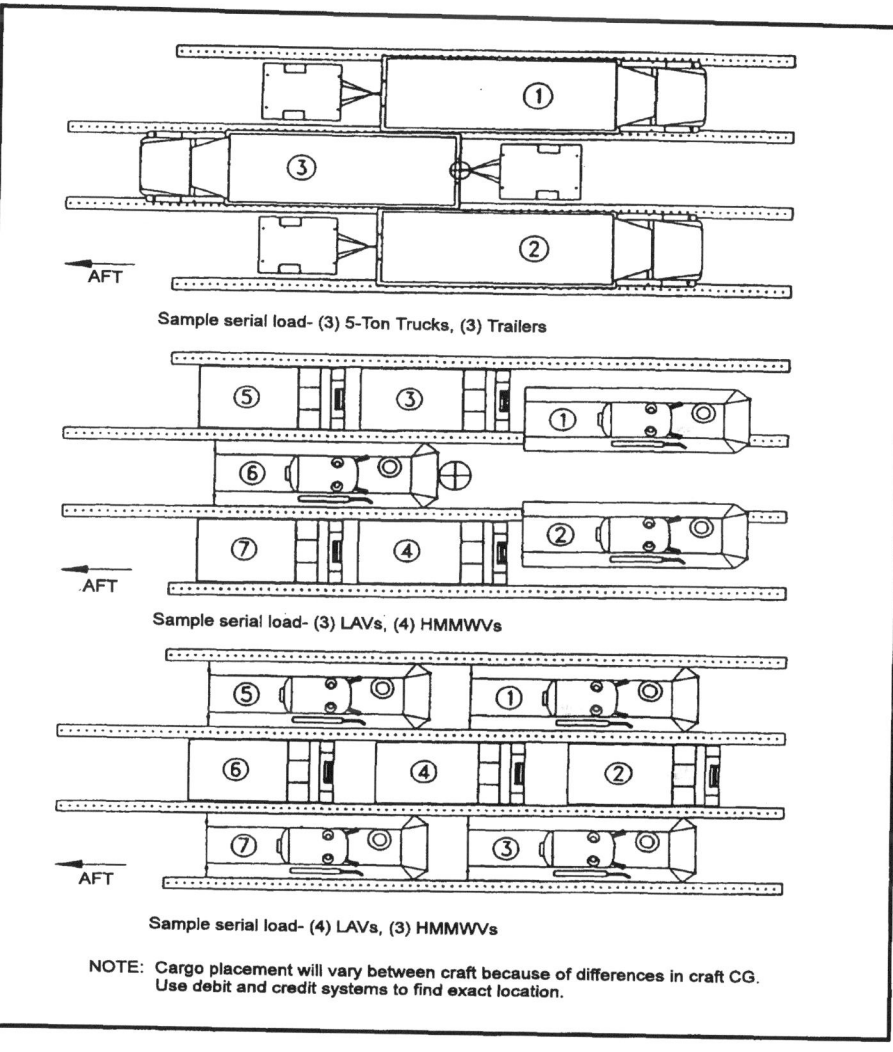

Sample serial load- (3) 5-Ton Trucks, (3) Trailers

Sample serial load- (3) LAVs, (4) HMMWVs

Sample serial load- (4) LAVs, (3) HMMWVs

NOTE: Cargo placement will vary between craft because of differences in craft CG. Use debit and credit systems to find exact location.

Figure C-7. LCAC Standard Loads and Standard Load Equivalents (Sheet 4 of 4)

LCAC Identification Lights, Markers, and Signals

D.1 GENERAL

LCAC do not display any amphibious-unique identification flags, lights, or insignia because of the FOD these devices could cause. LCAC are fitted with navigation lights and a special ACV light. LCAC beach operations can be supported by the use of distinct markers. Hand signals may be used to communicate with LCAC on the beach and in the vicinity of support ships.

Appendix C of NWP 3-02.2M, "Ship-To-Shore Movement," identifies the full range of flags, insignia, markers, lights, and signals used in waterborne ship-to-shore movement. This annex identifies those lights, markers, and hand signals that are LCAC related.

D.2 LCAC NAVIGATION LIGHTS

At night and during periods of limited visibility, LCAC display normal navigation lights as the tactical situation permits. LCAC's navigation lights includes an amber, all-around ACV light which flashes 120 times per minute.

D.3 LCAC BEACH MARKERS

Distinct day or night beach markers can be erected to support LCAC operations. The flanks of the CPP and the beginning of the ingress route to the CLZ can be marked with orange or infrared strobe lights affixed to poles at night and 6-foot by 6-foot markers with inverted international orange triangles during the day. Figure D-1 depicts LCAC beach markers viewed from seaward.

D.4 HAND SIGNALS

Due to the volume of noise generated by LCAC when the craft engines are operating, hand signals may be used in place of or as a supplement to voice radio to communicate with the craft. Hand signals are used to control LCAC maneuvers into and out of CLZs, CLSs, and support ship well decks. Figure D-2 depicts LCAC hand signals.

An additional set of hand signals are used to control vehicles and cranes during LCAC onload and offload operations. Wheeled and tracked vehicle and crane maneuvering hand signals are shown in the "Safe Engineering and Operations (SEAOPS) Manual for Landing Craft Air Cushion (LCAC)" Volume IV, Part I (LCAC Loadmaster Manual).

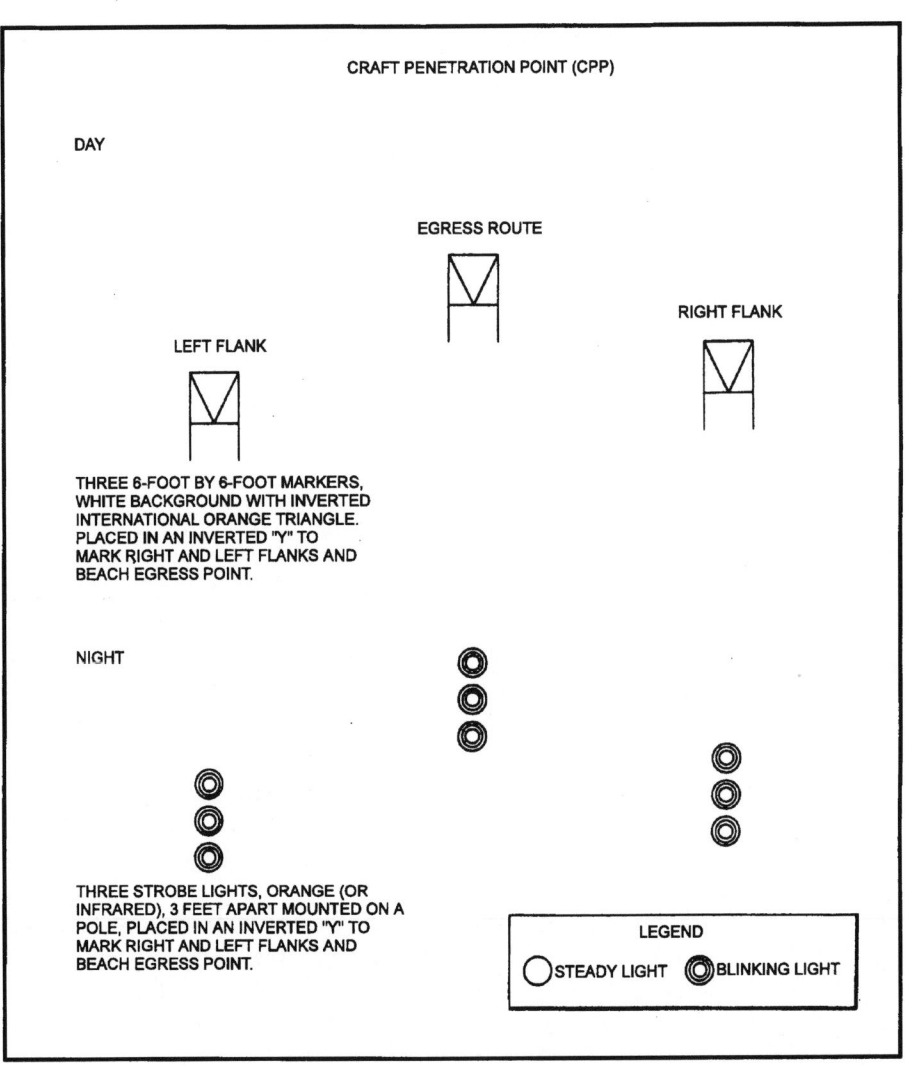

CRAFT PENETRATION POINT (CPP)

DAY

EGRESS ROUTE

RIGHT FLANK

LEFT FLANK

THREE 6-FOOT BY 6-FOOT MARKERS,
WHITE BACKGROUND WITH INVERTED
INTERNATIONAL ORANGE TRIANGLE.
PLACED IN AN INVERTED "Y" TO
MARK RIGHT AND LEFT FLANKS AND
BEACH EGRESS POINT.

NIGHT

THREE STROBE LIGHTS, ORANGE (OR
INFRARED), 3 FEET APART MOUNTED ON A
POLE, PLACED IN AN INVERTED "Y" TO
MARK RIGHT AND LEFT FLANKS AND
BEACH EGRESS POINT.

LEGEND

◯ STEADY LIGHT ◎ BLINKING LIGHT

Figure D-1. LCAC Beach Markers (From Seaward)

ORIGINAL

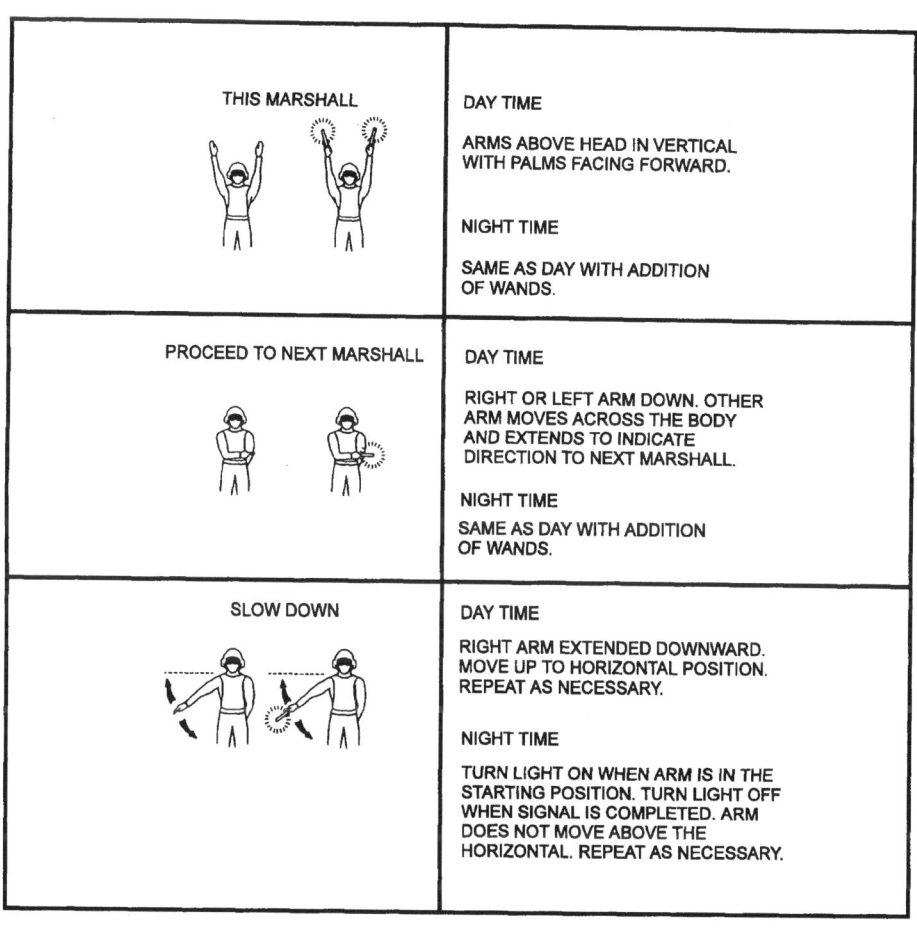

THIS MARSHALL	DAY TIME ARMS ABOVE HEAD IN VERTICAL WITH PALMS FACING FORWARD. NIGHT TIME SAME AS DAY WITH ADDITION OF WANDS.
PROCEED TO NEXT MARSHALL	DAY TIME RIGHT OR LEFT ARM DOWN. OTHER ARM MOVES ACROSS THE BODY AND EXTENDS TO INDICATE DIRECTION TO NEXT MARSHALL. NIGHT TIME SAME AS DAY WITH ADDITION OF WANDS.
SLOW DOWN	DAY TIME RIGHT ARM EXTENDED DOWNWARD. MOVE UP TO HORIZONTAL POSITION. REPEAT AS NECESSARY. NIGHT TIME TURN LIGHT ON WHEN ARM IS IN THE STARTING POSITION. TURN LIGHT OFF WHEN SIGNAL IS COMPLETED. ARM DOES NOT MOVE ABOVE THE HORIZONTAL. REPEAT AS NECESSARY.

Figure D-2. LCAC Maneuvering Hand Signals (Sheet 1 of 7)

MOVE AHEAD	DAY TIME
	ARMS ARE EXTENDED IN FRONT OF BODY AT A SLIGHT ANGLE TOWARD THE DECK WITH PALMS OF HANDS FACING UPWARD. HANDS ARE THEN BROUGHT IN TOWARD BODY BY BENDING ARMS AT ELBOWS.
	NIGHT TIME
	ARMS ARE USED IN SAME MANNER AS DAY SIGNAL EXCEPT WANDS ARE USED, EXTINGUISHING THE LIGHT BEFORE THE DOWNWARD STROKE.
TURN TO PORT	DAY TIME
	ONE ARM STRAIGHT OUT TO SIDE ON WHICH TURN IS TO BE MADE. OTHER ARM RAISED STRAIGHT UP, PALM FORWARD.
	NIGHT TIME
	LIGHTED WAND IN EACH HAND, ONE OUT, THE OTHER STRAIGHT UP.
TURN TO STARBOARD	DAY TIME
	ONE ARM STRAIGHT OUT TO SIDE ON WHICH TURN IS TO BE MADE. OTHER ARM RAISED STRAIGHT UP, PALM FORWARD.
	NIGHT TIME
	LIGHTED WAND IN EACH HAND, ONE OUT, THE OTHER STRAIGHT UP.

Figure D-2. LCAC Maneuvering Hand Signals (Sheet 2 of 7)

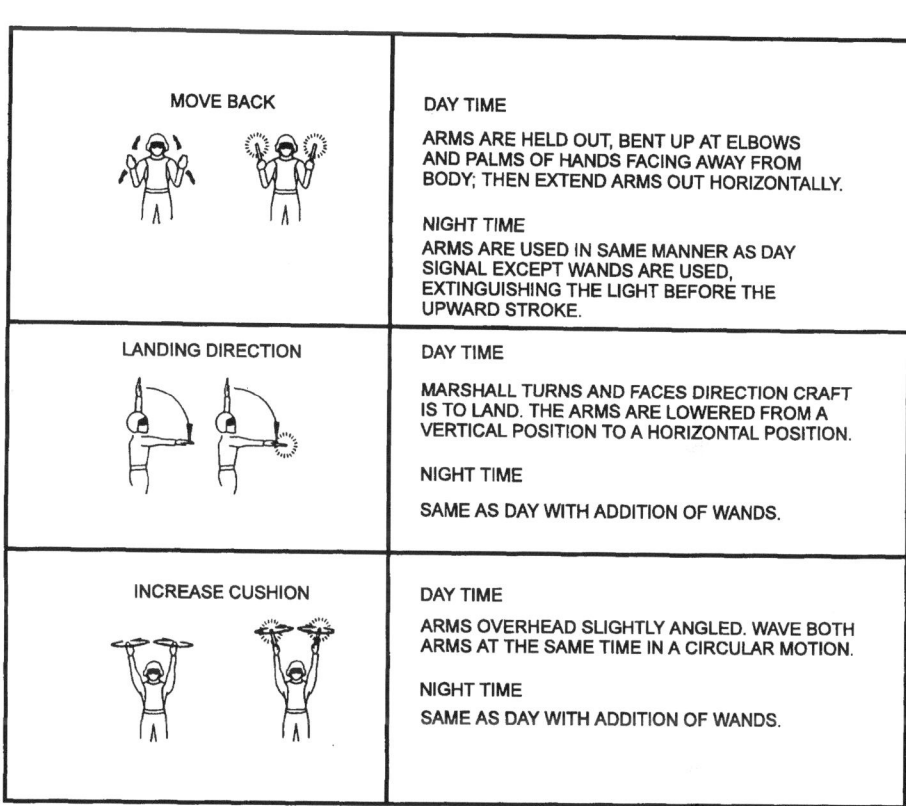

MOVE BACK	**DAY TIME** ARMS ARE HELD OUT, BENT UP AT ELBOWS AND PALMS OF HANDS FACING AWAY FROM BODY; THEN EXTEND ARMS OUT HORIZONTALLY. **NIGHT TIME** ARMS ARE USED IN SAME MANNER AS DAY SIGNAL EXCEPT WANDS ARE USED, EXTINGUISHING THE LIGHT BEFORE THE UPWARD STROKE.
LANDING DIRECTION	**DAY TIME** MARSHALL TURNS AND FACES DIRECTION CRAFT IS TO LAND. THE ARMS ARE LOWERED FROM A VERTICAL POSITION TO A HORIZONTAL POSITION. **NIGHT TIME** SAME AS DAY WITH ADDITION OF WANDS.
INCREASE CUSHION	**DAY TIME** ARMS OVERHEAD SLIGHTLY ANGLED. WAVE BOTH ARMS AT THE SAME TIME IN A CIRCULAR MOTION. **NIGHT TIME** SAME AS DAY WITH ADDITION OF WANDS.

Figure D-2. LCAC Maneuvering Hand Signals (Sheet 3 of 7)

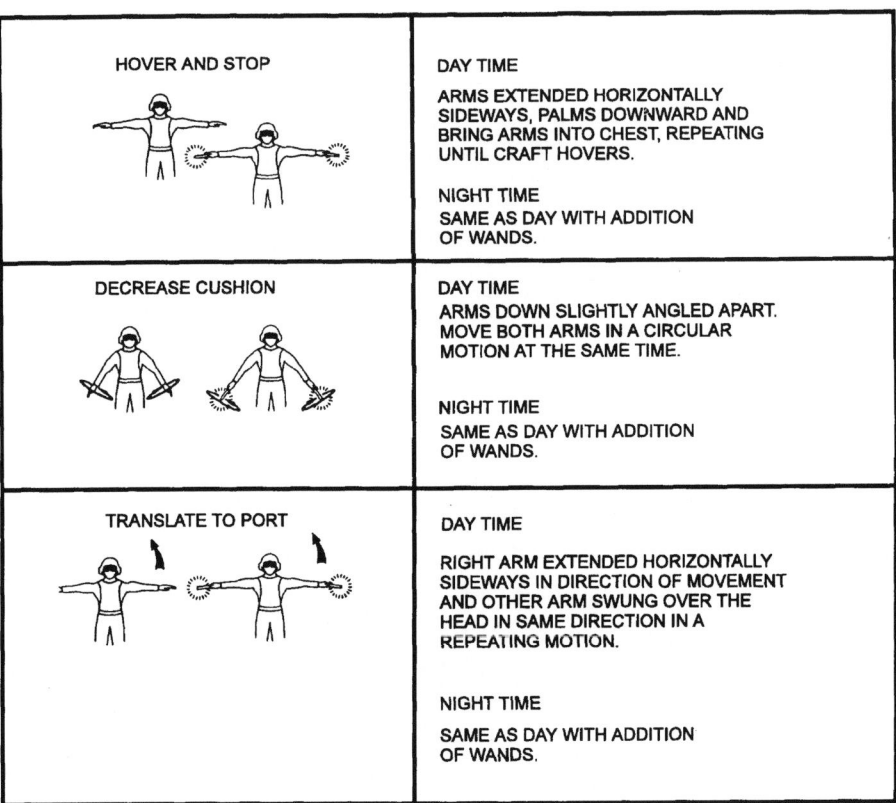

HOVER AND STOP	**DAY TIME** ARMS EXTENDED HORIZONTALLY SIDEWAYS, PALMS DOWNWARD AND BRING ARMS INTO CHEST, REPEATING UNTIL CRAFT HOVERS. **NIGHT TIME** SAME AS DAY WITH ADDITION OF WANDS.
DECREASE CUSHION	**DAY TIME** ARMS DOWN SLIGHTLY ANGLED APART. MOVE BOTH ARMS IN A CIRCULAR MOTION AT THE SAME TIME. **NIGHT TIME** SAME AS DAY WITH ADDITION OF WANDS.
TRANSLATE TO PORT	**DAY TIME** RIGHT ARM EXTENDED HORIZONTALLY SIDEWAYS IN DIRECTION OF MOVEMENT AND OTHER ARM SWUNG OVER THE HEAD IN SAME DIRECTION IN A REPEATING MOTION. **NIGHT TIME** SAME AS DAY WITH ADDITION OF WANDS.

Figure D-2. LCAC Maneuvering Hand Signals (Sheet 4 of 7)

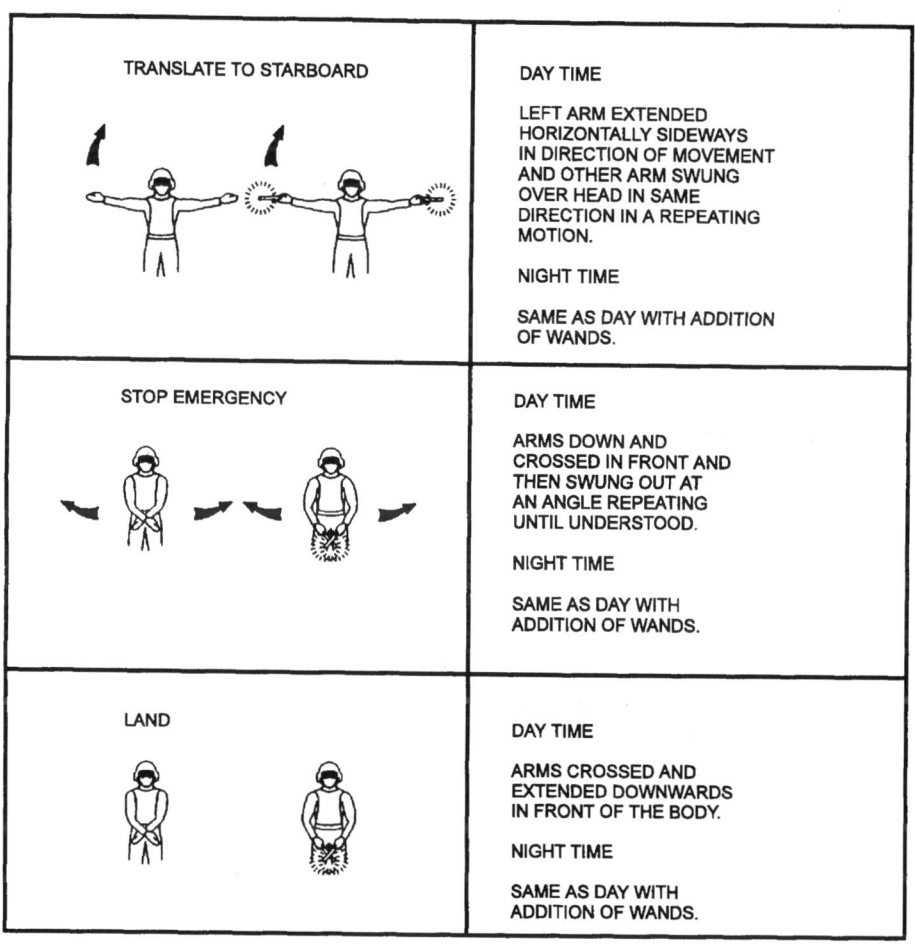

TRANSLATE TO STARBOARD	DAY TIME LEFT ARM EXTENDED HORIZONTALLY SIDEWAYS IN DIRECTION OF MOVEMENT AND OTHER ARM SWUNG OVER HEAD IN SAME DIRECTION IN A REPEATING MOTION. NIGHT TIME SAME AS DAY WITH ADDITION OF WANDS.
STOP EMERGENCY	DAY TIME ARMS DOWN AND CROSSED IN FRONT AND THEN SWUNG OUT AT AN ANGLE REPEATING UNTIL UNDERSTOOD. NIGHT TIME SAME AS DAY WITH ADDITION OF WANDS.
LAND	DAY TIME ARMS CROSSED AND EXTENDED DOWNWARDS IN FRONT OF THE BODY. NIGHT TIME SAME AS DAY WITH ADDITION OF WANDS.

Figure D-2. LCAC Maneuvering Hand Signals (Sheet 5 of 7)

ORIGINAL

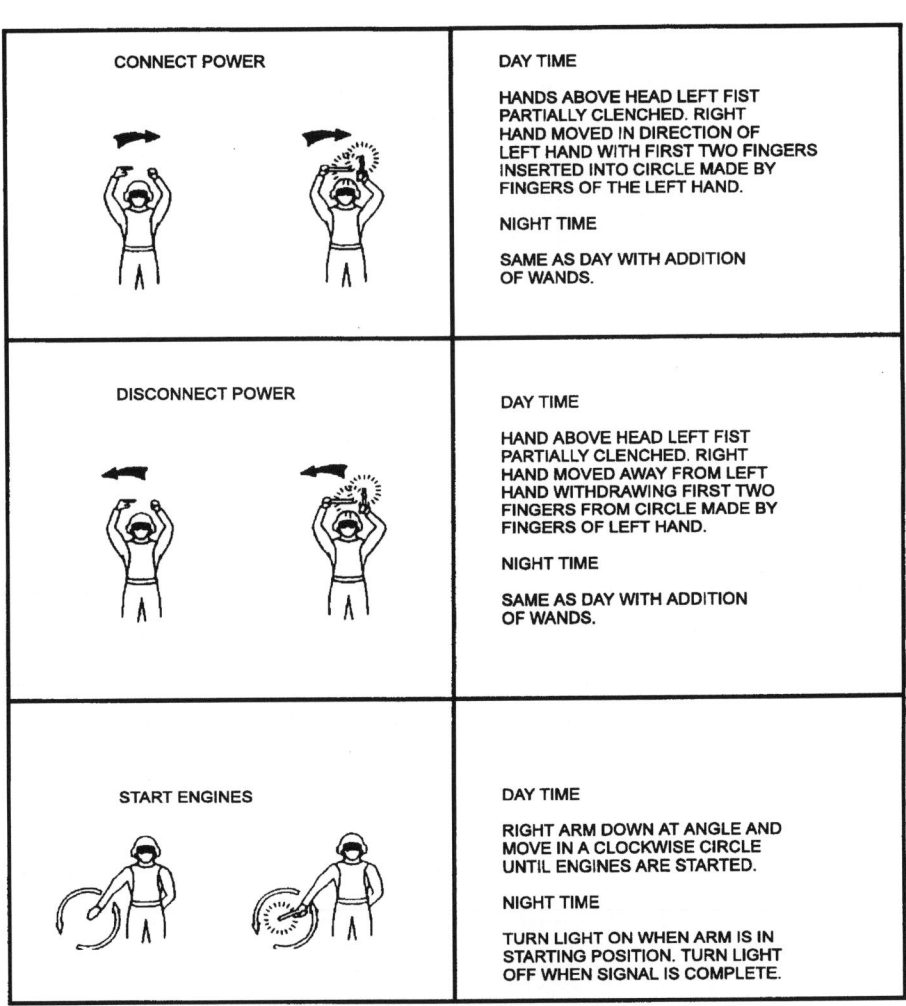

CONNECT POWER	DAY TIME
	HANDS ABOVE HEAD LEFT FIST PARTIALLY CLENCHED. RIGHT HAND MOVED IN DIRECTION OF LEFT HAND WITH FIRST TWO FINGERS INSERTED INTO CIRCLE MADE BY FINGERS OF THE LEFT HAND.
	NIGHT TIME
	SAME AS DAY WITH ADDITION OF WANDS.
DISCONNECT POWER	DAY TIME
	HAND ABOVE HEAD LEFT FIST PARTIALLY CLENCHED. RIGHT HAND MOVED AWAY FROM LEFT HAND WITHDRAWING FIRST TWO FINGERS FROM CIRCLE MADE BY FINGERS OF LEFT HAND.
	NIGHT TIME
	SAME AS DAY WITH ADDITION OF WANDS.
START ENGINES	DAY TIME
	RIGHT ARM DOWN AT ANGLE AND MOVE IN A CLOCKWISE CIRCLE UNTIL ENGINES ARE STARTED.
	NIGHT TIME
	TURN LIGHT ON WHEN ARM IS IN STARTING POSITION. TURN LIGHT OFF WHEN SIGNAL IS COMPLETE.

Figure D-2. LCAC Maneuvering Hand Signals (Sheet 6 of 7)

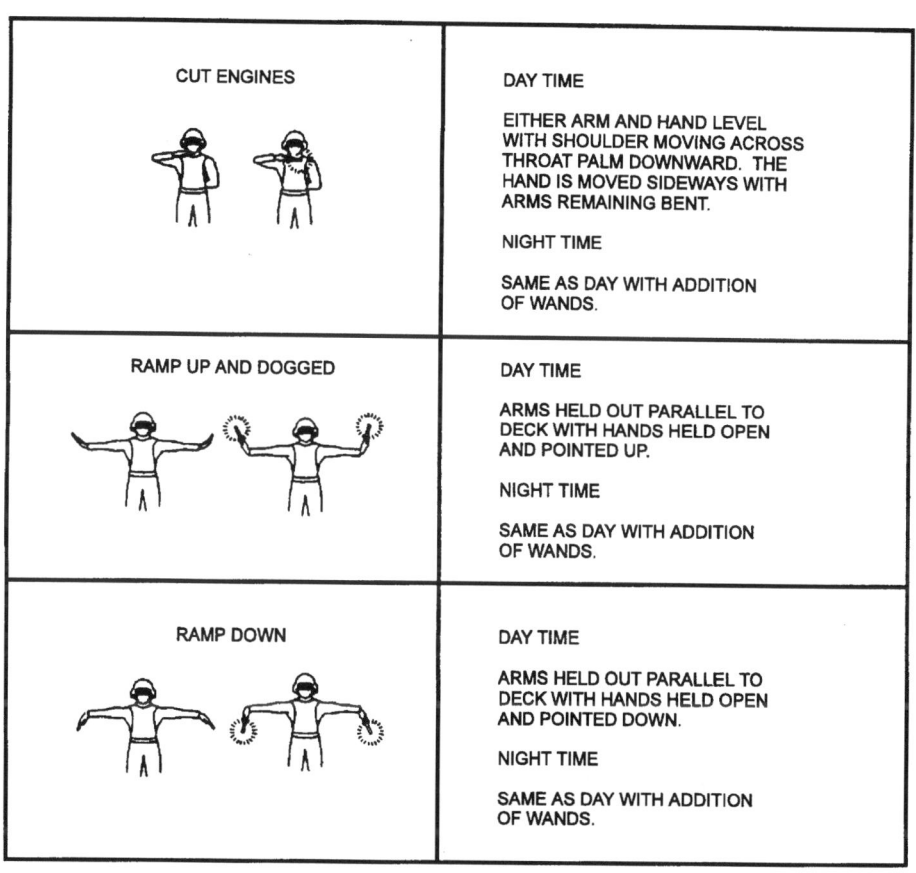

CUT ENGINES	DAY TIME
	EITHER ARM AND HAND LEVEL WITH SHOULDER MOVING ACROSS THROAT PALM DOWNWARD. THE HAND IS MOVED SIDEWAYS WITH ARMS REMAINING BENT.
	NIGHT TIME
	SAME AS DAY WITH ADDITION OF WANDS.
RAMP UP AND DOGGED	DAY TIME
	ARMS HELD OUT PARALLEL TO DECK WITH HANDS HELD OPEN AND POINTED UP.
	NIGHT TIME
	SAME AS DAY WITH ADDITION OF WANDS.
RAMP DOWN	DAY TIME
	ARMS HELD OUT PARALLEL TO DECK WITH HANDS HELD OPEN AND POINTED DOWN.
	NIGHT TIME
	SAME AS DAY WITH ADDITION OF WANDS.

Figure D-2. LCAC Maneuvering Hand Signals (Sheet 7 of 7)

INDEX

Page No.

A

Administrative Organization
   Assault Craft Unit (Air Cushion) A-12
   Naval Beach Group A-7
Aircraft Relay Platform 4-8
Amphibious Assault Vehicles
   Launch at Sea from LCAC 3-4
   Use in LCAC Configured for
     Personnel Transfer 7-1
Amphibious Objective Area
   Enlargement 1-15
   Mine Countermeasures Support 7-14
Amphibious Raids 3-3, 3-4
Amphibious Ship Classes 1-3, 1-4
Amphibious Task Force
   LCAC Support of Choke-Point Transit . . 7-12
   Surface Offload B-1
Anchoring A-11
Areas
   Beach Operating 2-5
   Craft Collection 4-4
   Craft Holding 2-5, 4-7
   Craft Launch 2-4, 4-4
   Inland Operating 2-5
   Inner Transport 2-4
   Outer Transport 2-4
   Sea Echelon 2-5
   Sea Operating 2-2
   Transport 2-4
Auxiliary Power Unit
   Cold Weather Operations 8-2
   Crew Day 1-12
   Launch Timetable 4-12
Aviation Intermediate Maintenance Depot
   Capability 1-3

B

Beach
   Approach 1-9
   Departure 1-10

Page No.

   Party 4-3
   Selection 1-14
   Separation 1-15
Beachmaster Unit 6-3
Boat Group Commanders 4-1
Boat Wave Commanders 4-1
Bow Thrusters 1-3, 4-16

C

Casualty Receiving and Treatment Ship . . . 6-5
Central Control Officer 4-1
Chemical, Biological, and Radiation
   Defense 1-16
   Weapons 5-2
Choke-Point Transit
   Extension of Radar Coverage 7-13
   Military Operational Deception 7-13
   Scouting 7-13
Close Air Support 5-6
Cold Weather Operations 8-1, 8-7
Combat Air Patrol Stationing 5-6
Combat Rubber Raiding Craft 3-1, 3-2
Components
   Hull System A-1
   Skirt System A-1
Considerations
   Amphibious Assault Vehicle Launch at Sea . 3-4
   Deception Van-Configured MCAC
     Employment 7-13
   Humanitarian Assistance and
     Disaster Operations 7-14
   Hump Transition 1-8
   LHA 1 Class Ship Surface Offload B-5
   Load Planning 2-7
   Loading C-1
   Mine Countermeasures-Configured LCAC
     Employment 7-14
   Noncombatant Evacuation Operations . . . 7-11
   Operating Over Ice 8-4
   Repair A-4
   Surface Offload B-1

Surf Zone Transitions 1-9
Transit 2-8
Vulnerability to Detection 5-1
Wave Maneuvering 4-14
Control
   Advisory 4-7
   AN/KSQ-1 Amphibious Assault
     Direction System 4-9
   Areas 4-4
   Independent 4-8
   LCAC Over-the-Horizon 4-8
   Officer (Central) 4-1
   Officer (LCAC) 4-1
   Officer (Primary) 4-1
   Officer (Secondary) 4-1
   Point (Craft) 2-4, 4-4
   Positive 4-8
   Ship (LCAC) 4-3
   Ship (Primary) 4-1
   Ship (Secondary) 4-1
   Ship-to-Shore Movement 4-7
   Team (Craft Landing Zone) 4-3
   Team (LCAC) 4-3
Craft Landing Site 2-5, 4-5
Craft Landing Zone 2-5, 4-5
Craft Landing Zone Control Team 4-3, 6-3
Craft Landing Zone Support Team 6-1
Crew Day 1-12
Crew Week 1-13

D

Dead Reckoning 4-8
Deception, Tactical 3-3
Disabled Craft Launch and Recovery A-7
Docking Blocks A-5

E

Electronic Attack 3-3
Embarkation Planning
   Docking Block Availability/Positioning . . A-6
   Use of LCAC 1-15
Emission Control 4-7, 5-1
Enemy Prisoners of War 6-3

F

Foreign Object Damage
   Amphibious Assault Vehicle Launch 3-4
   Cargo Securing and Protection 1-3, C-5
   Reduction of Hazards 7-15
   Use of Embarked Vehicle/Troop Weapons . . 5-5
   Visual Communications 4-9
   Vulnerability to Small Arms/Direct Fire
     Weapons 5-2
Fuel
   Capacity 1-3
   Consumption in High-Heat Environments . . 8-7
   Heating 8-2
   Management 1-10, 1-11
   Type 8-7

G

Gas Turbine Engines (Main)
   Cold Weather Operations 8-2
   Filtration System Clogging 8-7
   Launch Timetable 4-12
Global Positioning System 4-7, 4-17

H

Heavy Weather Operations
   Sea State 4 8-9
   Sea State 5 and Higher 8-11
   Over Land 8-11
   Wave Impact 8-8
Helicopter
   Escort 5-6
   Landing Zone 2-5
High-Heat and High-Airborne Particle Environments
   Effects on LCAC Performance 8-7
   Personnel Effects 8-8
   Well Deck 8-8
High Mobility Multipurpose Wheeled Vehicles
   Use in LCAC Configured for Personnel
     Transfer 7-2
Humanitarian Assistance and Disaster Relief
   Operations 7-15
Hump Speed 1-8

I

Icing (Craft and Cargo) 8-4
Identification Friend and Foe 4-18, 5-2
Initial Terminal Guidance 4-3
Infrared
　Strobes 3-2
　Vulnerability to Detection 5-1
Interior Voice Communications System 4-9
International Standards Organization
　Containers 7-9, C-5

L

Landing Area
　Organization 2-2
　Selection 1-14
Landing Area Organization 2-2, 2-5
Landing Craft Air Cushion
　Advantages Over Landing Craft Utility . . . B-2
　Casualty Mission Impact 1-11
　Characteristics and Capabilities 1-1, 1-3
　Components and Characteristics A-1
　Control Areas 4-4
　Control Officer 4-3
　Control Ship 4-3
　Control Team 4-3
　Craftmaster 4-3, A-14
　Cycles 2-8
　Cycle Time 2-8, B-2
　Deceleration and Acceleration Distances . 4-15
　Detachment A-13
　Efficient Employment 2-9
　Fuel Management 1-10
　Human Performance Guidelines and
　　Health Standards 1-12
　Hump Transition 1-6
　Lifts 2-8
　Lights, Markers, and Signals D-1
　Limitations 1-6
　Maintenance, Repair, and Docking A-1
　Manning A-14
　Maximum Displacement 1-6
　Mooring and Anchoring A-7
　Operating Limits 1-6
　Operational Impact 1-13
　Overview 1-1

　Plow-in Boundary 1-9
　Sea Conditions for Launch 1-9
　Sideslip 2-4, 4-15
　Standard Distance 4-15
　Standard Load 2-7, C-7
　Standard Load Equivalent 2-7
　Standard Turn Rate 4-15
　Structural Limitations 1-6
　Support Requirements 1-3
　Surf Zone Transition 1-9
　Tactical Diameter 4-8
　Transit Considerations 2-8
　Transit Lane 2-4
　Waves 4-12
　Wave Commander 4-3
Landing Craft Air Cushion Control Areas . 4-4, 4-7
Landing Craft Air Cushion Control Officer
　Responsibilities 4-3
Landing Craft Air Cushion Debarkation
　Sequence and Procedures 4-10
　Well Deck Operations 4-10
Landing Craft Air Cushion Formations . 4-12, 4-14
Landing Craft Air Cushion Waves
　Formations 4-12
　Maneuvering Considerations 4-15
Landing Craft Air Cushion Launch and Recovery
　Considerations 4-11
　Checklist and Timetables 4-12
Landing Craft Air Cushion Operations
　Amphibious Raids 1-17, 3-3
　Choke-Point Transit 7-12
　Cold Weather 8-1
　Extreme Environmental Conditions . . 1-18, 8-1
　Heavy Weather 8-8
　High-Heat/High-Airborne Particle
　　Environments 8-7
　Humanitarian Assistance and Disaster
　　Relief 7-15
　Landing Force Sustainment Ashore . . 1-17, 6-1
　Loading and Unloading C-1
　Maritime Interception Operations 7-13
　Mine Countermeasures 7-14
　Noncombatant Evacuation Operations . . . 7-11
　Personnel Transfer 7-1
　Preassault Operations 1-17, 3-1
　Salvage, Towing, and Disabled Craft . . . A-6
　Ship-to-Shore Movement 1-17, 4-1

ORIGINAL

Landing Craft Air Cushion Over-the-Horizon Control
  Aircraft Relay 4-8
  Aircraft Relay Platform 4-8
  Independent Transit 4-8
Landing Craft Air Cushion Protective Support
  Measures
    AH-1 Cobra Helicopter Escort 5-6
    Antiair Warfare/Antisurface Warfare . . 5-6
    Close Air 5-6
    Naval Surface Fire 5-6
Landing Craft Air Cushion Self-Defense . . 5-4, 5-5
Landing Craft Air Cushion Vulnerability
  to Detection 5-1, 5-2
Landing Craft Air Cushion Vulnerability
  to Enemy Attack 5-2, 5-3
Landing Craft Utility
  Advantages over LCAC B-4
  Lift Capability 1-3, 7-1
Landing Force
  Offload B-1
  Support Party 6-1
  Sustainment 6-1
Landing Force Support Party 6-1, 6-3
Landing Force Sustainment 6-5
Landing Zones
  Craft 2-5, 4-5
  Helicopter 2-5
Lift Fans 1-3, 1-9
Light Armored Vehicles
  Use in Amphibious Raids 3-3
  Use in Defense 5-5
  Use in LCAC Configured for
    Personnel Transfer 7-1
Limitations
  Casualty Mission Impact 1-11
  Firefighting with Cold Weather Kit
    Installed 8-3
  Fuel Management 1-10
  High Heat Environments 8-7
  Human Performance Guidelines and
    Health Standards 1-12
  Hump Transition 1-6
  Maximum Craft Displacement 1-6
  Operating Limits 1-6
  Operating Over Ice 8-4
  Plow-In Boundary 1-9
  Sea Conditions for Launch 1-9
  Structural 1-6

Surf Zone Transitions 1-9
Linear Demolition Charges 7-14
Line of Departure 4-4
Loading and Unloading Operations
  Characteristics C-1
  Considerations C-1
  Griping B-2, C-4, C-6
  Locations and Means C-7
  Standard Loads C-7

M

Maintenance and Repair A-1, A-3
Maneuver Warfare 1-13
Man-on-the-Move Voice Radio System . . 4-7, 4-11
Marine Corps Expeditionary Shelter System
  Assembling and Securing 7-3
  Capacity 7-5
  Configuration Options 7-4
  LCAC Configuration 7-1
  Medical Emergency Evacuation 7-6
  Modifications 7-3
  Use in Noncombatant Evacuation
    Operations 7-12
Marine Expeditionary Force (Forward) 2-1
Marine Expeditionary Unit (Special Operations
  Capable)
    Humanitarian Assistance and Disaster
      Relief 7-15
    Missions 1-13
Maritime Interception Operations
  Factors in LCAC Support 7-13
  Medical Emergency Evacuation . . 6-5, 7-2, 7-5
Military Operational Deception
  Cover and Deception Van 7-14
  Deception Van-Configured MCAC
    Considerations 7-14
  SSQ-74 Van 7-13
Military Vans 1-3, A-9
Mine Countermeasures 7-14
Mission Planning Procedure
  Cold Weather Kit Installation 8-3
  Craft Factors 2-10
Mooring A-7
Multipurpose Craft Air Cushion
  Deception Van-Configured 7-14
  Minesweeping and Minehunting 3-3
  Personnel Transport Module-Configured . . 7-8

Page No.

Surf Zone Breaching 3-3
Tactical Deception 3-3

N

Naval Surface Fire Support 1-14, 5-6
Navigation
  Considerations 4-17
  Electronic Suite 4-15
  Over Sea Ice 8-6
  Visual 4-17
Night and Low Visibility Operations 2-11
Noncombatant Evacuation Operations . . . 7-12

O

Operational
  Deception (Military) 7-13
  Maneuver From the Sea 1-13
  Security 4-10
  Tasking Amphibious 2-1
Overloading
  Operational Impacts 1-6
Over-the-Horizon
  Operations 1-13
  Tactical Surprise 1-15
  Transit in a Restricted Emission
    Control Environment 4-17
  NSFS Difficulty 5-5

P

Personnel Transport Module 7-8, 7-11
Planning
  Amphibious Operation 2-1
  Background 2-1
  Chemical, Biological, and Radiation
    Defense 1-16
  Command, Control, and Communications
    Systems Support 1-15
  Efficient LCAC Employment 2-9
  Embarkation 1-16
  Intelligence 1-15
  Landing Area Selection 1-14
  Logistics/Combat Service Support 1-15
  Mission Planning Procedure 2-10
  Night and Low Visibility Ship-to-Shore
    Movement 2-11

Page No.

Organization of the Landing Area 2-2
Preparation of Documents 2-2
Procedures to Reduce Cycle Times 2-9
Rate of Combat Power Buildup Ashore . . 2-9
Ship-to-Shore Movement 1-15, 2-6
Supporting Arms 1-15
Point
  Craft Control 2-4, 4-4
  Craft Departure 2-4, 4-4
  Craft Penetration 2-5, 4-4
  Decision 4-4
  Dropoff 3-1
  Insertion 3-4
  Recovery 4-7
  Rendezvous 2-4
Position Location Reporting System 4-9
Preassault Operations
  LCAC Control 3-4
  Mine Warfare 3-2
  Planning 3-4
  Reconnaissance and Special Warfare . . . 3-1
  Tactical Deception 3-3
Primary Control Officer Responsibilities . . . 4-1
Primary Control Ship 4-1
Propellers 1-3, 1-9

R

Return to Force Options 4-18
Rough Terrain Capabilities 1-7
Routes
  Egress 2-5, 4-7
  Ingress 2-5, 4-7
Rudders 1-3

S

Safety
  Inspections C-6
  Navigation over Sea Ice 8-6
  Personnel 5-2, 8-6
  Loading and Unloading Guidance C-6
Salvage Operations A-6
Sea-Air-Land Teams 3-1
Seabasing 6-5
Secondary Control Officer Responsibilities . . 4-1
Secondary Control Ship 4-1

Page No.

Selection Factors
  Beach 1-14
  Craft Landing Zones 2-5, 7-16
  Landing Force Landing Area 1-14
  Navy Landing Area 1-14
Shallow Water Mine Threat 5-3
Ship-to-Shore Movement
  Communications 4-9
  Communications Nets 4-10
  Control 4-7
  Control Areas 4-4
  Debarkation 4-10
  Dispatch to the Beach 4-1
  General Unloading 4-19
  Low Visibility 2-11
  Navigation 4-15
  Night 2-11
  Organization 4-1
  Planning 2-6
  Turnaround at the Beach and Return
    to Force 4-18
Ship-to-Shore Movement Control 4-7, 4-8
Ship-to-Shore Movement Organization . 4-1, 4-3
Ship-to-Shore Movement Planning
  Cycle Time 2-8
  Environmental Conditions 2-7
  LCAC Available 2-6
  Load Considerations 2-6
  Operational Implications 1-13
  Standard Load Equivalents 2-7
  Total Lifts Required 2-8
  Transit Considerations 2-8
  Vehicle Weight and Area Requirements . . 2-7
Spray Suppression Techniques 5-5
Support
  Administrative A-12
  Antiair Warfare 5-6
  Antisurface Warfare 5-6
  Close Air 5-6

Page No.

Command, Control, and Communications . 1-15
Electronic Warfare 5-1
Logistic/Combat Service 1-15
Naval Surface Fire 5-6
Reconnaissance and Special Warfare 3-1
Supporting Arms Coordination Center 5-6
Surface Offload Operations B-1, B-5
Surf Zone
  Breaching 3-3, 7-14
  Mine Clearance 3-3
  Mine Threat 5-3
Towing Procedures A-7
Transit
  Considerations 2-7
  Independent 4-8
  Lanes 2-4, 4-5

V

Vehicle Weight and Area Requirements 2-7
Very Shallow Water
  Mine Clearance 3-2
  Mine Threat 5-3

W

Well Deck Operations
  Alignment 4-10
  Cargo Restraint C-6
  Communications 4-10
  Docking A-4
  High-Heat Environment 8-7
  Ice Missile Hazards 8-6
  Launch and Recovery Considerations . . 4-10
  Launch/Recovery Checklist
    and Timetables 4-11
  Safety 4-10
  Surface Offload Usage B-1
  Temperature 8-6

LIST OF EFFECTIVE PAGES

Effective Pages	Page Numbers
Original	1 (Reverse Blank)
Original	3 (Reverse Blank)
Original	5 (Reverse Blank)
Original	7 (Reverse Blank)
Original	9 thru 17 (Reverse Blank)
Original	19 thru 28
Original	1-1 thru 1-18
Original	2-1 thru 2-12
Original	3-1 thru 3-4
Original	4-1 thru 4-19 (Reverse Blank)
Original	5-1 thru 5-6
Original	6-1 thru 6-6
Original	7-1 thru 7-16
Original	8-1 thru 8-11 (Reverse Blank)
Original	A-1 thru A-14
Original	B-1 thru B-7 (Reverse Blank)
Original	C-1 thru C-11 (Reverse Blank)
Original	D-1 thru D-9 (Reverse Blank)
Original	Index-1 thru Index-6
Original	LEP-1 (Reverse Blank)

UNCLASSIFIED

NWP 3-02.12
MCRP 3-31.1A